The Parents' & Teachers' Guide to Helping Young Children Learn:

Creative Ideas from 35 Respected Experts

edited by
Betty Farber, M.Ed.

P p
Preschool
Publications, Inc.

Preschool Publications, Inc.
Cutchogue, New York, U.S.A.

The Parents' & Teachers' Guide to Helping Young Children Learn:
Creative Ideas from 35 Respected Experts
Edited by Betty Farber, M.Ed.

Cover Design: Lester Feldman
Book Illustrations: Susan Eaddy
Book Design: Arthur Farber

Material adapted from articles that appeared in
Parent and preschooler Newsletter issues prior to 1997.

For information about quantity purchases contact:
Betty Farber, President
Preschool Publications, Inc., P.O. Box 1167
Cutchogue, NY 11935-0888, U.S.A.
Voice: U.S.A. 1.800.726.1708 • International 1.516.765.5450
Fax: 1.516.765.4927 • e-mail: preschoolpub@hamptons.com

Library of Congress Cataloging-in-Publication Data
The parents' & teachers' guide to helping young children learn :
    creative ideas from 35 respected experts / edited by Betty Farber.
        p. cm.
    "Material adapted from articles that appeared in Parent and preschooler Newsletter"—T.p. verso.
    Includes biographical references.
    ISBN 1-881425-05-3 (pb)
    1. Early childhood education—Activity programs—United States.
2. Creative activities and seat work. 3. Cognition in children—United States.
4. Learning, Psychology of—United States.
I. Farber, Betty
LB1139.35.A37P37   1997
372.21—dc21   97-6282
                                                          CIP

Foreword

Within these pages lies a cache of riches for you and your preschool child (and/or children) whether you are a parent or a teacher, or both. On every page there are treasures — information, ideas, resources — that will enhance your daily lives with children.

Do you wonder how your preschoolers *really* learn, or why certain things/events/people are more interesting than others? It's all there in the first section — how children learn through their senses, how to appreciate differences in learning styles, how play fosters learning, how to select appropriate toys.

Would you like to encourage your youngster's emerging literacy? Just turn to sections two through four and find a myriad of ideas for fun ways to play with language, engaging activities for reading and writing and natural, everyday opportunities for learning math concepts like shape, size, weight and number.

And lest you think that play and make-believe have gone out of style (or are useless) — think again and read on! Section five is a tribute to the power of children's imagination and its close connection to their ability to think. Find in this section great ideas for dramatic play and make believe games. No need to buy elaborate equipment, just use stuff that's already in most homes — hats, shoes, pots, pans, lengths of cloth and other common objects.

Nothing has been left out of this "encyclopedia" of ideas, from art, music, movement, neighborhood excursions, and museums to the splendid world of nature and outdoors — all are included. To cap it off, each section ends with Resources such as wonderful lists of good books for both children and adults or museums for children (by state).

For parents, chances are that this book will become your constant companion throughout your children's early childhood years and will provide many varied, enjoyable and memorable times for the whole family. Teachers will be reaching for this book on a daily basis to enhance and refresh your lively classroom.

Nancy Balaban, Ed.D.,
Director, Infant and Parent Development and Early Intervention Program,
Graduate School of Education, Bank Street College, New York City

CONTENTS

SECTION FOUR
SHARING LITERATURE

SECTION FIVE
IMAGINATION - CREATIVITY

SECTION SIX
MUSIC - MOVEMENT - ART

SECTION SEVEN
SCIENCE - NATURE

SECTION EIGHT
TRIPS WITH YOUR PRESCHOOLER

SECTION NINE
SCHOOL

SECTION TEN
COMPUTERS

Section One
How
Young
Children
Learn

Section One
How Young Children Learn

Introduction

Watch young children as they maneuver wooden blocks to build a castle. They try a certain size and shape, find it doesn't balance, look for another, set it atop the structure, step back to make sure it works, and smile with a feeling of mastery. When observing youngsters absorbed in play, as the authors point out in this section, you see that play is the natural state of children and the primary way that children learn.

Children learn best about numbers, letters, sizes and shapes in ways that have meaning for them in their own world. They learn about colors while choosing clothes to wear that day, about math as they set the table with one napkin and one spoon for each place, about science as they prepare a meal with you. Children take in information through all of their senses; they explore and discover.

Children are individuals and will differ in their learning styles and their strengths. The chapters in this section give the reader some insights into young children as they play, learn and grow.

SECTION ONE

HOW YOUNG CHILDREN LEARN

Chapter 1
Children are Natural Learners

Carol B. Hillman

The essential idea is that
learning comes through play,
in a relaxed, natural,
uncomplicated, enjoyable,
and meaningful way.

Jenny, who will start kindergarten in the fall, spends about an hour each day dressing up and pretending. She puts on high-heeled shoes and a flowered hat — and drapes a scarf around her shoulders. With a pocketbook casually placed on her arm and a scribbled "list" in her hand, she clomps about the house pretending she's on the way to market.

Children learn through play

Play is a natural state of childhood. It is the primary way that children learn. When Jenny scribbles a "list" on a piece of paper, she is doing what she has observed her mom or dad do. It is not important for her to write real words — that will come later. It is not important for her to write "b" for bread or "m" for milk at this point in her life — that will come later, too. What is important is that Jenny is observing the world around her and translating what she sees into her own terms.

Jenny can find out about numbers and letters in a way that has meaning for her. When her mother teaches Jenny which numbers to dial to get grandma or grandpa on the telephone, Jenny is learning number awareness. When her father points out traffic signs on the way to daycare, she is learning letter and word recognition. The essential idea is that learning comes through play, in a relaxed, natural, uncomplicated, enjoyable, and *meaningful* way.

Children are natural learners

Young children, because they have a natural curiosity, are eager to explore the world about them. They want to touch every object within their reach. They want to turn things over and inside out. They use all their senses to gather information. They then use these bits and pieces of knowledge to ask a multitude of questions. Often young children need the interpretation of an adult to help them process all their new information.

When they walk along a sandy beach, a piece of green glass can hold the same allure as a salmon-colored scallop shell. A child may ask, "How did the broken glass get on the beach?" or "Why are there so many shells on the sand?" An adult can explain to a child that someone could have broken a bottle while they were picnicking, and left it there, or that it could have washed ashore. In either event, a child can be told that a piece of broken glass, even though it's pretty, is not a safe object with which to play. The adult can also explain that shells are like houses for small animals that live in the ocean, and that the waves bring them up onto the sand. He can then say that it's fine to collect them because the animals are not living in them anymore.

Parents create learning environments

A child's home is her first and most significant learning environment. It is there that her lifelong attitudes about learning begin. Much of what a young child learns is not conveyed in words, but rather by the everyday activities which make up the pattern of family life.

Going to the library on a regular basis can be a richly rewarding experience. It can be exciting for young children to know that there are books written only for children, and that they have their own special section in the library. It can be a valued outing to attend a "story hour," where a trained storyteller brings a book or story to life through a dramatic presentation.

When parents and children *spend time together each evening, reading a story and sharing ideas about the pictures,* the youngsters are learning more than what the story says. They are learning that reading is a pleasurable experience. They are learning that words and books are essential parts of life.

When a family *comes together to share a meal and talk about each person's day,* parents are setting priorities not only for the family gathering, but also for the role of communication through words.

Ways to encourage children's learning

• *Provide an environment where children feel safe.* Adults who work with children can foster intellectual development by establishing ground rules and routines which make children feel physically and emotionally protected. At home, in nursery school or daycare, children need to feel that there are reasonable rules to be followed, and that there are caring adults to protect them. They learn best in a climate in which they can focus their attention on creative play and social interaction.

• *Avoid questioning to "test" children's knowledge.* Parents often, in their eagerness to teach young children, ask them too many questions. Questions are often used to "test" children's knowledge. Questions put children on the defensive and open up the possibility for negative responses. In place of questions substitute statements; they create a whole different atmosphere in which parents and children can share knowledge comfortably with one another. Instead of asking, "Do you know what word is in the middle of the red and white sign?" simply say; "Look at the red and white sign, it says stop." Instead of asking, "Do you know how many uncles you have?" simply say, "Uncle John and Uncle Thomas are your two uncles."

• *Use hands-on experiences.* Preschoolers learn differently from adults. They learn best by *doing,* by working with real objects. For most young children the more direct the involvement in activities the greater the likelihood for learning. Early childhood educators call these "hands-on experiences." If a child is learning about growing plants, give him a container and let him fill it with soil, put a seed in, cover it up, gently pat down the earth, and water and tend it each day thereafter. This would be considered a "hands-on experience." Actually young children like to involve their whole bodies in what they are doing. You may have seen a child walk directly through a rain puddle and splash water all over himself, and another youngster, bundled up in her red snowsuit, roll down a small snow-covered hill. You may also have observed a child who, as she creates her own designs with fingerpaint on top of a table with a plastic surface, moves gracefully like a dancer. All of these would be considered "hands-on experiences." 🎔

Hands-on Activities for Learning

Carol B. Hillman

• When your child is getting dressed in the morning, let her count the number of pockets on her clothing, or barrettes in her hair.
• When you are cleaning a room let your youngster work with you — supplied with a small dust cloth and a child-size broom. When you are finished, talk about what he did **first, next,** and **last**.
• When helping your youngster straighten up her room let her pick a number so you can each put **six** things away, then **four,** until the job is done.
• Give your child a plastic drinking straw. (This activity is best for four year olds and older.) Place a feather, a tissue, a marble, a block, etc. on the floor and let your youngster discover which objects he can move across the room by blowing at them through the straw.
• On your trips to the library, let your preschooler decide if she can carry **four** or **five** books inside by herself. Then allow her to make a few selections of new books to borrow.
• If you are taking a walk to the mailbox, count the number of steps it takes to get there and back.
• Plan a "nature walk." Make up a list in advance of things to look for on the ground: for example, three leaves, two bird feathers, four acorns and one piece of bark.

- Use a magnifying glass. For younger preschoolers, look for a magnifier with thick, easy-to-hold wooden handles. Look at objects such as shells, leaves, insects, sand, and your own fingers and toes under the magnifying glass and observe their details.
- "Paint" with water. (This activity is best done outside on a warm day.) Using large paint brushes and a bucket of water, let your child "paint" the garage, fence, steps, etc. with water.
- Explore the ways of water. (Another activity for a warm day.) Place a large plastic tub of water on a bench or low table so that your child, standing next to it can easily reach in with his hands. Provide unbreakable cups, squeeze bottles, funnels, strainers, egg beaters, etc. and let your child explore the ways the water acts, using the different materials.
- When you're driving in the car see if you can spot a license plate which has a number five, the letter "J," or the color blue.
- Sit together on a large rock or park bench with your eyes closed. How many sounds can you identify?
- Lie down on the grass and look up at the clouds. See what different shapes you can both see.
- As your child is on the way to the sandbox ask her to make you a birthday cake with five candles, and a cup of tea.

Chapter 2
There's a Concept Behind that Apple

Neala S. Schwartzberg

*Did you ever think
about how you know
that an apple
is an apple?*

Did you ever think about how you know that an apple is an apple? Or what the color red looks like? Or what happens at a birthday party? Or what it means to be "honest"? Fruits, colors, actions, values, all these and more are forms of *concepts*. Some concepts are fairly easy to describe in words; others are nearly impossible. Yet children learn them, as a natural part of their life. They learn because human beings are designed to do just that, extract meaning and information from the surrounding world. But our children also learn because parents and teachers provide experiences, the raw material for their learning.

Learning is as natural as breathing
Babies and children find learning as natural as breathing. They are inquisitive and curious, always looking, exploring, and trying to understand the world around them.

It starts with babies seeking stimulation. They stare long and hard at us, learning what we look like. Babies don't just glance at things, they study them intently until they have extracted whatever meaning they can.

They delight in pushing and pulling and swiping at things, learning causal connections. They begin to understand cause and effect. Baby swipes at a mobile, and her actions cause the colorful bears to move. She is delighted with this and does it again and again. It's as if she is thinking "When I swipe at that mobile, all the colorful bears twist and bob around. Neat!"

They learn how to make balls roll on the floor and that round things roll but square things don't.

Objects as thinker toys
Youngsters "think" with things. They experience and experiment not with ideas but with concrete objects from the world around them. They explore to see what each can do and then take those new ideas and try them out on something else. So a cardboard cylinder (from a paper towel roll) can be more interesting than a toy which "plays by itself." The child can watch the toy, but after a while he has simply learned all he can. The cylinder, on the other hand, allows him to try out his new actions. John has learned to play peek-a-boo with his hands, but he can also play peek-a-boo with the cylinder. He rolls his ball, but now sees he can roll his cylinder too.

John can also learn new actions from playing with the cylinder. He discovers how odd things look when he peers through the tube and sees just a little piece of things, like a bit of the couch or his father's nose when he climbs up on his lap. He also learns how funny his voice sounds when he talks into the tube.

Once John has discovered this, he can apply that new idea to other objects. Will his voice sound funny talking into his juice cup? Will it work if he talks into his hand?

Kids need a variety of things to play with and explore in order to develop these new concepts, ideas, and actions. How would children learn about "sticky" if they didn't have stickers or glue — or learn about stacking and balance if they didn't have blocks? We need to make sure they have a variety of things to explore and the benefit of our time and interest to help them discover some of the neat things they can do.

Parents also teach through language

Although time spent with our children helping them play with toys is crucial, we do much more than give our children interesting toys and help them play. We directly teach them through language. As children develop language they become able, with our help, to grab each piece of experience and label it. They become verbal; their concepts become more abstract and they gradually develop the ability to use language to learn. This starts gradually and takes years to develop, but at some point they will no longer be dependent on what they can touch and feel to explore. At some point, they will be able to learn things from words alone. And we are crucial to that effort.

Almost from birth we provide a steady stream of conversation about what we are doing. We talk as we change their diapers or give them breakfast. "Now, I'm going to put this nice clean diaper on you," or "Here's some delicious cereal —ready?" We point out things like stop signs and delivery trucks as we go for walks. We play games like "Where's Your Nose?" When we read to them we point out the objects in the book and identify them.

Language also helps concepts and objects become more differentiated and abstract. For example, at first almost everything with wheels is a car. "Look at the big car," says Alison as she looks out the window. "No," says her mother, "that's a truck. The Ellisons are moving and the truck is going to take their furniture to their new home. See how many wheels it has? Cars can't carry a lot of furniture and they don't have as many wheels." And Alison learns how cars differ from trucks and what trucks do that is unique.

This happens over and again. All dogs start out being "dogs," but end up — as children learn to refine the different categories — as cocker spaniels and sheepdogs, or frisky puppies. In fact, for many kids, cats also start out by being dogs. But parents explain "dogs bark while cats purr or say meow."

Concepts which are difficult to describe and explain are acquired through the give-and-take of our conversations. Just consider how you would stumble describing the concept of color, for example, or how one knows that something is made of plastic. But in conversation we begin to lay the groundwork for the development of these more abstract ideas. Red acquires meaning through its association with the red car but not the blue car, the red ball not the yellow ball. When we are preparing to go to the beach or lake we may say "Let's bring the plastic car to take into the water. The metal one will rust."

As they get older we supply our children with even more information as part of our conversations. We give them facts and details. "Isn't that a beautiful tree? It's a maple tree. Do you know we get maple syrup from trees? Do you remember the syrup we poured on the pancakes this morning? That came from maple trees."

Scripts

Children also develop generalized expectations of the events and experiences in their lives. These are often called scripts because they indicate what everyone is "supposed" to do. For very young children there are scripts: for bedtime activities (and just try to change that script and see what happens), for getting ready in the morning, and even game scripts like how we play peek-a-boo. Scripts help children make predictions about their world and the actions of the people within it. They are based on the sameness and consistency of experiences. Without them, children would be unable to predict what would happen next. We tend to take scripts for granted, but imagine being at a ceremony which you have never attended before. Even as adults our first thoughts are often "What's going to happen?" "What should I do?"

We can see our children's scripts in action by watching their dramatic play. How do they play house? What happens when they play supermarket? One common script is a child's birthday party. If we asked a youngster "What happens when you go to a birthday party?" we might hear... "You get all dressed up. Everyone brings a gift. We play games, eat cake and candy and watch the birthday child open his gifts."

Scripts are very useful. It means that when Sara goes to a birthday party she knows what to expect. It may be very different from what her mother expects from an adult birthday party. So different in fact that Sara may easily be confused when attending the adult version. "Where are the games?" she might think to herself. "This isn't party food."

Helping kids learn concepts

Children learn best through first-hand experiences. They are not sophisticated enough to use language as a substitute for experience. Language can only reflect and expand children's experiences, not replace them. Adults can understand a story from a book. We can learn about gardening from the newspaper and apply that information to our vegetables or flowering plants. We can read a magazine article about why we should recycle plastic and decide that recycling makes sense. Young children cannot. They need to develop the concepts through experiences, then acquire the "word label" from us.

• *Talk with your child when reading or watching television.* When looking at a picture book ask your youngster open-ended questions to discover what she already knows and supply additional information. Your child may not be able to watch cloth being made, but if he sees a program about it on television, or reads about it in a book, you have the opportunity to ask questions and provide information. You can take a piece of cloth and examine it together seeing how it is woven...and how it can become unwoven.

• *Teach your child concepts with actual materials.* It means nothing to a youngster to hear that blue and yellow make green. Even if he can patiently repeat it back to you. But, if you mix blue paint and yellow paint and create green, that means quite a lot.

• *Talk to your children about what you are doing and why.* Don't take it for granted that your children know what you are doing when you are baking, pruning bushes, putting out seeds for the birds, or working on the car. Whatever you are doing, it is an opportunity to explain and teach.

• *Provide a variety of experiences and materials.* Collect shells along the beach; watch how plants grow in a garden; supply colored paper, paints, and glitter; find child-sized musical instruments. Encourage family sing-a-longs and participation in preparing family picnics. All these things and more are the raw materials our children use to develop concepts, try out new ideas, and learn about the world around them.   ▩

Chapter 3
Learning Through Everyday Experiences

Amy Laura Dombro

*There is no better way of showing
her respect and helping her
feel good about herself
than by making her your partner
in everyday activities.*

Living and Learning
Most adults find the routines of daily life to be tedious. We get dressed, set the table, clean the living room and go to the supermarket because these are the jobs that must be done. We give little thought to these familiar chores except perhaps to wish someone else would do them for us.

Yet for your children, these everyday tasks are fascinating opportunities to explore and to learn about themselves and the people and things in their world. They are predictable enough — happening more or less the same each time — so that children can understand and master them: an important step in learning. And, as your child grows, the very same experiences reveal new meaning and offer new challenges.

Look Through a Child's Eyes
To help you look through her eyes to see the wonder of the ordinary, ask yourself, "What is my child experiencing?" For example, let's look at the daily activity of getting dressed.

Becky at one year old, loves playing, "Show me your tummy" with her parents as they dress her. She is learning the names of parts of her body. When Becky's parents hold her to put on her clothes, she feels safe and secure in their arms. For Becky, dressing is a lesson about trusting and loving another human being. When her mother talks about her green shirt and yellow pants, she begins to learn about colors.

As she approaches two, Becky uses dressing as an opportunity to define herself as separate by declaring, *"Me* do!" and refusing her parents' help. Days when her parents offer her a choice, "Would you like to wear your blue shirt or the one with red stripes?" she can practice making decisions. Zippers, buttons, snaps, and Velcro® straps offer her the opportunity to refine the skill of using her fingers.

By three, Becky laughs at her "silly Daddy" when he asks if her shoes go on before her socks, and if she wants to go to the day care center in her pajamas. His questions are funny only because she knows from years of everyday experiences how some things in the world work. She feels proud and competent when she puts on her own coat and zips it herself.

At five, Becky is an accomplished dresser when she wants to be. Yet getting dressed is still filled with learning for her. Last week she added "chartreuse" to her list of colors and her most recent challenge is trying to tie her own shoes.

Support Your Child's Learning

When possible, include your child in daily routines. Because you are the most important person in her life, she is interested in the things you do and is eager to participate. There is no better way of showing her respect and helping her feel good about herself than by making her your partner in everyday activities.

Expect that there will be times things won't go smoothly. A child's idea of "helping" may be your idea of making a mess. You won't appreciate her "help" when she dumps the freshly folded towels out of the laundry basket onto the floor. Some days your reserve of patience will hit empty and you'll end up shouting at her or sending her to her room. This is part of life and there's an important lesson here: even though people may get angry, they still love each other and can work things out.

Most important of all, remember there is nothing you can buy your child, no class you can enroll her in that is more important than the experience she will get from participating in everyday family life. ⬞

Daily Activities for Learning

Amy Laura Dombro

Offer Choices

Whenever possible, offer your child realistic, manageable choices such as, "Would you like to eat a pear or a peach?" or, "Would you like to take your bath before or after supper?" Learning to be a good decision-maker takes lots of practice.

Assign Tasks
Give her "real" jobs to do such as setting the table, carrying the bag of paper towels home from the store, and fluffing up the sofa pillows when you clean the living room. She will feel proud and competent to be a valued and contributing member of the family.

Taking a Bath
• The bathtub is a laboratory that invites children to explore and experiment with water, a fascinating substance. Toys such as plastic funnels, margarine containers, and measuring spoons encourage pouring, and can help to illustrate such concepts as *full, half full,* and *empty.* Corks and metal spoons invite discoveries about what floats and what sinks.
• Bathtub conversation lends itself easily to naming body parts. Children begin by learning the basics such as: *head, legs* and *arms.* When these are mastered, introduce *elbow, eyebrow* and *forehead.*

** **Safety Note:** The bathtub can be a dangerous place. Drowning is a leading cause of death among young children. Always keep an eye on your children as they bathe. *Never* leave a young child alone in a bathtub.

Setting the Table
• Let toddlers carry unbreakables such as napkins or place mats to the table.
• Encourage older preschoolers to help you count out how many people will be eating and how many plates and cups you need. This helps with the concept of number: children will learn to place one of each item for each person.
• Children 3 to 5 years will enjoy folding napkins into different shapes. Younger children will enjoy it too if you don't mind some napkins being crumpled into balls or torn into shreds.
• Setting the table is a perfect opportunity for older preschoolers to begin learning about "right" and "left" as they set out the silverware.

Going to the Supermarket
• Name the foods you see. Words such as banana, cashew, broccoli, and cinnamon are fun to say.
• Children 2 to 5 years old enjoy having their own shopping list. Write the name of an item you want to buy such as "yogurt" on a piece of paper. You may want to illustrate the list or have children draw a picture of the item they are going to look for. If the item is easy to reach and unbreakable, let your child take it from the shelf and place it in your cart or basket.
• Encourage children to help you count pears, peaches, or apples as you take turns dropping them in a bag.

• The produce department presents countless opportunities to categorize by size, shape, and color. And its large hanging scales are an open invitation to discuss the property of weight as well. Let them see how much 8 apples weigh compared to 8 plums.

• Point out signs hanging over the aisles, labels on cans, print on boxes to children beginning to identify letters and sound out words.

• Discussions about the fact that Denise likes cauliflower and Sammy doesn't, convey the important message that people are unique individuals — each to be respected for who they are.

Doing the Laundry

• Working together to carry the filled laundry basket to the machine is a terrific lesson about cooperation.

• Talk about textures of clothes. Words like "scratchy," "silky," and "knobby," are fun to say. They can easily lead to rhymes or silly songs conveying the message that language is pleasurable.

• Encourage children ages 3 to 5 to help sort the items to be washed. Afterward, let them try to pair up the socks.

• Older preschoolers are developing a sense of ownership. You may want to ask them to help deliver each family member's clothes to the right bedroom. This is a real life "matching game."

Chapter 4
Different Learning Styles

Diana Stanley

As parents you can help your preschoolers become "well-rounded'"so they can meet their future learning experiences with success.

Before bedtime Jake's mother reads him *The Gingerbread Man.* Jake concentrates on the pictures in the book to help him remember to retell the story to his mother. Jake might be thought of as a *visual learner.*

Maeve and her mother listen to instrumental music on the car radio. "That sounds like a giant snoring," and, "I hear a piano playing in this song," are just some of Maeve's comments as she listens. Maeve might be thought of as an *auditory learner.*

Linsey is learning to count. When she and her father count her stuffed animals, she touches each one on the head as she counts. Linsey might be thought of as a *kinesthetic learner.*

"Visual learner," "auditory learner," and "kinesthetic learner" are three ways to describe how an individual child learns best.

A visual learner uses his *sight* to comprehend and store knowledge. An auditory learner gains information through *listening*. A kinesthetic learner must *touch* or *feel* as a way of gathering knowledge.

By observing the activities your child enjoys you can determine which type of learning is most *dominant* in your child. For instance, a youngster who can work a challenging multi-piece puzzle without frustration might be described as a "visual learner."

But what happens if a visual learner wants to play the piano which requires listening skills? Or what if an auditory learner wants to type on the computer which requires a sense of touch? Children use all three types of learning in varying degrees. For example, a child must use the sense of touch, sight and hearing to acquire just the basic writing and reading skills.

Children can learn through all the senses. As parents you can help your preschoolers become "well-rounded" so they can meet their future learning experiences with success. The skills they will need for academic achievement are developed during the preschool years.

Throughout the day your child is surrounded by sounds, smells, sights, and textures but these experiences alone are not enough. He must also have simple information to help his mind *organize* what he receives through his senses. This information allows him to compare differences, similarities, and degrees. It helps him become aware of and appreciate the world around him. Dr. Maria Montessori, who developed the Montessori method of teaching, called this, "education of the senses."

Chapter 5
Learning Through the Senses

Norma Nathanson & Tara Greaney

Just by eating an apple,
a child experiences
a variety of sensations.

Just by eating an apple, a child experiences a variety of sensations. Children use all five senses: smell, sight, hearing, touch, and taste. They not only learn through them all — but they also enjoy the various experiences. By looking around your environment, you can find many ways to enhance their development.

Dr. Maria Montessori, the first woman doctor in Italy, noted in her studies of childhood that there are certain sensitive periods for particular learning accomplishments, especially from birth to six years. During this period of exploring the world through the senses, the child forms "sensorial concepts." By focusing on one sense at a time, such as "touch," children learn the vocabulary for that sense, with words like *hot, cold, sharp*, etc. These actual experiences are the foundation of the child's ability to understand more difficult concepts in the future.

THE FIVE SENSES

Sight
More than eighty percent of information about our world comes to us through our eyes. From the moment a seeing child is born he collects, reflects, and attempts to make sense out of what he has perceived. He begins to recognize the *familiar* — people who love him; the *pleasing* — bright colors of toys and mobiles; the *responsive* — the nurturing care-giver; the *physical shape* of his surroundings — what is too far to reach, too high to jump, too dark or "scary."

Ultimately, each slight difference he sees will have meaning. Each curved or straight line will have similarities and differences. As these become recognizable, he will eventually learn to read.

Taste
From the time infants are able, they put everything into their mouths. Take advantage of this fact. Remove everything (small or dangerous items) that should *not* go into your preschooler's mouth, but expose him to the things that he *may* taste. Make him aware that food is something that should not just be eaten, but should be enjoyed for its variety of tastes. Make him aware that there are four distinct taste sensations: *sweet, sour, salty, bitter.* Teach your child that he tastes with his tongue. Let your child taste new foods and learn about the words that describe them: *wet, dry, crunchy, mushy, soft, hard, chewy, minty, hot, cold.*

Children are reassured to know that as we grow our taste buds change, and if they do not like a food now, it's worth trying again in six months or so to see if one's taste buds have "grown up."

Smell

Make your child aware of her sense of smell. Help her become aware by exposing her to various odors and giving her the vocabulary to describe these new odors. Initially, things smell "nice," "yucky," "like a flower," "like the pizza place." Through vocabulary enrichment she can become more aware of the various odors and can start to label them: "That smells like cinnamon." "Are you baking bread?" "Someone must be barbecuing." Preschoolers are fascinated by the fact that it is one's nose that smells and want to know how it works.

Blowing one's nose becomes a more important thing to master when the child realizes he cannot "smell" at his best with a clogged nose.

Hearing

Hearing begins in the womb. The newborn is often calmed by the first internal sounds he hears, such as the heartbeat and the sounds of liquid. As the child grows, clues that he hears are essential in determining the emotional tone of a situation, the physical boundaries of a space, and the presence of oncoming dangers. These clues also provide a basis for learning language. The joys of sound include laughter, music, and poetry.

When older preschoolers are interested in learning how the ear actually works, there are books that are specifically designed for young children. (See Resources on page 61.)

Touch

It is natural for children to want to touch *everything*. Infants instinctively reach and grasp, and learn the consequence of their actions. Children love to snuggle with their favorite "blankie." They learn what kind of touching is appropriate and what kind is unacceptable. Let them touch everything *that is safe to touch*. Keep all unsafe or breakable objects out of reach. Children should not be constantly exposed to things that are visually attractive but may not be touched.

Children instinctively incorporate all new information through as many senses as possible. That's why babies see an object, grab it, notice if it makes a noise, eat it, and smell it, before tossing it aside. On the next five pages, you will find a variety of sensory activities that will be fun for you to enjoy with your preschooler.

Family Fun Activities

Norma Nathanson, Tara Greaney & Diana Stanley

SIGHT

Beginning with peek-a-boo and loving looks, you can help to provide visual experiences for your growing child.

• When showing colors, shapes, and textures to your child, say to her, "This is a circle and it is green." In a colorful magazine picture, ask, "What can we find that is green?" Reinforce the color names at every opportunity, using items in nature (grass, leaves) and personal items, "Your sweater is green."

• Use fingerpaint or watercolors to show how two colors can be mixed together to produce a third color.

• Turn refrigerator magnets into a learning game. Ask questions like, "Can you find the magnet with the letter — M?" Or, "Can you find two square magnets and three circle magnets?" This game will help your child look carefully for specific details. Try magazines for a different version of this game. Tell your child, "Somewhere in this magazine, there's a picture of a (little boy brushing his teeth, a rabbit or other known item), can you find it?"

• Grade sizes. Spread out a set of stackable measuring cups on the table. Ask your child to stack them together. Try measuring spoons once she has mastered the cups. In this type of game, your child's eyes must discern the difference in size.

• Play a matching game. On a table, spread plastic containers and matching lids in a variety of sizes. Ask your child to match the lids to the containers. For a young preschooler, use just 3 containers in extremely different sizes. For older preschoolers, try 4 or more containers in similar sizes.

TASTE

At the food store:
• Each time you go shopping, have your child play detective and find a few fruits (fresh, dried, or canned), vegetables or cheeses that he has never eaten.

• Point out the difference between the raw product (an apple) and a processed food (apple sauce).
• Tell your preschooler about the five food groups: breads and cereals, fruits, vegetables, meat or meat alternative, and dairy. See if he can guess which group an item belongs to.

At home:
• Let your child become involved in food preparation and cleanup. Preschoolers love to spread (with butter knives), mix and shake, and present their own creations for you to taste.

• When preparing food, let your child taste each ingredient as you add it in, then again as it is mixed with other ingredients. Finally, let her taste the cooked product. Often the individual items do not taste anything like the end product. *(For safety's sake, do not let children taste raw foods that may not be safe to eat — such as eggs.)*

• Have your preschooler make her own combinations of foods and experiment with the outcome. For instance, truly nutritious snacks can be made of various combinations of mashed bananas, peanut butter, oatmeal, raisins, cinnamon, apple sauce, and shredded cheese.

• Experiment with taste. Set out a few taste experiments so your child can discover how foods similar in appearance can taste very different. Compare water and vinegar, salt and sugar, bitter and sweet chocolate.

Mealtime:
• Name that taste. During dinner, take turns naming the taste of foods on your plate. Give your preschooler the opportunity to experience all four tastes — sweet, sour, bitter, and salty.

Meals should become a time to enjoy and share both the food and the company without pressure to finish everything. Discuss interesting facts about the food: milk comes from cows, bananas are grown in Central and South America, chocolate tastes sweet, etc. This not only promotes social development, but also language development and sensory awareness.

SMELL
• Have your child close his eyes (or use a blindfold) and identify the odors from food.

• Walk your youngster to different rooms in the house and have him tell you what he smells: flowers, the laundry soap, bread in the toaster, etc.

• Let your preschooler smell the spices in your kitchen cabinet. Tell him the names of each spice. Make him aware of the variety in life.
• Have your child smell things in the bathroom such as: soap, toothpaste, and tissues.

• Take the opportunity to point out to your child the array of smells in this world — a bakery, a lumberyard, a park, the ocean. Memories are often recalled by a whiff of a specific odor, such as the smell of a pine forest.

<u>HEARING</u>

Activities that develop your child's sense of hearing prepare her to distinguish the small differences in the similar sounds of our alphabet such as **p** and **b, s** and **z, m** and **n**. This skill is needed for writing words and reading.

• Begin a tape collection for your child. Most variety stores carry inexpensive tapes. Choose some music with solo instruments to help your child become acquainted with the sound of specific instruments. Share simple information about the composer, for instance, Mozart wrote music when he was five — a preschooler! An easy-to-use tape player will help your child gain independence as she selects music and masters the controls on her own.

• Learn a new language. Children, six and under, have the ability to learn a foreign language easily. Some foreign language tapes are produced specifically for children. You can also check out foreign language books for beginners at your library. Begin with a few words each week and progress according to your child's interest.

• Find the bell. This is the perfect game to play before bedtime because your child must quietly concentrate and move cautiously. To play, slip a blindfold (a wide terry cloth head band works well) over your child's eyes. Ring a bell from across the room. Ask your child to move towards the sound until she finds it. The blindfold will isolate your child's hearing so she must rely only on this sense to find the sound.

• Tell a story without pictures. In our extremely visual society, children often have limited opportunities to create their own mental images. Help your child visualize the stories she hears or reads. Ask her to close her eyes while you read. Encourage her to create pictures for the story in her mind.

• Listen and identify sounds of common objects outside the house: trucks, fire engines, animals, etc. Inside the house, listen for sounds such as dishwashers, running water, and closing doors.

• Draw or paint to music for a creative use of the senses.

• Read poems and stories to your preschooler and listen to records with him. This is so important to creative thinking, as it helps him to use his imagination.

<u>TOUCH</u>

• When preparing food, let your children put their clean hands into everything! Have them close their eyes and feel the lettuce, pudding, flour, etc. Ask them how it feels. Is it hard, soft, rough, smooth, cold, wet, dry, smooth, bumpy, sticky? Discuss it later. Have them close their eyes again and see if they can recall the feel of the flour, pudding, etc.

• A feather's touch. Some items your child will want to feel or handle require a delicate touch. To demonstrate this "feather touch" stroke your child's arm or hand with a feather. Talk about how light and gently the feather touches her arm. Delicate sea shells, a pet hamster, and holiday ornaments all require a feather's touch.

• Discovering weights. Ask your child to hold her hands palms up with elbows off the table. Place one can of fruit, vegetable or other canned items in each hand. Instruct, "Put the heaviest (or lightest) one down first." Try cans or boxes of food that are equal in size but drastically different in weight.

• Point out that you can touch with other parts of the body such as toes, or elbows.

• With your finger trace a shape, number, or letter on the back of your older preschooler — can he identify what it is?

• Make your child's name in sand or sprinkles. On a sturdy paper or board drip glue to form his name, shake sand, glitter, corn meal, popcorn, or dry alphabet noodles on top of the glue. When it dries—have him "feel" his name. Make a collection of various versions of the name.

• Match textures. Before you toss out worn clothing, cut 2 squares from the fabric. (Remove all of the buttons for the next activity.) Collect a variety of textures like felt, satin, cotton and flannel. Blindfolded, your child can find the matching pairs by feeling the fabric with her fingertips.

• Match sizes. For this activity, you will need about 3 sets of 2 matching buttons. *(Caution: Buttons are a choking hazard. Use only with older preschoolers under supervised conditions.)* Each set should vary greatly in size or shape. Put the buttons in a bag. Ask your child to put her hand inside the bag and pull out one button. Then pick another that feels the same. Add more sets, once your child has mastered the first three.

These games and exercises are learning experiences that add to the delight of living. As your preschooler learns through all of his senses, he can truly explore the wonder of the world around him.   ❖

Chapter 6
Using Both Sides
of the Brain

Elizabeth J. Webster

Both left and
right brain are right

While the research into left and right brain dominance is fairly new —
this section will 1) explain how children's behavior is influenced by the
dominant side of their brain, and 2) offer parents and teachers activities to
help develop both sides of the child's brain.

Throughout this discussion of dominance, it is necessary to keep in mind
that both sides of the brain are important.

Both left and right brain are *right*
The preschool years are a crucial time for the development of brain
functions. During these years each child develops a unique way of
perceiving his own world, *thinking* about it, and *interacting* with it.

In addition to differences in personality and temperament, children have
been classified into two groups on the basis of how they perceive and think.
The groups are "left-brain dominant," or "right-brain dominant."

Because the largest part of the brain (the cerebrum) is divided from front to
back into two parts, the halves are referred to as left and right. Although
both sides of the brain are used, (the halves are connected) the half that is
used most comfortably will be dominant over the other.

*Dominance of one side of the brain is not better than dominance of the
other. Each is extremely useful, each produces different behaviors, and each
must be developed as the child grows.*

What does each side's dominance mean?
*Gary, Michael, and Hanna — all age 5 — were playing in the same room. Hanna
asked both boys to look at her crayon drawing of a bright red house, a totally green
tree, and a yellow sun. Gary responded immediately, "Oh, you've made a pretty
sunshine day!" Michael studied the picture a moment, then said, "The tree should
have some brown here (pointing to the trunk of the tree) and the house is bigger
than the sun, but that's okay, it's pretty."*

When Gary and Michael first saw the picture it *registered* on the left side of
their brains —because that is where sight and sounds are first registered.
However, although both Gary and Michael saw the same picture, their
reactions to the picture were totally different. Gary saw the whole picture
and it reminded him of a "sunshine day" (right brain). Michael, however,
did not see the entire picture before he saw its details (left brain).

Summary of left brain abilities

What is seen and heard is understood first in the left brain. This half contains the area which enables the child to understand language and to speak. Without the left brain, there would be little understandable language and speech.

Left-brain activity is essential for analytical thinking. It enables the child to learn about differences between categories, for example: that dogs are different from cats.

Left-brain children can recall and work with detailed information. This ability helps them to remember instructions, learn to recognize words to form sentences, and later to remember the order of letters to spell words.

Because as they develop they can think more and more analytically, they may be very good later on at such educational tasks as arithmetic, algebra, and logic. It is likely that successful practitioners in fields such as accounting, law, and engineering have left-brain dominance.

Summary of right brain abilities

The right brain is responsible for creative, imaginative, theoretical thinking, and it can conceive of a larger viewpoint and of possibilities for action.

Right-brain children create unusual sentences, tell imaginative stories, think of new and interesting ways to use toys, create new games, and are able to visualize possibilities.

The right brain is where artistic expressions begin: it is responsible for the creation of painting, music, and literature. It also seems to be the center for spontaneous appreciation of the artistic expressions of others (as in the example of Gary's response to Hanna's drawing).

In later educational endeavors right-brain children may have to work hard to learn the detail required of memorizing, spelling, and arithmetic. However, as adults, they may have rich and varied vocabularies by which to express themselves and will be good at activities such as creative writing, theoretical mathematics, and creative architecture.

The task of helping to develop brain functions
Both left and right brains are essential for learning the tasks necessary for human development. At the preschool level much attention and reinforcement are focused on left-brain skills, for example, learning to say the letters of the alphabet, to count, to remember and follow instructions. Children to whom such skills come easily are often considered the "smart" ones. Parents and teachers need to recognize that both left and right brains are essential to human development.

The activities on the following pages are designed to work from a child's strength to stimulate the other half of her brain.

Activities for Developing the Less Dominant Side of the Brain

Elizabeth J. Webster

How to help the right-brain child utilize the left brain

If a child finds it difficult to remember details, it is probably because she is right-brain dominant. The adult—parent or teacher—has the task of activating the right brain, *and then asking the child to give left-brain responses.* It is important to keep instructions simple and to the point.

Activities:
• *Listen to music together.* Have her tell you when she hears a certain instrument: drum, piano, guitar, etc. Because right-brain children enjoy just *listening to* music, rather than *analyzing it*, use this activity sparingly.

• *Have her tell you what happened on TV.* After she watches a TV program such as *Mr. Rogers Neighborhood* or *Sesame Street* ask her to tell you about it. (She will use the left brain to remember details.)

• *Have her tell you what happened in a story you just read to her.* This is similar to the previous activity.

• *Have her act as a "helper" in one of your activities.* When cooking you can ask her to bring you a variety of kitchen utensils (spoon, strainer, etc.) This allows her to create the role of helper (right brain) and then carry out the details (left brain).

• *Let her decide how the two of you play together.* Let her take the lead in directing the play, within acceptable limits, of course. For example, when Karen was at her grandmother's they often played what Karen called "going grocerying." As they walked around each room Karen first pretended she was driving a car, then pretended that one or the other was pushing a shopping cart. She would instruct her grandmother about what to select from imaginary shelves. After much walking her grandmother would become tired, and Karen would lead her to a chair and say to her, "You wait in the car; I'll finish up." Karen's imagination (right brain) could be active here, while her instructions were left-brain activity.

How to help the left-brain child
utilize the right brain

The left-brain child will need experience with creating, imagining, and getting in touch with his non-analytical side. The adult — parent or teacher — has the task of activating the left brain, *and then asking the child to give right-brain responses.*

Activities:
• *Listen to music.* In addition to knowing which instruments are used, it is important to ask him *how the music makes him feel.* If he cannot tell you how he feels, both of you should act out what the music makes you feel like doing: marching, dancing, clapping, etc.

• *Find unusual uses for familiar objects.* Make a game of thinking up new uses for everyday objects. For instance, a toothbrush can be used to a) give a doll a bath, b) polish intricate silverware, c) put shoe polish in seams of shoes, etc. Free up your imagination.

• *Use props for imaginative play.* Michael asked his father, an airline pilot, what he did when he flew a plane. The father put two kitchen chairs side by side, and with Michael as his copilot asked him to pretend that there were instruments and a windshield in front of him — and passengers behind him — just like in an automobile. Then Michael and his father took an imaginary plane ride. At first Michael had difficulty imagining this play experience, but later in the week he played his father's role with his younger sister, and *they* flew a big plane with hundreds of passengers.

• *Use large and small muscles to become more creative.* Blocks, cars, dolls, toy animals, and trains can be used with boys, girls, and adults for imaginary play.

• *Encourage creativity in art.* Let the child determine how a house or a tree should look. When he shows you a drawing, instead of asking him what it is, your response could be, "My, you've used lots of bright colors."

To summarize, the purpose of these suggested activities is to build on what the child does well to help him experience what is harder for him to learn. These everyday types of activities are just as useful and more enjoyable to both children and adults than those that are contrived solely for children's learning.

Chapter 7
Cooking = Learning

Anne Moriarity

12 Ways Preschoolers Learn Through Food Preparation

Cooking equals learning in many forms

A group of preschoolers are clustered around the snack preparation table, preparing muffin batter. Robbie holds an egg carefully, remarking that it is smooth, cold, and breakable. He waits while Keisha measures out a cup of flour and pours it into the bowl. Mei comments that the batter is harder to stir than it was before the cup of flour was added. Then Lexi holds the bowl still, while Justin takes a turn stirring the batter.

Initially, such a messy and often lengthy activity may seem daunting to parent and teacher alike. However, if parents and teachers knew that this one activity fosters at least 12 types of learning experiences, they probably would be enthusiastic to schedule it at home and at school.

12 Ways Preschoolers Learn Through Food Preparation

1) *Science concepts* are introduced and expanded during food preparation and cooking activities. Children learn how foods change when mixed together, as Mei did when flour was added to the muffin batter, or how food changes when it is heated or cooled. Just as a scientist does, children will use their five senses (sight, hearing, smell, touch, and taste) to make observations, such as Robbie's comments about the egg. They can observe various characteristics of foods, including color, shape, texture, and taste.

2) Health issues are discussed during food preparation, such as how foods are divided into five basic groups (Breads and Cereals, Fruits, Vegetables, Meat or Meat Alternatives, and Milk and Milk Products) all of which we must eat each day to remain healthy. Another health issue, that of good handwashing practices, is naturally introduced during food preparation.

3) *Math concepts* can be introduced or reinforced during the preparation of food. When measuring and weighing ingredients, children are learning about volume (1 cup of water) and weight (6 ounces of gelatin) and the concepts of "more than" and "less than." Some cooking projects also require dividing, such as dividing batter into 12 muffin cups or cutting a stick of butter in half. Using a timer to measure baking time fosters children's understanding of the concept of time.

4) *Sequencing* (what comes first, next, and last) is not only an important skill in math, but is also important in itself, as an aid in processing instructions and as part of general problem solving. Sequencing is reinforced by using a step-by-step process in assembling the ingredients and utensils, then following the recipe, and finally, cleaning up.

5) *Reading* a recipe is a language development activity. Rereading and rechecking the procedure outlined in the recipe shows children the process a good reader uses in reading recipes.

6) *Language development* can be stressed during food preparation by encouraging descriptions of ingredients, and using alternate descriptive words to describe the process of preparation. For example, you can describe mixing as blending, stirring, whipping, etc.

7) Both the *left brain and right brain* can be utilized in food preparation projects. As detailed on pages 33 and 34, measuring, sequencing and counting are left-brain activities, while designing a beautiful platter of food or creating a new recipe are right-brain activities. Food preparation activities can be structured to build on an individual's *strengths:* for example, the child whose right side of the brain is dominant can help others with arranging the food. It can also be used to encourage children to *increase their use of the non-dominant side:* for example, the child whose right brain is dominant can be encouraged to measure ingredients.

8) Children also learn the art of *cooperation* through cooking projects. Group food preparation necessitates taking turns, sharing tasks, and helping others, such as when Lexi holds the bowl so Justin can stir effectively. Cooperation also can be introduced by having each child bring one item needed for the recipe. Discussion can be initiated about such ideas as how turns will be taken, how the recipe would have differed if one child hadn't contributed, and how to serve the food.

9) Being a *food taster* can be learned. Being an adventurous food taster comes naturally to some children. But for those who hesitate, being involved through preparing the food, or by contributing an ingredient may be the only incentive need to spur children on to taste a new food item. The focus is not on asking children to <u>like</u> all foods, but on encouraging them to try new foods.

10) *Learning to cook,* which is a real-life skill, is important for both boys and girls. Children can master many culinary skills if given the chance and some patient guidance. Four year olds can learn to slice most fruits and vegetables using "pumpkin cutters" (small knives with large but dull teeth).

11) *Creativity* can be fostered in food preparation, by altering a recipe when an ingredient is unavailable or unacceptable to the children, or when a specific utensil is missing. Naming a new recipe is especially enjoyable for young children.

12) *Both large-motor and small-motor development* are addressed through routine food preparation. Kneading, rolling dough, and stirring a stiff dough all engage large muscles, while measuring, cutting and pouring enhance fine-motor control (using the small muscles in the fingers). The many tasks involved in measuring, slicing, mixing, and pouring help preschoolers with eye-hand coordination — useful when learning to write later on.

Whether in a one-on-one situation at home or in a one-on-seven situation in a preschool room, food preparation can be an exceptionally valuable learning experience. As our preschoolers wash, peel, mash, stir, measure, knead, pour, read, discuss and, of course, taste during cooking activities, they are learning naturally, by being involved in a meaningful activity.

Be creative, talkative, and flexible (and be ready for a mess, which your child can help clean up). And above all, have fun as you introduce your preschooler to a host of learning experiences.

Favorite Foods to Prepare with Preschoolers

Anne Moriarity

The following food preparation activities encourage *muscle development* as children cut, pour, or stir; *math concepts* as they measure ingredients and time the baking; and *language development* as they describe the food they are preparing.

Children are also involved in *science experiences* as they discuss food groups and observe changes made when heating the food. They are learning *cooperation* as they take turns and share the snack; and they become *food tasters,* as they try new foods. In addition, these activities are delicious fun!

Graham Cracker Smash
graham crackers
apple sauce
small plastic bags

Place graham crackers in plastic bag. Push air out. Close bag and have child smash graham crackers using fist. Spoon apple sauce into small bowl or cup. Have child open bag and pour graham cracker bits over apple sauce.

Mini Pizzas
pizza crust (pita bread, English muffin,
sliced French bread, pizza dough,
or prepackaged refrigerated biscuits)
spaghetti sauce, grated mozzarella cheese,
grated Parmesan cheese, or other toppings if desired

If using unbaked dough, press into small circles and bake as directed. With adult help, children can grate cheese. Let children spread a tablespoon of sauce on each pizza crust, sprinkle cheese on top, and then add grated Parmesan cheese or toppings. Bake at 425 degrees for 8-12 minutes, until cheese is melted and bubbling. Cut into quarters to serve.

Peanut Butter Balls
1 cup peanut butter
5 Tablespoons nonfat dry milk
4 Tablespoons honey (note: do not feed honey
to children under 2 years of age)
Optional Ingredients: shredded coconut,
wheat germ, sesame seeds, raisins

Mix together ingredients. Form into balls. Let children choose items they would like from the optional ingredients. Balls may be rolled in sesame seeds. Eat at room temperature, or refrigerate.

Cereal Crunch
Ingredients: various crunchy cereals
(low-sugar types preferred)

Parents: Look through your pantry for different cereals and have your child mix a variety of them for a new taste.

Teachers: Ask each child to bring in 1/2 cup of any crunchy cereal. Each child pours his/her cereal into a large bowl and stirs it. This recipe serves as many children as participate.

Shake a Salad
A variety of tossed salad ingredients,
cut into small pieces: various greens, carrots, celery, green pepper,
cucumber, tomatoes, broccoli, cauliflower, zucchini, croutons

This is another cooperative snack. Children may take turns adding an item to a large, clean, plastic bag and shaking it. Put on plates and add salad dressing if desired. (In the preschool, teachers may assign each child to contribute one salad item.)

Friendship Fruit Salad

May be created in the same manner. Children wash fruits. Adult quarters and cores fruit. Three year olds may slice soft fruit, such as bananas, with a butter knife; older preschoolers may cut fruit into bite-sized pieces, using a "pumpkin cutter" a knife with a large, dull serrated edge. (With any cutting activity, however, close supervision is a must.) When fruits are cut, place in a large bowl, mix, and enjoy.

Chapter 8
The Benefits of Play

Betty Farber & Louise M. Ward

*Play...is the major way in which
young children learn about the world
and how they can cope with it.*

We grownups often think of play as frivolous, or even useless. Sometimes we look at play as "busywork" — something we accept in young children because they are not yet ready to take on the really serious business of going to school or working for a living. However, play is the child's dominant activity during the preschool years — one of life's most rapid periods of learning. Child development experts say that play is really the "work" of childhood.

Play can be a rich creative experience and is the major way in which young children learn about the world and how they can cope with it. Play is invaluable in the young child's development: emotionally, physically, intellectually, and socially.

Play Helps With Emotional Development

Play is valuable emotionally, as a way of overcoming the anxieties of childhood, as well as working through traumatic experiences, such as illness or loss. It is a way your preschooler can work through his fears and conflicts, by pretending to be someone else -— even by being the monster he is afraid of!

The child development authority Erik Erikson, in discussing play and emotional development, points out that children can play out their fears, angers, disappointments, and other hard experiences when they are not yet able to talk them out as adults do. The wise adult recognizes that when children play out such experiences they are able to cope with their emotions more constructively.

Play Helps With Self-esteem

First and foremost, play is <u>fun</u>. And, when you are having fun you tend to feel good about *yourself,* your *interactions with others,* and *the world around you.* In play a child can experience his greatest chance to be in control of his environment and activities. This promotes an "I can" rather than an "I can't" approach to life, and enhances a sense of competence and openness to learning.

Play Develops Motor Abilities

When your child rides her tricycle or climbs on the jungle gym she is developing her large muscles and enhancing her coordination and strength. When she puts pieces into a puzzle she is using her fine motor skills and aiding her eye-hand coordination.

Play Benefits Intellectual Development

Play gives your child the chance to try out new ideas, to problem solve, and to meet new challenges. In play, children are buffered from the ordinary consequences of making mistakes ("You did it wrong") and therefore are willing to try things they have not yet mastered. Play gives your child the chance to examine an object, such as a toy, to see what it can do, to explore how many ways he can manipulate it. It is a way in which your child can practice a skill until he can master it. It is for this reason an authority on play said, "Play is the trampoline on which children spring to their highest level of thought."

As your preschooler interacts with blocks, for example, any way he builds his towers is correct. As he progresses, he learns to make more imaginative and complex structures.

When he pretends to be another person, such as a police officer, teacher, or astronaut — he is learning how it feels to be those persons and how to act in many different roles. When he plays games, in order to play well, he must learn strategies. For example, when playing "hide and seek," he must continually find places to hide so that he won't be found easily.

Play Aids In Communication And Social Skills

Communication is first of all a social phenomena. One of the first social acts observed in very young children is to show a toy to an adult saying non- verbally that they expect a response. ("Oh, is that your new duck ?") Infant games such as patty-cake begin the learning of turn-taking. Communication skills and social skills continue to be closely linked. Children don't just talk. They talk about what they do, and play is the major vehicle through which the early development of these skills occur.

When your child plays, her speaking, listening, and social skills are enhanced as she talks, listens, and interacts with others. For example, when playing house, words must be used to act out roles like mother or father.

Now that you have seen its many benefits, you can observe your child at play with the happy thought: "My child is doing something very important — he's playing!"

Stages of Play

Betty Farber

Prepare for landing —

Your child begins to play in infancy and will continue to play throughout his adult life.

Jean Piaget, the famous child psychologist whose research contributed greatly to ideas about child development, divided play into three general stages: *sensorimotor play, symbolic play,* and *games with rules.* The age when a child enters a new stage varies with each individual child. However, the stages remain in this sequence, each stage building on what has gone before.

Sensorimotor Play
At the earliest stage, your infant becomes aware of the materials in her environment without deliberately meaning to put them to constructive use. She may, for example, at a few months old, start to swat at a mobile over her crib. As she hits the mobile and it moves, she repeats her actions, tries new actions, and then imitates those actions.

As she advances in this stage, your baby starts to manipulate objects deliberately, shaking a rattle or pushing a train that is attached to her crib railing. She learns that her actions have a consequence.

The social uses of play begin. Your baby starts to interact with people: play activities take place between you and your child, such as peek-a-boo or patty-cake.

Later in this stage, your child begins to use manipulative toys, such as wooden cars or plastic sorting blocks, for longer periods of time. At this point, if there are other children playing in the same room, she may engage in "parallel play," playing near the other children without interacting with them. This is the forerunner of actually playing with other youngsters.

Symbolic Play

In this stage, your preschooler begins to encode his experiences in symbols. A symbol is something that stands for something else; for in-stance, your preschooler can pretend that a block is a truck. Symbolic play is based on imagination. It begins as a very personal expression of your child's experiences. For example, if your child has been on a plane trip, he may arrange chairs in a row to make an airplane and have all of his stuffed animals join him on the journey, while he flies the plane himself.

In this stage of play, your child can acknowledge the real world and at the same time substitute an imaginary situation that satisfies his personal needs and wishes.

As children develop, they become able to think about and symbolize not only their own experiences, but also the experiences of others. Cooperative dramatic play emerges in which your preschooler pretends to be various persons, (Mommy, Daddy or Baby; pilot, Superhero, etc.), with the action continuing for an extended period of time. In this way, your preschooler is learning how one might act in many different roles.

As she pretends, your youngster may imitate what she thinks is adult speech, or she may use words to explain an imaginary situation: "I'll be the Mommy and I'm driving to the supermarket to buy food for supper." As children play, they talk about what they are doing; they communicate with others; they plan events. Symbolic play is the basis for language and intellectual development.

Games with Rules

This is the final stage in play development. Games with rules are most important *after* the preschool years. In this stage, your child accepts prearranged rules in games such as checkers or baseball. Your youngster learns to control her behavior, wait her turn, move within given limits, and react to other players' actions. This is the principal form of play that carries into adult life.

Preschoolers often feel upset when they lose at a game, even when adults try to explain that someone has to win and someone has to lose. But young children might not be ready to understand that idea. They are not being "poor sports." Young children are called "egocentric" by Piaget. They cannot see the world from another person's point of view. To congratulate the winner when he wanted to win himself, would not go along with the young child's egocentric thinking. If he is not the winner himself, he will have difficulty in seeing the game from the winner's perspective.

More About Stages of Play

The stages of play described here may overlap, but at any given time one stage of play appears most prominent. For example, a toddler in the sensorimotor stage might take his daddy's hat, put it on and say, "Me Daddy." This is an example of symbolic play. But in most of his play, your toddler will manipulate materials such as pegs and pull-toys and he will not engage in symbolic play for any extended period of time. Your older preschooler will continue to enjoy manipulative toys while being able to use them in more imaginative ways as he enters the stage of symbolic play. Late in that stage, he will gradually move into playing some games with rules.

The stages in play listed above are true for children in a general way. As always, it is important to remember that your child is an individual, with individual preferences and needs. That fact will be reflected in his play. ▨

Parental Role in Making Play Better

Betty Farber

When can I find time to play with my child?

Children can find much joy and learning while playing alone or with other children when no adult is involved. Nevertheless, adult involvement, whether in small or large amounts of time, can make what is good about play better.

Although it is difficult for many parents to find <u>time</u> to play with their children, there are many moments when you can include play along with the routine of the day. If you drive your preschooler to school in the car, you both can think of some of the ways imagination can make the trips more lively. While you are preparing dinner and setting the table your youngster might like to pretend to be an assistant cook or a waiter. When you are watching him in his bath, can you think of ways in which imaginative play can be part of that time you have together?

How can I interact with my child during play?

Many adults find it difficult to develop an attitude of playfulness. They are more comfortable with adult-directed play, and they say, "Let's build a house with the blocks," or "Here's what this toy is supposed to do." There is certainly a place for this kind of adult function but very much of it takes the playfulness out of play for the child and he may quickly lose his enthusiasm.

Adults can make their biggest contribution to play when the play activities are child directed. The child chooses the activities, determines how the activities are to proceed, and controls the direction of the conversation. (Of course, adults must set the limits that protect the safety of persons and property.) The child is the creator, the experimenter, and the major problem solver. The adult follows the child's lead, responding to what she can understand of the child's world of meaning. This kind of adult involvement is especially important for imaginative play.

When you are joining your child in imaginative play, remember to address her as the character she is pretending to be. For example, if your youngster is holding her doll, you could ask, "How is your baby feeling today?" If your preschooler answers in her role as the "Mommy," "Oh, she has a little cold, and I took her to the doctor," you can continue the conversation. If she does not take up the role play, you should drop the conversation. The important point is that you follow your child's lead.

What more can I do to make play better?

Sometimes a prop can help. For example, paper "tickets" can make being a "train conductor" more real to your child. Or a piece of material for a cape can be just what is needed for a "Superhero." An old sheet thrown over a bridge table makes a wonderful "house" or tent or cave for a small child. A large cardboard box can become a boat or a car or a rocket ship.

PROPS FOR PRETEND PLAY

Pretend play gives children a chance to use their imaginations, take on different roles, and try to understand the world around them. You can put together a variety of materials for all different kinds of pretend play. Props can be grouped together so that children can use their imaginations to play at: supermarket, post office, train, hospital, cleaning service, etc.

Supermarket Props: Cash register, play money, paper bags, empty cartons, food boxes and cans. *(For safe play, check that cans have smooth edges.)*

Post Office Props: Pencils, holiday stamps, rubber stamps, stamp pads, envelopes, canvas bag for delivering mail, shoe boxes as mail boxes.

Train Props: Conductor's hat, tickets, play money, hole puncher, chairs in a row for seats.

Hospital Props: Doctor's white coat, candy pills, stethoscope, bandages, cotton balls.

Cleaning Service Props: Apron, child-sized brooms, dust cloths, mops, sponges, soap, paper towels, dish towels.

Tea Party Props: Dress-up hats and clothes, unbreakable pitchers, cups and saucers, napkins, tablecloth, spoons, flowers in a vase, juice, cookies.

Chapter 9
Guidelines to Help You Choose Toys

Michael K. Meyerhoff

*...there is still a 50-50 chance
that whatever you select
for your child
will be less appealing to her
than the box, paper, and ribbon
in which it was wrapped.*

Choosing toys for young children can be a trying and tricky experience, and many first-time parents end up investing a lot of time, energy, and money in the process of purchasing playthings for their preschoolers. However, experienced parents will tell you that even with the best of luck, there is still a 50-50 chance that whatever you select for your child will be less appealing to her than the box, paper, and ribbon in which it was wrapped. Therefore, in order to keep your fussing, frustration, and financial strain to a minimum, focus on the following factors.

Safety

Safety is the <u>first</u> consideration when choosing toys for preschoolers. During the last few years, the federal government has gone a long way to protect young children from their playthings. There are now regulations which prohibit toys manufactured for preschoolers at certain ages from having *lead-based paint, removable parts that are less than 1 1/4-inch in any dimension* (which could be swallowed and choked upon), *sharp edges, corners, or protrusions, flammable elements, dangerous projectiles,* and various other hazards. However, it still is wise to double-check all items yourself to be sure — especially imported products, hand-me-downs, and garage-sale specials. *(Information may be obtained from the United States Consumer Product Safety Commission, Washington, D.C. 20207. 1-800-638-2772.)*

Durability

While older children can be instructed to take care of their playthings, this generally is an unrealistic admonition for toddlers and younger preschoolers. Regardless of how the toy was designed to be used, young children will chew on it, pull at it, bang it, drop it, and otherwise heap abuse upon it — and they will do so with a strength that will surprise their parents. Recently, several toy manufacturers have begun to offer lifetime guarantees against breakage on some of their products. However, you would be well-advised to open up all boxes and check out for yourself just how tough the toys really are before you buy them. Washability is important too. Just as a toy that is broken easily will soon become a worthless safety hazard, a toy that cannot be cleaned regularly will soon become a worthless health hazard.

Play Value

The fundamental factor in determining whether or not a toy will ultimately be a worthwhile investment is the degree to which it matches the abilities and interests of the child for whom it is purchased. Due to the power of novelty, virtually any new plaything will capture the attention of a preschooler, and most will probably please her for a few minutes. However, it is a relatively rare item that will turn on a young child repeatedly and keep her entertained for long periods of time.

In general, preschoolers appreciate items that feed into the development of their sensory capacities *(such as sand or water play),* large muscle skills *(such as a ball or a tricycle),* hand-eye coordination *(like bowling pins or ring toss),* concept formation *(for example, puzzles or lotto),* and imagination *(like dress-up clothes or puppets).*

They are also drawn toward toys that allow them to achieve a feeling of mastery through challenges that are not so difficult as to be frustrating — yet not so simple as to be boring. And finally, preschoolers like to have fun. No matter how safe, durable, and appropriate an item is, they won't continue to play with it unless they derive a fair measure of pure enjoyment from doing so.

Since development proceeds so rapidly during the early years, and since each child has a unique pattern of development and a distinct personality, it is practically impossible to find a toy that will be stimulating and suitable for all preschoolers at all times. Therefore, in order to determine which items will have the most play value for *your* child, it is important for you to be thoroughly familiar with *her* specific abilities and special interests of the moment, as well as those she is likely to develop in the coming months. This won't make you infallible, and you may sometimes be confused by some common misconceptions and misleading information, but it certainly will give you the best shot at success.

Play Value Pointers

Michael K. Meyerhoff

Recommended Age Ranges

Because of the federal regulations, the recommended age ranges that are printed on toy boxes usually are reasonably reliable guides when it comes to *safety* considerations. However, there are no regulations regarding *play value*, and these recommendations often are extremely misleading in this area. Because the interests and abilities of preschoolers change so quickly, most toys will be appropriate and appreciated only for very brief and specific periods of time. But because they are in the business of selling as many toys as possible, many manufacturers routinely stretch their recommended age ranges to ludicrous limits. If you put too much faith in the manufacturers and neglect to take adequate note of your child's actual behaviors and tendencies of the moment, you may miss the mark by many months on many occasions.

Adult Perspective

Preschoolers don't buy toys for themselves, and younger ones aren't even adept at articulating their preferences. Consequently, many toy manufacturers have a tendency to design and market their products in ways that will appeal primarily to adult purchasers rather than child players. A good example of this is the routine use of Disney, Sesame Street, and other such characters to decorate toys for little toddlers. The manufacturers spend a fortune for the rights to use these famous figures, and the cost is passed along in the price of the product. However, the pleasant associations we have with these characters are developed in later childhood, and toddlers usually don't know — nor do they care about — the differences between such "stars" and generic figures. Therefore, when selecting playthings for your preschoolers, make sure you try to look at items through her eyes rather than your own.

Educational Claims

The educational progress of their preschooler is of central concern to parents, and consequently, many toy manufacturers are almost shameless when it comes to touting the educational benefits of their products. However, as long as they have ample opportunities to exercise their emerging sensory (use of the 5 senses), motor (use of the large and small muscles), and mental capacities, children will be learning constantly throughout the early years — and they will learn a lot from virtually any item with which they have an inclination to interact. In other words, there is no toy that has a special or unique power to teach a preschooler anything, and there is no particular toy that any child must have in order to develop any important skill or concept. As far as the preschool period is concerned, educational value is completely synonymous with play value, so unless your child is going to have fun with it, there is no need to purchase any item — despite what the manufacturer claims.

Adult Involvement

Throughout the preschool period, even though she will become increasingly comfortable playing alone and with peers, you will remain your child's favorite playmate. As a result, toys that encourage and enhance interactions with you will be especially appreciated by your preschooler. However, it is important to note that she will want to be an equal partner and not just a passive observer in these interactions. Therefore, make sure that beyond an initial demonstration or two, your involvement will be welcomed but not necessary for your child to use a particular item.

Homemade Alternatives

There are a number of excellent toys on the market. However, it is a rare commercial item whose play value cannot be easily equalled or surpassed by simple items that can be found in a typical household. For instance, several commercial bath toys will be appropriate and appealing for your preschooler because they provide ample opportunity for her to pour, splash, and squirt while she's in the tub. On the other hand, she will have just as much fun — if not more — with a set of plastic measuring cups, a sponge, and a nonbreakable turkey baster. Therefore, when searching for stimulating and suitable playthings for your child, you might try looking through your own closets and drawers before you head for the toy store shelves.

Expense

Spending a lot of money on a toy for a preschooler rarely makes sense. The *cost* of a toy usually increases with the number of things that it does, whereas the *play value* of a toy increases with the number of things that a child can do with it. For example, as impressive as it may be at first, an elaborate, battery-operated robot will soon become boring. On the other hand, a small collection of snap-together blocks probably will be used many times and in many different ways over the course of many months. Therefore, contrary to what adults often assume, simple, versatile items that lend themselves to varied activities will be far more appropriate for and appreciated by preschoolers than their fancy, highly structured, and relatively expensive counterparts.

Numbers

The notion that "more is better" does not apply to toys for preschoolers. Since they are getting into it and around it for the first time, the world we live in is an extremely exciting and invigorating place for young children; and they spend a lot of time having fun with and learning from play involving cardboard cartons, pots and pans, stacks of freshly-folded laundry, trash baskets, sidewalk puddles, and a variety of other "every-day" things that we adults take for granted. While an occasional commercial toy may effectively capture your child's attention and challenge her growing abilities, it is likely to be the case that the more toys she has, the more toys she will ignore — not the more toys she will play with.

Suggested Toys
for
Different Age Groups
and
Reasons for Choosing Them

Betty Farber

1 to 2 years

• *Push toys, pull toys, balls, climbers* (Toddlers enjoy action. They are learning to use their big muscles to walk, climb, and throw.)

• *Puzzles with just a few pieces with knobs, simple shape sorters, wagon with wooden blocks, nesting blocks, pegboard with large pegs, sand and water toys* (Young children like to experiment with objects, and to dump and fill. Toys such as pegs and blocks encourage use of fine muscles in the fingers.)

• *Stuffed animals, soft dolls* (Toddlers like something to hold and hug.)

• *Broom, pots and pans, shopping cart, doll carriage, unbreakable dishes, hammer toys, toy telephone* (Toddlers enjoy imitating adult behavior in play.)

• *Large books with colorful pictures and simple stories, small books they can carry around easily* (Young children are fascinated with the hinged pages of books. They like pictures of ordinary objects they can identify, or stories with just a few words on each page. Small books they can carry from room to room are often favorites with toddlers.)

• *Records with songs and rhymes, bells to ring, a drum* (Young children respond to music, are interested in sounds, and love to dance with you to music.)

• *Fat crayons, large pieces of paper* (Scribbling is not only fun but also is the first step in drawing and writing.)

2 to 3 1/2 years

• *Wagon, wheelbarrow, trucks, wagons, tricycle, large ball, large cardboard box* (This age is always on the go. They like to test their physical capabilities in large muscle play. This kind of play helps develop motor coordination and strength.)

• *Wooden unit blocks, snap-together blocks, puzzles with up to 20 pieces, sewing cards, pegboards, sand and water toys* (Children of this age are gaining more control of hands and fingers. These kinds of toys give them practice in mastering their small muscle skills.)

• *Soft, washable doll with a few clothes. Crib, cradle, doll carriage, clothes for dressing up, hand puppets* (Young preschoolers like to act out familiar events in their world.)

• *Books with simple stories that relate to their own lives, books with lots of repetition in language, poems about familiar things. Stories like The Three Bears that have some fantasy* (Vocabulary is expanding rapidly. Young children have a short attention span and need stories that are simple, with some surprises, and illustrated with colorful pictures.)

• *Records and cassettes of children's songs such as* Old MacDonald *and finger- plays such as* The Eensie Weensie Spider (Children of this age sing parts of familiar songs and love to move to music.)

• *Crayons, markers, fingerpaint, tempera paint, wide brushes, blunt scissors, paste, dough clay* (Young children enjoy learning new skills and love to experiment with creative art processes.)

3 1/2 to 5 years

• *Tricycle, bowling pins, balance beam, jump rope, ring toss, plastic bat and ball, roller skates* (Preschoolers have a need for active play. They get a sense of accomplishment through their physical abilities.)

• *Wooden unit blocks and accessories, puzzles with 20 or more pieces, beads to string, woodworking bench with hammer and nails* (This age has a longer attention span. A child can explore a toy and see how many ways he can manipulate it. Blocks are used to build elaborate constructions.)

• *Simple board games* (Preschoolers enjoy playing with friends, but they do not like to lose, and competitive games where there is a winner and loser are usually difficult for them.)

• *Play kitchen with food, puppets, dress-up clothes, miniature houses, farms, airports, stuffed toys, dolls and accessories, doctor's kit, model vehicles* (Dramatic play helps children pretend to be various people and see how they might act in different roles. It is valuable emotionally as it helps children to act out their fears and anxieties.)

• *Clay, tempera paint, various widths of brushes, crayons, chalk, markers, blunt scissors, construction paper, paste, collage materials* (Preschoolers' drawings seldom resemble a real object. Parents and teachers help by offering encouragement through acceptance of preschoolers' explorations in art. Working with art gives children a sense of their own uniqueness and creativity.)

• *Books with simple, direct plots, folk tales like The Gingerbread Man, simple science books, poems, stories on tape, wooden numbers and letters, flannel board with pictures and letters* (Preschoolers love picture books with interesting plots and characters and words that rhyme or repeat. Also interesting are wordless books where children tell the stories illustrated in the pictures, and toy books, where the reader opens flaps to find an object underneath.)

• *Rhythm instruments, tapes of children's songs, folk songs, marches, ethnic music* (Preschoolers may sing complete songs from memory; they love word play and rhyming words. They love to dance and move to music.)

5 to 6 years

Children of this age usually show interest in toys that are similar to those described above in the 3 1/2 to 5 age range. They may also enjoy riding scooters and bicycles, playing with puzzles with more pieces, joining their friends in more difficult board games, reading some books with chapters, painting with watercolors, drawing with charcoal, playing with science toys, and taking photographs with a camera.

Resources for Section One: How Young Children Learn

FOR ADULTS

Is the Left Brain Always Right? by Clare Cherry, Douglas Godwin, and Jesse Staples. Fearon, 1989. A very detailed discussion of the brain and its functions, as related to education.

The Hurried Child: Growing Up Too Fast Too Soon, by David Elkind. Addison-Wesley, 1981. An insightful look at the stress placed on young children as we hurry them to grow up.

How To Talk So Kids Can Learn At Home and In School, by Adele Faber & Elaine Mazlish. Rawson Associates/Scribner, 1995. The bestselling authors discuss what parents and teachers need to know in order to handle the problems that interfere with learning.

Before the School Bell Rings, by Carol B. Hillman. Phi Delta Kappa Educational Foundation, 1995. This paperback discusses child's play and other important topics in early childhood to help caregivers to fill young children's lives with healthy and joyful experiences. It is written by an author of two chapters in this book.

Learning Through Cooking Activities, by Amy Houts. Preschool Publications (1-800-726-1708), 1993. Amy Houts shows how cooking is not only fun for young children — but a way of learning math, science, vocabulary, and social skills.

Selecting Toys for Infants and Toddlers, by Michael K. Meyerhoff. The Epicenter, Inc. (PO Box 81326, Wellesley Hills, MA 02181), 1995. The author, an early childhood authority, has written an informative booklet to help parents and caregivers choose toys wisely. Dr. Meyerhoff is also an author of several chapters in this book.

Resources for Early Childhood, a handbook edited by Hannah Nuba et al. Garland, 1994. This important resource book includes essays and annotated bibliographies by respected experts on all aspects of child development and early childhood education.

The Best Toys, Books, Videos & Software for Kids 1997, by Joanne Oppenheim and Stephanie Oppenheim. Prima Publishing, 1997. (Oppenheim Toy Portfolio, 1-212-598-0502.) Updated every year, this book rates 1000+ products for newborns to age 10.

FOR CHILDREN

Short Train, Long Train, by Frank Asch. Scholastic Cartwheel, 1992. Designed with humor and simplicity, this book illustrates exactly what *long* and *short* mean. Youngsters turn each page to see, for example, a short car and then unfold the page to see a long car, then a short dog and a long dog, and so on, giggling as they read.

Alphabet Times Four: An International ABC, by Ruth Brown. Dutton, 1991. Here is an ABC book in four different languages: English, Spanish, French, and German, including a simple pronunciation guide.

It Begins with an A, by Stephanie Calmenson. Hyperion, 1994. Preschoolers will enjoy the riddles in this alphabet guessing game in rhyme, with cheerful illustrations by Marisabina Russo.

Where's the Fly? by Caron Lee Cohen. Greenwillow, 1996. The illustrations in this intriguing book show increasingly distant perspectives, from a fly on a dog's nose to the earth itself — introducing young children to the concept of spatial relations.

The Shape of Things, by Dayle Ann Dodds. Candlewick Press, 1994. With simple rhymes and colorful illustrations, this book can help children identify shapes in the world around them.

Now Soon Later, by Lisa Grunwald. Greenwillow, 1996. The concept of *time* can be difficult for young children to understand. This book takes a little girl through the day's activities, describing in terms preschoolers can understand, what is happening *Now,* what will happen *Soon,* and what will happen *Later.*

Animal, Vegetable, or Mineral? by Tana Hoban. Greenwillow, 1995. The photographs of this famous photographer/author will arouse children's curiosity as they guess which category fits each picture.

I Read Signs, by Tana Hoban. Mulberry Edition, 1987. Color photographs of familiar signs appear on each page of this book, with words that children can learn to recognize.

Animal Sounds for Baby, by Cheryl Willis Hudson. Scholastic Cartwheel, 1995. In a book with heavy cardboard pages for the youngest preschooler, a little African-American boy listens to the sounds of familiar animals.

Eating Fractions, by Bruce McMillan. Scholastic. 1991. In this tasty introduction to fractions, two children cut a banana into halves, rolls into thirds, and pizza into fourths, eating their way through the parts of a whole. The author's colorful photographs illustrate the book. Recipes are included.

Growing Colors, by Bruce McMillan. Lothrop, Lee & Shepard, 1988. Bright color photographs show luscious fruits and vegetables and how they grow in nature — above, in, or below the ground.

I Spy: a Book of Picture Riddles, by Jean Marzollo. Scholastic/Cartwheel, 1992. With vivid, detailed photographs by Walter Wick, this book challenges the reader to find hidden objects in the pictures.

Can You Guess? by Margaret Miller. Greenwillow, 1993. "What do you comb in the morning?" There are several silly suggestions along with a full page photograph to illustrate the correct answer. A book to reinforce logical thinking, while giving the reader many moments of fun.

I Can Tell by Touching, by Carolyn Otto. HarperTrophy, 1994. This Let's-Read-And-Find-Out-Science® book tells how we can use our hands, feet, or our whole body to discover information using the sense of touch.

Left or Right? by Karl Rehm and Kay Koike. Clarion, 1991. "The concept of left or right can be tricky for young children to master." By using much repetition, and clear color photographs, the authors help to clarify this difficult concept.

Color: a poem, by Christina Rossetti. HarperTrophy 1994. With beautiful paintings by Mary Teichman, this book uses the delightful poem by Rossetti, first published in 1871, to introduce children to colors and to poetry.

Ears Are For Hearing, by Paul Showers. Crowell, 1990. This book is in the Let's-Read-and-Find-Out Science Book series. It explains, using scientific illustrations and terms an older preschooler can understand, how our ears are able to process sound.

Do Pigs Have Stripes? by Melanie Walsh. Houghton Mifflin, 1996. With bright childlike illustrations and simple text, the author/illustrator asks questions that make young children want to think about the answers. Then they can turn the page and find out!

Section Two
Language
Development

Section Two
Language Development

Introduction

When a baby begins to babble and coo, the adults in the family are overjoyed and eagerly await the emergence of the child's first words. Yet, how do children progress from sounds like ba-ba da-da to making words and sentences? While scholars are fascinated by the acquisition of language, how it occurs remains something of a mystery.

The chapters in this section provide information about the progress of language learning in the first five years of life. While "no one has ever figured out how to teach a baby to talk," the authors discuss ways adults can *enhance* language development during early childhood. In addition, one article speaks to parents' concerns about their child's language and speech.

SECTION TWO
LANGUAGE DEVELOPMENT

Chapter 10
The Miracle of Language

Betty Farber

---

*...it is truly a miracle
that in five years,
human babies progress
to become
active communicators.*

Recently, I listened to tapes of my grandchild's voice from when she was an infant to her current age of four. I wondered how she grew from repeating sounds like ba-ba-da-da to putting together complex sentences. (Even the experts don't agree on exactly how it happens.)

The miracle of language becomes powerfully apparent when you listen to the cries and babbling of a seven-month-old baby on a tape, and then play an interview with the same child — now a chatty preschooler — who tells you a long story about what happened at her birthday party.

We do know that babbling (repetition of sounds) starts in most babies at about 4 months of age, and that it is inborn, not learned by hearing others. And the babblings that babies make are so universal that in infancy, at least, we are able to talk each other's language with ease: French, English and Japanese babies all sound alike.

Infants learn to attract attention through sounds. Gradually your baby learns how to communicate meanings through intonations. At seven months, through an insistent cry, my granddaughter, Emily, communicated the demand: "Take me out of this playpen!" And it worked because on the tape you can hear her mother say, "You want out of there?" And then peaceful silence when she picked up her baby. Communication may have begun to make sense to my infant granddaughter because others were listening and trying to interpret her sounds. She, in turn, like other babies, gradually learned to interpret other people's meanings.

At about one year old, your baby usually says his first meaningful word. Usually, these first words are related to familiar people and objects: mother, father, bottle, cookie; or words that deal with needs like: more, up, open and no.

At about one to two years old, toddlers develop a vocabulary of about 50 words, but understanding the language comes before being able to express the words. Therefore Emily understood a question like, "Where's the ball?" (especially if we started searching as we spoke) before she was able to say all those words.

At age two to three, children combine two words to form short sentences or phrases. Emily used phrases like, "All right," "A duck" and "My ball."

While *language* is the thoughts, experiences and feelings you express in words, *speech* is the manner in which you pronounce them. Emily's words were not always easy to understand except in context. (It helped to see a picture of a duck when she said those words.) A two or three-year-old's speech has not yet developed to the point where her words are understandable at all times. Some speech sounds are not acquired clearly and consistently until age six or seven.

Between three and four years old, youngsters begin to combine three or more words together to form more complex sentences. As they do, they seem to learn the rules of the language, such as: add an "s" to make a plural and add "ed" to talk about the past. Young children often overgeneralize these rules and come up with words of their own invention, such as "He comed here yesterday." When Emily talked about her drawing, she said she drew "Fingers and foots."

The four-to five-year-old child can tell a long story, but may confuse the facts. Emily told me that she wanted a particular doll and then talked about having a baby of her own. *After five years of age,* most children can be understood easily by family as well as unfamiliar persons. One could say that it is truly a miracle that in five years, human babies progress to become active communicators.

Chapter 11
Enhancing
Language Development

Michael K. Meyerhoff

*...no one has ever figured out
how to teach a baby to talk.*

I once observed a young mother diligently attempting to induce her one-year-old to say his first words. Over the course of the previous few months, she and her husband had been urging the child to "say Mama" or "say Dada" on a regular basis; and on this particular day, she was kicking the effort into high gear.

As this woman moved about the kitchen preparing the evening meal, she repeatedly passed in front of the infant who was propped in a seat nearby; and each time she captured his attention, she would lean forward and cajole, "Say Mama, say Mama, say Mama." However, despite her perseverance, each one of her overtures continued to be met by a cheerful but silent smile.

Then all of a sudden, while transferring a dish from the stove to the table, she accidentally spilled some hot gravy which splattered across the floor below; and without thinking, she let out a loud "Damn it!" To her surprise and chagrin, the infant looked up, smiled again, and repeated "Damn it!" with perfect intonation and diction .

While this incident caused considerable embarrassment and effectively prevented the child's parents from telling a delightful "first words" story to their relatives and friends, it does help to illustrate a key point about the teaching and learning of language during the early years.

Perhaps no other event of this period has received as much attention and acclaim as the onset of speech. Philosophers and theologians have expounded upon its significance for separating humans from other mammals; psychologists and educators have noted its importance not only for communication, but for the development of higher mental abilities as well. For thousands of years, mothers and fathers have anxiously and eagerly awaited the emergence of their children's first words.

Yet, despite all this, the fact of the matter is that no one has ever figured out how to teach a baby to talk.

That does not mean, however, that we know nothing about *enhancing* language development during infancy and early childhood. While the process of inducing the initial production of speech remains a mystery, we have learned that it is relatively not that important. Some children who eventually exhibit superb language skills start speaking a word or two as soon as seven or eight months of age, but some remain largely silent until they are almost two years old — at which time they often start speaking in complete sentences.

On the other hand, it is clear that all such children begin to understand a few words sometime between the sixth and eighth month — and parents who focus on this early "receptive" capacity (*understanding* language) along with the later "expressive" components (*using* language) can do a lot to insure that their child will make excellent progress in language learning.

The following are some language-enhancing practices that parents should consider using on a regular basis.

• *Talk a lot to your child, right from the beginning.* This may seem like obvious advice, but few parents actually carry it out. Human nature evidently makes us reluctant to talk to things that don't talk back. We don't regularly converse with chairs, doors, and fire hydrants, so why should it be considered natural to talk to little babies? All parents speak to their infants — even newborns — from time to time, but it may take some effort to make sure that your baby is exposed to language at every opportunity.

Interestingly, it also is apparently important that a baby be exposed to a lot of "live" language. Sitting a child next to a radio or in front of a television set, even if "Sesame Street" or some other special program is being aired, evidently just does not have the same impact as actual human speech during the early years.

• *Monitor your child's ability to hear clearly.* Profound deafness during infancy and toddler-hood is rare, and is almost always noticed during a competent medical examination. However, mild to moderate hearing losses due to ear infections, allergies, or congenital defects are comparatively common, and they often go undetected. Children who *can* hear but cannot hear *clearly* sometimes are misdiagnosed as "stubborn" or "slow" and consequently, they miss out on many months of important language processing before the real problem is corrected.

You can check your child's ability to hear quite easily, beginning at about four months of age, by standing in various positions off to the side and behind her and calling her name in a soft voice — most of the time, she should turn her head, accurately locate the source of the sound, and smile. After the first year, monitor her receptive vocabulary for steady progress — she should show signs of understanding at least a dozen words by one year of age, and about two-thirds of all everyday language by three; and once she starts talking regularly, watch for prolonged episodes of slurred speech when using even simple words.

If, for any reason, you are convinced that a problem exists, then a trip to the pediatrician is in order. Up until a few years ago, some pediatricians were reluctant to become alarmed over mild-to-moderate hearing losses because the conditions that cause them are rarely life threatening and children often "grow out" of them eventually. However, recent evidence indicating the potentially devastating consequences for language development has made them much more inclined to pursue a diagnosis and arrange proper treatment immediately.

• *Focus and expand upon what your child is interested in at the moment.* As with any instructional situation, it helps to have a highly motivated student. Once your child starts showing signs of understanding several words and begins actively exploring and investigating her environment on her own, many wonderful opportunities to teach language to an eager pupil open up.

As your child pursues her independent activities, you will find that she will approach you from time to time in order to receive comfort (if she has bumped her head or pinched a finger), to obtain assistance (if she can't find a missing puzzle piece, for example), or to share the excitement of some discovery she has made (such as a crinkly, dust-covered candy wrapper she found under the sofa). When she comes to you on these occasions, it should not be too hard to figure out what is on her mind, even if she is not yet speaking a great deal.

As you are taking care of whatever need she has indicated, simply talk to her about it in plain language (not "baby talk"), and throw in a related idea or two while you're at it. For instance, if she is excitedly exhibiting the aforementioned candy wrapper, you can say something like, "My! That's a pretty piece of paper. It's yellow. Your shirt is yellow too. And your pants are blue. Do you think we can find a blue piece of paper?" It may be only a few seconds before your child shows an inclination to resume her independent activities, but it has been demonstrated that repeated episodes of such relaxed, relevant, and *child-initiated* verbal interchanges contribute significantly to optimal language development.

• *Be careful to provide a good model for your baby.* Once children do begin to speak, their favorite method of increasing their word power is through imitation of the people around them. Therefore, it is a good idea to be conscious of your vocabulary and grammar to the extent that you can without becoming too self-conscious and unnatural in your speech spatterns.

Also, you can gradually urge reasonable improvements in your child's language output, but don't demand perfection. Many children are simply unable to master certain specific sounds until they are six or seven years old, so saying , "thilly" instead of "silly" is quite normal for preschoolers.

Similarly, in addition merely to mimicking what they hear, children eventually begin to construct phrases and sentences from their own minds; and it takes them a little time to recognize and incorporate all the intricacies and irregularities of English. Consequently, although they may seem like dreadful lapses in language learning — statements such as, "I wented to the store," represent a phase of real developmental progress. These sentences show that the young child is trying to learn the rules of language. In doing so she may overgeneralize these rules and come up with words of her own invention. In such instances, gently repeat the phrase correctly *without criticizing.*

• *Keep the process of language learning as enjoyable as possible for your child.* It is understandable that some parents become overly-anxious when it comes to promoting such an important aspect of development; however it is essential to remember that in order to be effective, any educational experience of the early years must be in tune with the individual child's interests and abilities as determined by her unique rate and pattern of progress. **Pushing too hard or too soon may occasionally produce impressive results initially — but ultimately will be counterproductive.**

For example, there is no doubt that books can play a helpful role in language learning. But reading complicated tales won't work with a one year old who does not yet have the attention span to sit still for several minutes, who does not have the ability to understand the plots, and who would much rather just turn the pages back and forth. Even an 18 month old is more likely to be amenable to simple pointing-and-naming games with picture books than long story sessions. Patiently waiting until your child herself shows genuine interest in and ability to deal with basic storybooks, and then choosing books that focus on *her* currently favorite topics and *her* apparent level of comprehension at the moment will allow the experience to have a far greater payoff.

It is never easy to stay completely calm about this subject, especially if the children of your relatives and friends start talking a mile a minute while your baby remains largely silent as the months go by. If your child passes her second birthday without speaking at all, it may be the case that she has an unusual problem and she should be checked by a pediatrician, or a speech-language pathologist. However, as long as there is no obvious cause for concern, the best policy is just to relax and pursue the practices outlined above. Before you know it, your child will be using words too — and using them well.

Activities that Stimulate Language

Betty Farber

•**Reading Aloud:** Read to your child every day. Use a variety of picture books.

•**Storytelling:** Learn stories by heart. It gives you a chance to look right at your youngster as you relate the tale. Attend story hour at the library.

•**Fingerplays:** Engage in fingerplays which combine language, music and gesture.

•**Interpreting Pictures:** Look at pictures from books, magazines, newspapers or your family photograph album and ask your youngster what might be happening in the pictures and how the people might be feeling.

•**Dictation Stories:** Let your child tell you a story to write down. Example: he can have you write a story about a trip he took or a party he attended — or just a tale out of his imagination.

•**Poetry:** Recite *Mother Goose Rhymes, A Child's Garden of Verses,* or other favorite children's poems.

•**Puppets:** Make puppets out of paper bags or socks and act out familiar stories.

•**Story Acting:** Act out nursery tales with you and your child taking the speaking parts. This works well when several children are involved. Use stories with repetition like: *The Three Billy Goats Gruff* or *The Three Little Pigs.* That way, your preschooler will be more likely to remember the words to say.

•**Wordless Picture Books:** Using a story without any words like *Moonlight* by Jan Ormerod, let your youngster tell *you* what is happening. Write it down. Use paper clips to clip her version of the story to the page.

Fingerplays: A Combination of Language, Movement, and Music

Lois Ross

Speaking as a music teacher and as a grandmother of a preschooler, I know by experience that children love to sing and dramatize their songs with fingerplays. (A fingerplay is a poem or song that is accompanied by gestures with the fingers or hands.) In addition to this being an amusing activity, it also stimulates the imagination and provokes curiosity.

What is this fascination with fingerplays?

I think it is the child's way of identifying with the creature or object of the song. Friedrich Froebel, called the father of the kindergarten, said, "What the child imitates he begins to understand." Children delight in imagining what it might be like to fly like a bird or creep like a spider. Fingerplays evoke that kind of pretending. Children enjoy the fact that fingerplays are a form of sign language too, a different way of communicating, through movement, music, *and* language.

Fingerplays can be a great pastime at home, on your doorstep, or sitting in the back seat of a car.

Fingerplays inspire questions.
Each song or poem, although short in length, can inspire many interesting questions. Take for example the beginning of one fingerplay I have sung many times, "The eensie weensie spider went up the water spout / down came the rain and washed the spider out." You and your youngster can observe these interesting creatures spinning their webs. Your preschooler probably will not know what a spout is and you could look up the meaning of the word in the dictionary together. You could read that wonderful story about a spider, *Charlotte's Web* by E.B. White (Harper, 1952). And you might look up books on spiders in the children's section at the library. All of this from one simple fingerplay!

Where to find fingerplays.
There are many good fingerplay books — some contain poems with illustrations of the gestures; others include musical accompaniment. I especially recommend the book, *Eye Winker, Tom Tinker, Chin Chopper* (See Resources, page 80). It has 50 musical fingerplays with piano arrangements and guitar chords along with easy-to-understand directions and illustrations.

If you have never tried fingerplays with your child, you're missing a delightful experience. Today would be a good day to start.

When to be Concerned About Your Child's Language and Speech

Betty Farber, Elizabeth J.Webster,
and Sallie Hillard

Each child is an individual, learning language at his own pace, and his speech may be easier to understand or more difficult to interpret than another child of the same age.

When should speech or language be tested by a professional?

A speech or language problem that affects how your child feels about himself, or how he gets along with others, or how well you yourself can understand him, is best brought to the attention of a speech-language pathologist for testing.

Who is a speech-language pathologist?

"A speech-language pathologist is a professional educated in the study of human communication, its development and its disorders. By evaluating the speech and language skills of children, the speech-language pathologist determines if communication problems exist and decides the best way to treat these problems." (From *Recognizing Communication Disorders*, see Resources, page 79).

What are the causes of speech and language disorders?

Most of the causes of disorders are unknown. Evaluation by a speech-language pathologist can assess the extent of the gap between what most children of that age are doing and what your child can do. Types of speech and language disorders are briefly described below. If you have a concern about your preschooler's speech or language, contact your local hospital, health department or university with a speech and hearing center.

LANGUAGE DISORDERS

Receptive Language Impairment:

Difficulties with *understanding* language. Children with these problems may be unable to understand or to process what is being said to them and may have difficulty in following directions.

Expressive Language Impairment:
Difficulties with *using* spoken language. Children with these problems may have a limited vocabulary. Their language may contain grammatical or structural errors. **Please Note:** It is normal for very young children to speak in one or two word sentences. Also, the language of young children usually contains some errors in grammar. Your child's language would need to be measured against the norms of that age to see if it is markedly different.

SPEECH DISORDERS

Stuttering: Disfluency in speaking. Child may prolong or repeat sounds, syllables or whole words. **Please Note:** Many young children experience stuttering-like behaviors. Between the ages of three and five years, children often exhibit normal disruptions in the smooth flow of speech. Such disruptions can take the form of repetitions of beginning sounds in words ("d-d-dog"), whole words ("Look, look, look, Mommy!"), or starter words ("Uh, uh, can I go, too?"). These breakdowns in the smooth flow of speech normally fluctuate and vary in length from several days to several weeks. Many speech-language pathologists suggest that these difficulties result from the child's attempts to master certain sound productions, to add many new words to his vocabulary, and to learn to use the complex grammatical structure of the language.

Voice Disorders: Problems with the quality of the voice. Children with these disorders may have very loud or very quiet voices. They may speak in a monotone, or with a nasal quality, as though with a cold.

Articulation Problems: Difficulty with speech sounds. Sounds may be left out ("Oop" for "soup") or distorted ("Yeh" for "let"). Or one sound may be substituted for another ("Foop" for "soup").

Please Note: Most children cannot master all the sounds in the language until about age seven. Therefore, a child of four who says, "wabbit" for "rabbit" does not necessarily need speech therapy.

Resources for Section Two: Language Development

FOR ADULTS

Brochure: Recognizing Communication Disorders. *Single copies available free from: American Speech/Language/Hearing Association,* 10801 Rockville Pike, Rockville MD 20852.

Wordsaroni: Word Play for You and Your Preschooler, by Linda Allison and Martha Weston. Little, Brown, 1993. This is a collection of delightful reading, writing, talking, and rhyming activities that parents and preschoolers can engage in any time they have a spare moment.

Language in Early Childhood Education, rev. ed., edited by Courtney Cazden. National Association for the Education of Young Children, 1981. A compilation of articles about language development in preschoolers, edited by an authority in the field.

Surviving Your Two-Year-Old, by Janet Poland. St. Martin's Paperbacks, 1995. In the series entitled, *The Magical Years,* this informative parenting book includes a chapter called: *A Way with Words: Language Development.*

Caring for Your Baby and Young Child: Birth to Age 5, editor-in-chief, Steven P. Shelov, M.D. Bantam Books, 1991. One of a series of child care books from The American Academy of Pediatrics, this comprehensive volume includes information on speech and language development as the child grows.

FOR CHILDREN

Finger Rhymes, collected and illustrated by Marc Brown. Puffin Unicorn edition, 1996. This book includes some favorite fingerplays, such as *There Was a Little Turtle,* and *Where Is Thumbkin?* Along with charming illustrations to the rhymes, the finger movements are clearly drawn in little boxes next to each line of text.

Too Many Rabbits and Other Fingerplays, by Kay Cooper. Scholastic, 1995. The 22 fingerplays in this book introduce children to scientific information and concepts about animals, nature, weather, and the universe. The imaginative cut paper collage illustrations are by Judith Moffatt.

Truck, by Donald Crews. Mulberry Books edition, 1991. As a truck rides along city streets and highways in this colorful Caldecott Honor Book, children will enjoy reading the signs along the way.

Eye Winker, Tom Tinker, Chin Chopper, by Tom Glazer. Doubleday, 1973. Includes 50 musical fingerplays with piano arrangements and guitar chords, along with easy-to-understand directions and illustrations.

Seeing, Saying, Doing, Playing: A big book of action words, by Taro Gomi. Chronicle Books, 1991. Each page illustrates a different scene (such as a schoolroom, a city street, or a swimming pool) in which many activities are taking place. The words to describe each activity are printed next to the person performing the action. For example in the schoolroom, children are: drawing, stretching, cutting, watching, and reading.

All About Where, by Tana Hoban. Greenwillow, 1991. The famous author/photographer uses her colorful photos to illustrate location words such as <u>above</u>, <u>behind</u>, <u>under</u>, and <u>around.</u> Preschoolers will have fun looking at the pictures and describing what is happening.

Just Look, by Tana Hoban. Greenwillow, 1996. A wordless book in which a cut-out circle on one page permits you to see partly into the color photograph on the next page. Children can predict what the picture might represent, and then turn the page to see if they are right.

Tell Me a Story, Mama, by Angela Johnson. Orchard Books, 1989. Winner of the 1991 Ezra Jack Keats award, this is a warm and loving dialog between a mother and her young daughter.

Alphabatics, by Suse MacDonald. Bradbury, 1986. Letters of the alphabet turn magically into the objects they represent in this imaginative ABC book.

Moonlight, by Jan Ormerod. Lothrop, Lee & Shepard, 1982. This wordless book depicts the evening hours of a child and her family.

My First Book of Words: 1,000 Words Every Child Should Know, illustrated by Lena Shiffman. Scholastic Cartwheel, 1992. With words and illustrations that take in a child's everyday surroundings, such as: my family, my clothes, and my town, preschoolers will love pointing out the objects in their world, and have fun adding new words to their vocabulary.

Who Said Moo? by Harriet Ziefert and Simms Taback. HarperFestival, 1996. Children love to imitate animal sounds, and this colorful book with sunny, humorous illustrations gives you many opportunities to do so.

Section Three
Reading
Writing
Arithmetic

Section Three
Reading - Writing
Arithmetic

Introduction

A news article in The New York Times told of 17-year-old siblings who were believed to be the first twins to get the highest possible score on their Scholastic Assessment Tests. Their mother was questioned as to how she prepared them to attain such excellent scores. She replied that she hadn't filled their days with lessons and tutors. Instead, as youngsters, she read to them at bedtime and naptime, and let them have time to be kids.

To foster a love of reading and writing in young children, adults need to surround them with books from the earliest age. The miracle is that persons from all economic backgrounds have access to these volumes — the shelves in public libraries are filled with beautiful picture books, and employ helpful librarians who can offer recommendations.

The authors in this section show how reading for young children can consist of just "looking at books," and writing can take place when a child uses a pencil to "make her own marks" and dictate their meaning to an adult. Practical, creative ideas are provided by the authors to encourage child to be successful readers and writers.

While schoolchildren sometimes dread math, to a preschooler math can offer the fun of "counting the napkins for the dinner table, the steps that lead to the house, or the number of raisins in her cereal." The author of the chapter on math describes many everyday activities to introduce different math concepts to young children.

SECTION THREE
READING - WRITING - ARITHMETIC

Chapter

Chapter 12
Encouraging a Positive View
of
Reading & Writing

Nancy F. Browning

She need not know the name
of each of the letters
in "elephant"
for that word
to have meaning for her.

In many ways, your child is already both a reader and a writer. When your preschooler turns the pages, looking at a book, he is a reader, and when he can tell you, "That's McDonald's," because he knows the symbol of the golden arches, he is also a reader. Your child is a writer when she tells a story for you to write down, or when she makes marks or letters on paper to tell her own story.

To help your child see himself as a reader and writer from the start, involve him with books at an early age: read to your infant from birth, look at picture books with your child and provide books made of plastic and cardboard for your baby to manipulate. As your child gets older, provide a variety of books for him to look at by himself and with others.

Importance of a Positive View of Reading and Writing

Most activities that will help your preschooler to love both reading and writing do not require any fancy materials or programs. Instead, you need some books, pencils and paper, and some time to share reading and writing experiences with your child. It is more important to foster a positive view of reading and writing as enjoyable and useful activities, than to have your youngster work at mastering a skill like recognizing and writing the letters of the alphabet.

Importance of Discovering Meaning

Researchers have found that reading is learned best through actual reading and that writing is learned best through actual writing, because reading and writing are complex processes that involve much more than the mastery of specific skills. Because the goal of reading is to create meaning, it is possible for a child to master many "reading skills" such as phonics (recognizing the sounds of the letters) and word recognition (memorizing words by sight) but still not work toward understanding the meaning of what she is reading.

As a preschooler, if your child will learn how to work toward meaning by knowing that an author tells a story, by predicting what might happen next, and by doing the other activities suggested in this book, she will be able to acquire the necessary "reading skills" as she searches for meaning. For example, your child may be able to read a difficult word like "elephant" if she has an interest in elephants, or if she has just taken a trip to the zoo and wants to write or dictate a story about elephants. She need not know the name of each of the letters in "elephant" for that word to have meaning for her.

Encouraging Writing

Children also learn reading by writing. Your preschooler can "write" stories by telling them to you and having you write them down. When she looks at this writing and then retells her story, she is reading because she is making the symbols mean something. Encourage your child to write her own stories too, even if her marks do not resemble the traditional alphabet, or if she uses her own "invented" spelling.

Try to provide experiences for your child that could be used as a basis for writing. After a picnic in the park, encourage him to write about what happened. You might talk about the trip first and suggest that your child draw a picture. Your preschooler could "write" a letter to grandma about the trip, or dictate a letter for you to write.

Print is Everywhere

Reading encompasses much more than books —print is everywhere. Explore traffic signs, phone books, advertisements, and food boxes with your preschooler. Read to your child daily, talk with your child frequently, and let him know that reading is important to you. If you enjoy reading and keep books, magazines and newspapers available, you will serve as a model which will be likely to influence your youngster's future behavior.

The Reading Calendar on pages 90-91 has many specific ideas for enjoying language with your child. It is a day-by-day set of guidelines for integrating the language arts and giving your child the feeling that he or she is both a reader and a writer.

Chapter 13
Children Who
Love to Read

Laura Daigen-Ayala

*...real reading readiness
is accomplished quite simply:
through exposure to language
and print in all their forms.*

Sitting on the couch, four-year-old Bryan was absorbed in his picture book. Suddenly he ran to his father, book in hand, and asked thoughtfully, "How do you do those words?" "What words, Bryan?" his father asked. "You know, the ones you read me in my books!" Bryan had just jumped headlong into the process of discovery that would lead him to reading.

Parents are often confronted with ads for computer software, videos, and workbooks suggesting that certain "pre-reading" activities are necessary in order for children to become good readers. However, real reading readiness is accomplished quite simply; through exposure to language and print in all their forms.

Think of reading as a process that is learned just like speaking. When babies babble and coo, we don't call them "pre-speakers," or require them to master specific pre-speaking skills. Quite the contrary, as soon as we hear something that sounds like a real word, we offer encouragement and praise, asserting that, "She's talking!"

If workbooks are not useful activities for reading readiness, how then are parents to help with the reading process? First, find encouragement in the knowledge that today many schools are trying to imitate what you as parents do by reading their favorite stories to students over and over, using big books (marketed as "Big Books") with large print so that the class can see the words being read to them. The aim is for children to come to recognize the words of the story, just as they often do while sitting in your lap hearing a favorite book.

Just by reading to your child you're taking the single most important step toward instilling in her a love of reading. And by all means, reread that story for the thousandth time if your child requests it. There's something in that book that she needs to hear again and again.

How parents can help preschoolers in the reading process
• One technique you can use to help draw your child's attention to the print is occasionally to point to the words as you read. This will help your child realize that the symbols you're pointing to are the words you are saying. It will also show your child that we read from left to right. Avoid overdoing this however. Love of the story and its illustrations are most important.

• From time to time, as you read aloud, pause before the last word of a line, and allow your child to complete the phrase. If the word he fills in is not the one on the page, let it go without correcting him. Your child is using the story line, his memory, and/or his ability to predict in order to find the meaning. That's what reading is all about.

• To encourage memorization and prediction, include in your read-aloud collection: 1) books with rhymes and repetition such as *The Very Hungry Caterpillar*, books of poetry, and 2) cumulative stories (stories that repeat phrases, adding new lines as the story grows) such as The *House That Jack Built*. When your child has memorized a book, this is a great step toward independent reading. Applaud your reader for this accomplishment, and let him read his book to someone. Be sure *not* to preface his performance with, "He's only memorized it." The words your child has memorized will become his first reading words as he begins to associate the symbols on the page with the words that have become important to him for their meaning.

• To help your preschooler discover that those squiggles on the page are just language written down, begin by writing down your child's own words. Not only does this lend importance to your child's thoughts and ideas, strengthening his developing self-image, it also makes it possible for you, your child, and others to read back these words later. Soon your youngster will come to understand the value and usefulness of print. You can have him dictate letters to friends and relatives, stories, songs, or poems, or the titles for his art work.

• Provide a notebook for your child to do his own "writing" which at first will be scribbles and drawings, and later may include marks resembling letters or words. Ask your child if he'd like to read you the story he's written, or tell you the story of his picture.

• Let your child see you using books of all kinds: telephone books, dictionaries, recipe books, and especially books you read for leisure. Make sure her books are easily accessible to her, and encourage her to get a book and read quietly when you do. Don't distinguish between "reading" and "looking at" a book. Looking at a book *is* reading for a young child, and you want your child to consider herself a reader from the beginning.

• Draw attention to the print that surrounds you. When you take out the milk container, point to the word, "milk" and read it aloud, or ask, "Can you guess what this says?" Other examples of what educators like to call "environmental print" are the signs on restaurants and stores, traffic signs, and the covers of favorite books and records.

continued on page 92

A Reading Calendar
(for Any Month)
Nancy F. Browning-Rahim

SUNDAY	MONDAY	TUESDAY	WEDNESDAY	THURSDAY	FRIDAY	SATURDAY
				1 Read a recipe. Refer to it, find the ingredients and cook together.	**2** Have your child teach you a song or jump rope rhyme. Write it down for him to read.	**3** Attend story hour at the library.
4 Invite your child's friends and tell a good fairy tale by candlelight.	**5** Open the mail together and talk about it.	**6** Send your child a card or letter through the mail.	**7** Dramatize a story using costumes or puppets, if desired.	**8** Leave a note for your child. (Use pictures as cues.) Encourage her to respond in writing.	**9** Tell your preschooler a favorite story without using a book.	**10** Explore the library, checking out books for yourself and for your child.
11 Investigate a topic of interest to your child (such as dinosaurs) by going to the library.	**12** While driving or walking, take turns reading signs to each other.	**13** Before reading a book, look at the cover and ask your child to predict the plot.	**14** Let your child choose one of his writings to read to you.	**15** Read some poetry together.	**16** While reading, stop a few times to predict what might happen next. Think of a few possibilities.	**17** Look at the family album and tell stories about your childhood.

18	19	20	21	22	23	24
Before taking a walk together, tell your child to remember all the things he sees, hears, smells, and touches. Have him dictate a story about the walk.	Let your child write her own story making her own letters or marks. Have her read it to you. To help you remember the story, write it using traditional spelling.	Let your child "read" a favorite book to you. Accept his version.	Let your child create a new ending for a story.	Explore a wordless picture book. Using paper clips, attach your child's version of the story to the bottom of each page.	Make one or more lists with your child. List things to do, things she wants, people you know, etc.	Explore books at a bookstore.
25	26	27	28	29	30	31
Using a photo album, or bound paper, make a book using cut up magazines, greeting cards, and drawings. Talk and write about the pictures.	Write an "I Wish" poem by starting every line with "I Wish...." No need to rhyme!	Help your child write and mail a letter to a friend or relative, or to an author whose book you like.	Set aside 15 minutes in which your entire family can read silently. Your preschooler can look through her picture books.	Share the reading of a known book by letting your child "read" one character's part (for example: the baby bear).	Look at pictures in newspapers or magazines and guess how the people feel. Write a story about the pictures.	Plan a menu with your child; make a list; shop together, and then cook together.

• Help your child to understand the concept of time sequence by discussing daily experiences. After a trip, for example, ask, "What did we do first? What did we do next? What did we do at the end of the ride?" Remember that there is no one "right" answer. Use a similar approach for activities you are planning, by predicting what you will do: "What will we do before we leave? What do you think you'll see on the way?" This talk about time sequence can be translated from daily experience to reading of books. You can discuss what happened first, next, and at the end of the book. You can also predict what might happen in books you are about to read.

Transition to School

Now is the time to learn what approach to reading is being used in the school your child will attend, so that you can determine how to become involved. Plan to be active in the PTA and push for a book drive or fund raiser for *classroom libraries.* If you have the time, volunteer to help out during language arts or storytime. Organize a parent/teacher workshop on reading to learn your school's approach and to see how you can best support it in school and at home. Finally, ask your principal, librarian, and teacher how they foster the love of reading and how you can help them to do so.

Chapter 14
Writing Letters
to Grandma

Ellen Javernick

*The following letters were sent
from Lisa's mother to
Lisa's grandmother
over a time period of three years.*

February 10, 1987
Dear Grandma B.,
What do you think of the valentine Lisa made for you? Not bad for a two year old! I've read that drawing is the earliest form of written communication. I know it's hard to understand what she's trying to communicate, but she says it means she misses her grandma.

Love, Janelle

August 3, 1987
Hi,
This is Lisa's thank-you for the books you sent for her "3 birth-day.'" She wrote my folks a thank-you letter too, and although I couldn't see much difference, she was adamant that this one was for you. You'll notice that she now distinguishes between writing and drawing. Even though she's used no real letter forms, don't the up and down lines resemble real writing? I've read that the scribbling of children in different countries resembles the alphabet of that country. She's beginning to recognize a few letters of the alphabet ("L" for Lisa and "M" for McDonalds), but she still represents them all the same way on paper. How she loves to "write!" I can entertain her anywhere with the pencil and paper I keep in my purse.

Love, Janelle

December 29, 1987
Dear Grandma B.
Lisa just loved the box of writing supplies you sent for Christmas. She's had fun experimenting with the pencils and markers. What a wonderful gift! She picked out the pretty pink paper for her note to you. Notice how she wrote the "B" at the top — for Grandma B. of course, and how she signed her "L" at the bottom. Writing is often a part of Lisa's play. She makes grocery lists, writes checks (on that long, narrow green paper you sent), and after a visit to Dr. Dreith's office, she wrote prescriptions. I think her writing compares favorably with his!

Love, Janelle

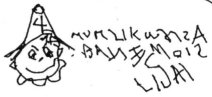

July 25, 1988
Dear Grandma B.
Lisa wanted me to mail you an invitation to her birthday party. Each clown looks different and was especially made for the friend for whom it was intended. Notice the "writing" and the signature. She seems to write the letters in her own name much more frequently than she writes other letters. Although some people — even a few teachers — say that children should be made to use upper and lower case letters right from the start, other educators don't believe in limiting children's writing. I agree. I can see that Lisa and lots of other kids don't have the fine motor control to make the lower case letters. I don't want to wait until she develops those skills. I'd rather encourage her to write as much as she wants, labeling her art work and signing her letters. Besides, she really doesn't recognize many lower case letters yet so why should I worry about her writing them. She does know that she'll be 4!

Love, Janelle

P.S. Wish Delaware and Denver weren't so far apart and that you could accept Lisa's invitation.

1. baby doll
2. drum
3. tea set
4. paints

December 5, 1988
Dear Grandma B.
I made you a photocopy of Lisa's letter to Santa. I knew you'd get a chuckle reading it, and besides you wanted some suggestions for what to send. This letter was a sort of "write and tell" activity. Good thing she told me what each item was so I could write it down. I'd have had trouble reading it on my own. Notice that Lisa uses some correct consonants to try to spell with — like "p" for paints.

Love, Janelle

D'AR GRANDMA'S ♡
THANK YOU FOR THE
DREZZ I LOVE IT PINK IZ MY BEST
COLOR LOVE LIZA

THANK YOU FOR THE DRESS I LOVE IT
PINK IS MY BEST COLOR LOVE LISA *

August 15, 1989
Dear Grandma B.
Lisa loved the birthday dress. She decided to save it to wear next month for the first day of kindergarten. Here's her thank-you. She wanted to dictate it to me and then copy it. She's going through a stage when she is hesitant to write on her own. At the kindergarten orientation the teacher, Mrs. Jewett, said this usually happens as children begin to notice written words. She said that there should be a balance between what a child dictates and what she actually writes. She also suggested that parents explain the writing process and "transitional spelling" (or "invented spelling") to grandparents so they'd offer lots of praise as their grandchildren progress. Of course you always have been good about responding appropriately to everything Lisa sends you. We'll take pictures in her "best color" dress.
                    Love, Janelle

DR GRMa B
DEAR GRANDMA I'M GON TO BE A DK
              I'M GOING TO BE A DUCK
4 HELOEN NDI WL GT LTZ
FOR HALLOWEEN AND I WILL GET LOTS
   OVKND.   LOVE
   OF CANDY   LIZA

October 15, 1989
Dear Grandma B.
You'll love this! Lisa suggested that I write "grown-up writing" under her own spelling*. "Just in case you can't read kindergarten spelling." You'll notice that she still runs words together, and reverses letters, but look at the period at the end of the sentence. Don't you love her spelling of candy? I'll write more soon.... I've got to get sewing on the duck costume or she'll have to go as a "gost."   Love, Janelle

* *Type has been substituted for the "grown-up writing" for legibility.*

February 11, 1990
Dear Grandma B.,
Remember the first valentine that Lisa sent? Hasn't she come a long way? This one is pretty close to conventional writing. She's leaving spaces between words and adding more vowels. I think that's because she's learning to read and also becoming aware of how written words look. She reads several sight words now like "love" and "you" and you'll notice that she's included them. Mrs. Jewett says she's making great progress. Isn't it wonderful to see that writing emerges naturally through several developmental stages when children practice a lot at home, and get encouragement from folks like us.

Love, Janelle

Ways to Encourage Your Child as a Writer

Ellen Javernick

Encourage your child to write.
Let your child see you write and encourage participation. Provide a variety of writing materials (such as pencils, pens, markers, crayons, etc.) Encourage your child to communicate by creating pictures. Suggest to your preschooler ways in which to incorporate writing into play activities. (Menus for a restaurant, signs to use with little cars, etc.)

Enjoy your child's inventiveness.

Remember how excited you were when your child began to talk? Praise early written language in the same way. "Daddy will like the picture you drew for him." "Look, how you wrote bunny (BNE). You're hearing lots of sounds." "I see you left spaces between words. You're learning a lot about writing." Remind yourself that the ability to write will improve as your child matures.

Don't emphasize correctness.

If you expect your child's beginning writing to meet adult standards, you'll both be frustrated. Your overemphasis on correctness may make your child reluctant to try to write. It will certainly inhibit what he writes. Instead of writing about a subject that interests him, (for example, his pet hamster), your child may feel compelled to write about a cat, only because he knows the spelling of cat and does not know how to spell "hamster."

Don't rush your child's writing progress.

Remember that writing as much as two sentences can be as hard for a child as writing an entire essay can be for an adult. Allow your child to write some sentences and then dictate some. When your child shares writing with you, encourage him to expand upon what was written in the story by asking questions like, "What does your hamster look like?" or, "What could happen next?" Become your child's secretary and take dictation for longer stories.

Answer your child's questions about spelling.

Try to balance your child's need to know with her need to develop independence as a writer. You can give clues like: "What letter sound do you hear at the beginning?" Remember — if it takes more than a few seconds for a child to spell the word, interest in writing won't be sustained. Give your child strategies for writing without knowing the correct spelling of words. Besides encouraging "transitional spelling" (or "invented spelling"), encourage your child to put a blank line on the paper to symbolize a word she can't spell. You can also help your child retrieve correct spelling from the environment by looking on a soup can to find "tomato," etc.

Save samples of your child's writing.

You will treasure it years from now, and your child will be able to see the progress that he has made over a period of time. But most importantly, he will see that you *value* writing.

Chapter 15
Math for Preschoolers

Janet Dengel

*Preschoolers are naturally
drawn to math.
Just ask any three year old
if she would rather have
two cookies
or one cookie.*

Long before 2+2=4 becomes a concrete concept in children's minds, they are learning mathematical principles every day.

Sorting objects (like buttons) by color — *recognizing shapes* in the rectangle of a door and the circle of a clock — arranging blocks in a row *by size* — *measuring* one's height against the door — *counting* the number of apples in a bag — all these preschool activities are the foundation for the later challenges of higher mathematics.

Preschoolers are naturally drawn to math. Just ask any three year old if she would rather have two cookies or one cookie. Young children will also enjoy "charging" their parents for groceries at their pretend stores and spending hours stacking a variety of sizes, shapes, and numbers of blocks into architectural wonders.

Numbers are useful
It may be fun for a four year old to learn to count to 50 by memory, but it's more important that she understands that numbers can stand for *objects* that can be counted. Preschoolers learn best from experiences with real objects. Let her count things that are part of her life: the cracks in the sidewalk, napkins for the dinner table, the steps that lead to the house, or the number of raisins in her cereal.

Numbers also have a special usefulness when your preschooler discovers that he can dial grandma's house with your help, or when he proudly announces, "I used to be 3 — but now I'm 4." Numbers have a personal significance when a child learns his address and telephone number or finds out he weighs 30 *pounds* or stands 40 *inches* tall.

Recognizing written numerals
Later in the preschool years, children may begin to recognize written numerals. Here again it is important for children to learn that each symbol corresponds to a specific amount. Books about counting always show *three ducks* or *five bears*, as well as printing the numerals 3 and 5.

MORE MATHEMATICAL CONCEPTS
THAT PRESCHOOLERS CAN LEARN ABOUT

Sorting: grouping objects by likeness. For example: a group of buttons can be organized by *color* — or grouped by *size* — or classified as to whether they have *2 or 4 holes* for sewing. *(Caution: buttons should never be used with younger preschoolers who might put them in their mouths.)*

Recognizing shapes: observing the shapes of real objects like a dinner plate or a window, starting with circles, squares, and triangles and working up to rectangles, ovals, and shapes with more than 4 sides.

Matching: pairing two things that are alike. For example, looking for matching pairs of socks or mittens.

Sequencing: arranging a group of objects in order. For example, arranging cans or blocks in size order from smallest to largest.

Measuring: using tools to find length, width, weight, or amount. For example, measuring ingredients for a cake.

Using hands-on math activities and games related to these concepts (such as the ones on pages 102-104) will promote learning and may prevent the "I hate math" syndrome that often occurs during the elementary school years.

Lastly, it is the responsibility of parents and educators to dispel the myth that girls are less capable than boys in mathematics. Studies have proven this to be false. Let's make sure that children of both sexes are encouraged to learn and enjoy mathematical concepts.

Activities

Janet Dengel

It is not necessary to buy expensive toys in order to have your preschooler discover his mathematical abilities. The following suggestions use inexpensive materials plus the added ingredient of your child's creativity and imagination.

Learn about shapes: Have a shape hunt. Look around the house or out-of-doors and let your preschooler find round plates, square windows, and eight-sided stop signs. Have your preschooler close her eyes while you place a square block in a box with a round ball and an orange. She can choose which object doesn't belong in the set. Or, put the shapes in a bag and ask your child to identify by touch alone.

String beads, macaroni, or cereal: Use a pattern such as one red, two blue, and three green beads, or one macaroni and two cereal circles — see if your child can follow the sequence and copy your pattern.

Do number rubbings: Place a piece of paper over a coin, your house numbers, or a car's license plate. Take the paper off a crayon and rub with the crayon placed horizontally on the object. See the pattern of numbers appear before your preschooler's eyes.

Get out the blocks: Blocks have been around for ages with good reason: children love them and without realizing it, they learn about size, space, balance, planning and logic from playing with blocks.

Use imaginary play: Let your preschooler sell stamps at a pretend post office, tell the dolls it's time for lunch, construct a neighborhood lemonade stand, build a fort with blocks, measure and weigh your pet at a pretend vet's office, and "fill up" his tricycle at a backyard gas station.

Combine household chores and math: Preschoolers enjoy setting the table, sorting silverware and laundry, and stacking plates according to size — household chores that are also educational.

Get out a tape measure: Use a tape measure or ruler to measure the length of your child's room, the width of her bed, and the height of her stuffed toys.

Make math magic in the kitchen: The kitchen provides endless opportunities to measure, divide portions, and introduce weight and size. Don't overlook other kitchen math such as oven temperature, counting down with the microwave, and setting timers.

Go to the store: Grocery shopping is an activity filled with mathematical challenges. Your preschooler can help compare sizes of cans and boxes, as well as prices. For older preschoolers, you can point out the difference between a digital scale in the deli section and the dial scale in the produce department.

Use rhymes, games and books: This Old Man, Five Little Monkeys, and the game of musical chairs contain the concepts of counting, addition, and subtraction hidden under all the fun. And, of course, there are countless books that teach just that — counting! (See Resources on pages 105-108.)

Make number recognition fun: Numerical symbols will become familiar to your preschooler as he grows older. Don't worry if he confuses a 6 for a 9, or if he learns numbers at a later age than other children. Keep learning fun with simple board games, bingo, hopscotch, or playing cards.

Start shuffling the deck: An ordinary deck of playing cards can teach the concepts of matching, number recognition, shapes, number sequence, greater than/less than, and can also sharpen your child's memory. Start out with the all-time favorites of Concentration, Go Fish, and Old Maid. It's also an activity that most grandparents would enjoy participating in with their grandchildren.

Math and me: Math will mean so much more to your young child if he experiences it on a personal level.

• Design a growth chart together and hang it on the wall to see how tall he is growing.

• Using the calendar, talk about the days she goes to school; circle her birthday and other special days.

• Look at a clock and discuss what time she eats dinner.

• Measure how far he can jump; or use a stop watch to clock how fast he can run.

• Measure her arms and legs.

• Cut a piece of string the length of her body so she can compare her height to a bush, door, or chair.

• Outline her body on a huge piece of paper and let her measure her shape.🎀

Resources for Section Three:
Reading
Writing
Arithmetic

FOR ADULTS

Read to Me: *Raising kids who love to read,* by Bernice E. Cullinan. Scholastic, 1992. This paperback is written by an authority in reading and writing, who has a love for books and a way with words. With unpretentious language, she shares ideas with parents on how to help their children learn that books are a source of knowledge and pleasure.

More Than 1,2,3: *The Real Basics of Mathematics,* by J.B. McCracken. NAEYC brochure #575 (1-800-424-2460). The author illustrates how math can be an exciting part of children's lives.

Whole Language Whole Learners, by Laura Robb. Wm. Morrow, 1994. Drawing on her thirty years' experience as a teacher and writer (the author of 4 chapters in this book), Laura Robb's work inspires as she shows how whole language philosophy can be applied from kindergarten through junior high school. Also included are 15 essays on the creative process by some of today's best known children's book authors and illustrators.

Literacy Begins at Home: *Helping Your Child Grow Up Reading and Writing,* by Judith I. Schwartz. Charles C. Thomas Publisher, 1991. This guide is designed for parents who want to foster in their children a love of reading and writing. The author discusses topics such as: creating an atmosphere for learning, capitalizing on print in the environment, and reading and writing through the day.

FOR CHILDREN

Have You Seen My Cat? by Eric Carle. Scholastic Blue Ribbon Book, 1987. A little boy goes on a world trip looking for his cat, and encounters a variety of cats: a puma, a jaguar, a cheetah—until he finds his own pet. This story is told with few words and much repetition, so that preschoolers can soon tell the story themselves.

The Very Hungry Caterpillar, by Eric Carle, Putnam, 1989. This tiny creature with its prodigious appetite eats its way through many foods over a week's time, until it is finally transformed into a beautiful butterfly.

Dear Annie, by Judith Caseley. Mulberry Books edition, 1994. From the time Annie is born, her grandfather sends her letters. Soon Annie is dictating answers to her mother to send back to Grandpa. Now that Annie is in school, she can read the letters herself and Grandpa is her pen pal. A story about a loving relationship that grows through letter writing.

Mouse in the House, by Michelle Cartlidge. Dutton, 1991. This board book, with heavy pages for the youngest readers to turn, says, "Mouse is in the house. What does she see?" The child can then point to and name a familiar object on each page, such as a cat, clock, or table. The final picture shows all of the objects in a room setting, for the child to identify again.

Jack's Garden, by Henry Cole. Greenwillow, 1995. A cumulative tale, similar to "The House that Jack Built" but starting instead with, "This is the garden that Jack planted." Each page brings a new addition to the garden, until you see it in full bloom.

Frank and Ernest, by Alexandra Day. Scholastic Blue Ribbon Book, 1988. Children recognize quite early that language is different in different surroundings. In this humorous story, Frank and Ernest manage a diner, and learn the vocabulary that goes with the business. For example, a hamburger with lettuce, tomato, and an onion translates to: "burn one, take it through the garden, and pin a rose on it."

City Street, by Douglas Florian. Greenwillow, 1990. With scenes of jumping rope, playing basketball, and sitting on the front stoop eating ice cream, children will recognize their city experiences as they read this book. The simple, rhyming text (City street/Jumping feet) will help preschoolers to guess which words come next.

Each Orange Had 8 Slices: A Counting Book, by Paul Giganti, Jr. Greenwillow, 1992. In this unique counting book, preschoolers will get an introduction to simple addition through the interesting questions posed by the author and the colorful illustrations by Donald Crews.

Guess Who? A Peek-A-Boo Book, by Taro Gomi. Chronicle Books, 1991. This board book pictures a different animal on each page, with two holes cut out for the eyes, making it easy to play peek-a-boo. A simple statement appears on each double page, such as: "I like to chase mice. I am a **cat**." (If you stop occasionally before the answer, your youngster can try to guess.)

Good Books, Good Times! selected by Lee Bennett Hopkins. Harper & Row, 1990. A collection of poems about the joys of reading. Each poem is a delight.

Let's Count Baby, by Cheryl Willis Hudson. Scholastic Cartwheel, 1995. In a book with heavy cardboard pages for the youngest preschoolers, a little African American girl counts everyday objects from one to ten.

Domino Addition, by Lynette Long. Charlesbridge, 1996. With colorful pages picturing groups of dominos, children can learn basic addition by counting the dots.

The Best Bug Parade (MathStart™ Series-Level 1), by Stuart J. Murphy. HarperCollins, 1996. Youngsters can compare bugs that are big, bigger, and biggest, and then choose others that are long, longer, and longest, in this appealing book about comparing sizes.

Give Me Half! (MathStart™ Series-Level 2), by Stuart J. Murphy. HarperCollins, 1996. To introduce the topic of "understanding halves," the author tells a story in rhyme about a brother and sister who need to learn to share. They also learn that $1/2 + 1/2 = 1$.

Beach Day; Good Night, Good Morning; Shopping Trip, by Helen Oxenbury. Dial Very First Books, 2nd edition, 1991. These three board books for the youngest preschoolers have no words printed on the pages, but the illustrations in each book tell a story that is in tune with a young child's experiences. You and your toddler can discuss what is happening in the pictures.

The Button Box, by Margarette S. Reid. Puffin Books/Frederick Warne, 1995. A little boy tells about the fun he has sorting the buttons of different sizes, shapes, and colors in grandma's button box.

Shapes, by John J. Reiss. Aladdin Books Editions, 1987. This book uses vivid colors to illustrate a variety of shapes from circles to octagons, identifying the uses for shapes in everyday objects, and introducing the concept of three-dimensional forms such as cubes and spheres.

Root-A-Toot-Toot, by Anne Rockwell. Macmillan, 1991. This simple, cumulative tale is about several animals who join a little boy as he marches along, playing a flute. Some of the words in the text are replaced by a picture — helping the child to read the story by himself.

Dinosaurs Are 568, by Jean Rogers. Dell Yearling, 1991. Older preschoolers and kindergarten children will enjoy this chapter book about Raymond, who is intrigued with books about dinosaurs (at the library, 568 is the number that identifies the book as being about dinosaurs). Raymond loves to read about interesting creatures, and becomes famous when he discovers a mistake in the encyclopedia!

Who Says That? by Arnold L. Shapiro. Dutton, 1991. Each page shows a different animal and the sound it makes in this simple, colorful book. But, every few pages, it is pointed out that human children make a different noise, and we see that, among other sounds, girls and boys whisper, chuckle, shout, sing, and laugh. Youngsters may enjoy making the sounds as they read the book.

The Pop-Up, Pull-Tab, Playtime House that Jack Built, by Nadine Bernard Westcott. Joy Street, Little, Brown, 1991. This is the classic story of the house that Jack built, that adds new lines as the story grows — with the addition of pop-ups and tabs to pull, making it more fun than ever.

Playtime 1 2 3, by Jenny Williams. Dial, 1992. Preschoolers can count from 1 to 20 children in these pictures, as they enjoy everyday activities, such as swinging, swimming, and listening to a story.

Section Four
Sharing
Literature

Section Four
Sharing
Literature

Introduction

A young child I know confided, "I wish I could creep inside that book and see what's going on." So many magical things go on inside of books! They can take you on a journey to any place on earth, or even out in space. They can open your mind to new ideas, and your heart to people all over the world. They can introduce you to the rich language and rhythm of poetry. Young children are eager for the discovery.

Reading a book aloud with a child curled up in your lap is satisfying to both the adult and the child, providing physical closeness, security, shared pleasure, and learning.

The authors of the chapters in this section offer a lively discussion about various types of books: picture books, fairy tales, poetry and nursery rhymes, multicultural books, and information books. Their articles include resource lists of books in every area. You will find many ways to share literature with the young children that you care about, encouraging them to care about books.

SECTION FOUR

SHARING LITERATURE

Chapter

Chapter 16
Sharing Literature:
A Love Gift

Ellin Greene

From
"Happiness"
by A.A. Milne

Sing or chant nursery rhymes,
Mother Goose rhymes and poetry
while feeding, bathing, or
dressing your young child.

To give children a love of literature is one of the greatest gifts a parent can bestow on a child. Lewis Carroll, the author of *Alice in Wonderland,* called stories, "love gifts." When you read aloud to your preschooler, you are saying, "I love you. I am taking time to do something special with you."

Literature as an important part of life
You can make literature a part of your child's life by taking time from a busy day to read to your child, showing pleasure in reading books yourself, going to the library for books and story hour, and having your preschooler's books in a special place, where she can reach them.

The preschooler who is read to and taken to the library usually learns to read earlier and enjoys books more than the child who has not had these experiences. While hearing stories and looking at books, your youngster will learn reading readiness skills such as: recognizing words, following events in sequence, and looking at the words on the page from left to right. He will begin to understand that pictures and words have meaning.

But do not think of sharing literature only in terms of teaching your preschooler to read. Most of all, your preschooler will develop a happy attitude toward books and reading that will help her to feel that literature is an important part of life.

Introducing your child to literature
The child's introduction to literature is through the ear. Sing or chant nursery rhymes, Mother Goose rhymes and poetry while feeding, bathing, or dressing your young child.

Try to read aloud every day. Establish a time and place for this special sharing time, such as at bedtime or before a nap. Reading aloud should be done away from distractions such as television. A big, soft pillow, a rocking chair, a comfortable stuffed chair are suitable reading spaces. The sound of your voice, the warmth of body contact, the enjoyable interaction that takes place between you and your child during the read-aloud times will become associated with books in your preschooler's mind.

Even when your youngster begins to read on her own, continue reading aloud to her on a regular basis. Try reading slightly longer books, that take a few sittings to read, such as *Charlotte's Web* by E.B. White (Harper, 1952). Children are ready for such books long before they can read them by themselves.

Encourage your youngster's involvement in the story through questions and comments, but never press for a response. The reading time should never become a "lesson." Encourage your preschooler to respond by asking such questions as, "What do you see?" "What is happening in the picture?" or "How does the picture (or story) make you feel?"

Involve your preschooler in other ways. Have your child make paper bag puppets and act out the story, draw a picture about how the story makes him feel, or help you prepare a recipe suggested by a story, such as *The Gingerbread Man*.

When you share stories with your youngster, you are saying books and reading are important. You are making literature a part of your child's life, and helping him to discover that books bring lifelong pleasure.

Books for Various Ages

Ellin Greene

Infants enjoy stories with interesting sound patterns and a lilting cadence. Read in a gentle, quiet voice.

Some time between eight and fourteen months, your child will reach out with her hands to touch the book you are reading aloud. During this stage, use books that have strong durable paper or laminated pages. Allow your baby to turn the pages for you; the child's first fascination with books is often the hinged page! Involve your youngster through singing, touching, identifying the object in the picture, or completing a rhyme.

Toddlers (about 15 months to 2 years) like small books — books they can carry easily — or large books that seem almost as big as the child. They enjoy books with pictures of ordinary objects that they can identify, books with humor and counting books Using wordless books encourages your toddler to talk about what is happening in the pictures.

Very young children usually enjoy books that they can interact with — books with pictures that have a flap to lift or a tab to pull, and books that surprise the reader with a picture that pops up! This may be a way to interest an active young child in enjoying a quiet time with books.

Preschoolers (about 2 1/2 to 5 years) easily move back and forth between reality and fantasy and look for this in their stories. In such a story as *The Three Bears,* for instance, the chair and the bowl of porridge are familiar to your preschooler. Having them belong to the bears adds mystery and adventure to the story, but the situation is simple, and there are enough everyday events in it so that children are not confused.

Three and four year olds are ready for simple folk tales, such as *The Gingerbread Man* and *The Three Billy Goats Gruff.* They enjoy the repetition of words and phrases in a set pattern, "Run! run! as fast as you can! You can't catch me, I'm the Gingerbread Man!"

Preschoolers like stories with suspense and characters with whom they can identify. Look for stories with simple, direct plots in which familiarity is mixed with surprise, short dialogue, action that quickly builds to a climax, and a satisfying ending.

By five and six, preschoolers are enjoying the traditional folk tales such as *Cinderella,* or simple myths, like *Pandora's Box.*

Picture books are your child's first introduction to art. Choose among the best. Ask your librarian to show you Caldecott Medal and Honor Books. The Caldecott Medal is presented annually by the American Library Association to the illustrator of "the most distinguished picture book for children published in the United States during the preceding year." Look for books in which both stories and pictures combine to delight the reader.

Benefits of Story Time: at Home and at the Library

Sandra Stroner Sivulich

You may have tangible love untold
Caskets of jewels and coffers of gold
Richer than I you can never be —
I had a mother who read to me.
(From *The Reading Mother*
by Strickland Gillilan)

Sharing literature and language with preschoolers during their formative years is a priority that should not be ignored.

A preschooler's mind without words and images filling it, remains like a sponge without water, hard and small and never even beginning to reach its capacity as a useful tool. That preschool mind must be filled with sounds, vivid images and words during the sensitive period of language development. Careful attention must be paid to *what* sounds, images and words are programmed into that fertile preschool mind.

Quality picture books are vital first impressions that will build the base for literary and art appreciation. It takes just as long to read a mediocre, trite story book with dull illustrations and monotonous language as it does to share an imaginative, beautifully designed, vividly colored picture book.

Hopefully, your local library board has used your tax money wisely and you have the benefit of a professionally trained librarian who knows the criteria that constitutes an excellent picture book and who has enough copies available for her preschool population.

Befriend your children's librarian, learn her name, introduce your child to her, ask her to recommend her favorites. If you make yourself and your child's interests known, you will be represented the next time she submits a book order.

The most satisfying way of sharing literature is the one-to-one, child-on-lap reading aloud experience between you and your child. The library group story hour is another important way of sharing the child's literature with her. As a social experience, as well as a language arts experience, library story hours have certain benefits that an isolated read-aloud doesn't.

It's part of the group dynamic to have others laugh, cry, or applaud at the same time. To have shared a similar "moment" cements the group together, for example, when Danny gives his mother the secret birthday present in Marjorie Flack's classic, *Ask Mr. Bear* (Macmillan, 1932), or when all the animals finally come to the little girl in Marie Hall Ets' story *Play with Me* (Viking Kestrel, 1955). The children in the group have a common denominator which could be the basis for other interactions. They are also following directions, hearing a more dramatic rendition of a story than a one-to-one experience allows, and are participating in one of the oldest art forms known to man — storytelling.

Most librarians take the group to another part of the library, away from distractions. The programs usually have a limited registration, last for one half hour, and have finger games and songs interspersed with book sharing. When the session is finished, I would expect, as should you, smiles of enthusiasm from your child and a request to return to library "school" (as so many call it) as soon as possible, along with a desire to take home the books that were shared.

For many children, this is not only a literary experience, but the first group experience away from mother, so the ambiance at the library should be gracious, calm, cheerful and above all **fun**. A lot of libraries are doing story hour at night — pajamas are the appropriate attire and milk and cookies are served — in consideration for working parents. Some libraries are doing experimental programming with children 6 months to 28 months featuring Mother Goose rhymes, and song and finger games instead of story books.

How active or inactive a library is as far as preschool involvement depends on the area you live in, how verbal the community is in expressing its needs, and the reality of the situation regarding personalities and dollars.

But no matter where you live or your particular situation, if you make a daily habit out of sharing good books with your preschooler during the important first years of her life, if you have a public library card and are aware of what your library system offers preschoolers, if you give your child the "roots and wings" that come with literature and belong to her because she is a member of the republic of childhood, then you are giving your child a treasure that cannot be taxed or taken away and you should congratulate yourself on a job well done!

Chapter 17
Once Upon a Time...

Ellin Greene

Fairy tales appeal to children because they embody a child's conception of the world.

"Once upon a time there were three billy goats who were to go up to the hillside to make themselves fat, and the name of all three was 'Gruff.' On the way up was a bridge over a river they had to cross, and under the bridge lived a great ugly troll with eyes as big as saucers and a nose as long as a poker. So first of all came the youngest Billy Goat Gruff to cross the bridge. Trip, trap! Trip, trap! went the bridge."

The young child listening to these words is swept into the story at once. In just three short sentences the principal characters have been introduced, the conflict set up, and the action begun. The plot is carried along as each of the two younger Billy Goats Gruff is challenged by the troll, building to the climax when the Big Billy Goat Gruff and the troll square off in a contest of strength. The conflict is resolved when the Big Billy Goat Gruff tosses the troll into the river. Everything is neatly tied together as we leave the three Billy Goats Gruff eating grass on a peaceful hillside, and "snip, snap, snout, this tale's told out."

Traditional tales—more familiarly called *fairy tales, folk tales, or nursery tales*— are part of the young child's literary heritage. These tales are very old, having been passed down by word of mouth from one generation to another over centuries. They were used to entertain, to educate, and to pass on the cultural values of the group. Today, fairy tales still satisfy the young child's dramatic instinct and offer comfort and assurance.

Fairy tales appeal to children because they embody a child's conception of the world

In an effort to understand their child appeal, the late educator André Favat analyzed the connection between the characteristics of fairy tales and the psychological characteristics of young children. He concluded that "the tales embody an accurate representation of the child's conception of the world." The child's interest in the fairy tale peaks between ages 6 and 8 when he goes to school and is adjusting to a world less familiar to him. He finds a safe haven in the more orderly world of the fairy tale.

Children identify with the hero or heroine of the fairy tale

The young child believes he is the center of his world (egocentrism) and that good forces (such as parents) act in his behalf just as the hero in the fairy tale is the center of his world and good forces (such as fairies and wizards) are there to help him fulfill his desires. According to child psychologist Jean Piaget, young children of approximately age 2 through 7 believe magical relationships exist in which objects, actions, thoughts, and words influence events. These same relationships exist in the world of the fairy tale — a kiss can waken a princess from an enchanted sleep *(Sleeping Beauty)*, wishes can come true *(The Three Wishes)*, and — if you know the name of your enemy — *(Rumpelstiltskin)* you have power over him.

The characters in folk tales help children to understand patterns of human behavior

Folk tales contain all types of people, but they tend to be represented as stereotypes rather than well-rounded human beings. The typical hero is generous, good-hearted, and kind to animals and old people. The heroine is beautiful (physical beauty is equated with inner goodness), resourceful, and, like her male counterpart, brave in the face of adversity and willing to go through trials to attain her goal. Witches, for the most part, are symbols of evil; while old women are symbols of wisdom. These one-dimensional characters help children at this stage of development to define acceptable behavior. Hearing folk tales from different cultures contributes to children's appreciation of the traditions and customs of various peoples, while helping them to understand that human beings all over the world have similar feelings and needs.

Fairy tales help children to cope with their fears

Bruno Bettelheim, in his book, *The Uses of Enchantment: The Meaning and Importance of Fairy Tales,* discusses how fairy tales help children cope by enabling the child to bring unconscious material into conscious fantasies and by giving the child a structure in which to deal with her inner fears. The story of *Hansel and Gretel,* for example, helps children cope with their fear of being abandoned.

The structure of the folk tale gives the young child a sense of security

The form of the folk tale is as pleasing as its content. There is a definite beginning, middle, and ending. This tight structure gives the young child a sense of security. Chants or rhymes "control" the violence which is so troubling to many parents. In telling folk and fairy tales, "Once upon a time" signals to the child that the actions take place in a time outside everyday reality.

Young children enjoy tales that blend fantasy with reality

Tales that enthrall young children most are the "wonder tales" and animal tales. In these tales birds and animals speak and humans understand their language, and ordinary objects act in extraordinary ways.

Choosing fairy tales

For their classroom library collections and story hour programs, teachers and librarians choose fairy tales that have wide appeal and are appropriate for different stages of the child's development. Toddlers and preschoolers enjoy nursery tales, such as *The Three Billy Goats Gruff* and *The Gingerbread Boy* for their simple direct plots, short dialogue, clear images, and pleasing rhythm that comes from the repetition of words and phrases in a set pattern. Older children (from 4 or 5) are ready for tales with more complex plots, such as *Vasilissa the Beautiful* (the Russian *Cinderella*) and *Why Mosquitoes Buzz in People's Ears.*

Every family will want to have one or more collections of traditional tales for parent/child reading times. In addition, there is available a visual feast of picture book editions of single tales.

In choosing an illustrated version of an individual folk tale remember that first impressions are lasting. Choose books that accurately reflect the culture or people from which the story comes, such as, *A Story - A Story.*▩

10 *Suggestions for Sharing Folk & Fairy Tales with Your Child*

Ellin Greene

1. Introduce your child to the traditional versions of the tales first. The version that a young child hears first is the one he thinks is the "correct" version. Older preschoolers and school age children enjoy the "fractured" retellings of the traditional tales (modernized renditions) such as *The True Story of the 3 Little Pigs,* as told by A. Wolf.

2. Toddlers and preschoolers enjoy acting out nursery tales. Join in the fun. A grandmother I know surprised her two-year-old granddaughter with her rendition of the little pig's house made out of a large cardboard box. The little girl giggled with delight when her grandmother knocked on the door and cried, "Little Pig, little Pig, let me come in, or I'll huff and I'll puff and I'll blow your house in."

3. Make simple puppets with paper bags, wooden spoons, or socks for the various characters in the tales to use in dramatic play.

4. Let your child "illustrate" the story after hearing it told. While very young children are not at the stage in art where they draw figures that look like people and animals, they may want to use a variety of colors to illustrate the story in their own way. If your child is into finger paints, encourage her to express her feelings about the story rather than depict the events in the story.

5. Don't be surprised if your toddler insists on having you read or tell the story in the exact same words *every* time. (Psychologists think repetition may satisfy the child's need for order during a period of rapid physical, emotional, and mental growth. Hearing the words repeated in the same order also helps your child learn sequence, a prerequisite to reading.)

6. Young children enjoy making up their own "fairy tales" using the pattern of the folk tale for continuing the adventures of the hero or heroine in a familiar story. Let your child dictate the story to you. Seeing the words on paper connects print with talk.

7. Picture books expose your child to different styles of illustration and help him develop an appreciation of art. Ask your librarian for folk and fairy tales that are Caldecott medal and honor books. The Caldecott award is given annually to the outstanding picture books published during the previous year.

8. Show your child different illustrated editions of the same folk tale. Let your child know that everyone sees a story in a unique way. Your child's ability to imagine will grow as he learns to "make pictures in the mind" while listening to a story.

9. Take your child to toddler storytimes and picture book programs at the library. Borrow the books used in these programs.

10. On a special occasion, such as your child's birthday, take him to a book store (if you are lucky, your community will have a bookstore that specializes in children's books). Let him choose a book for your home library.

Chapter 18
Poetry for
Young Children

Ellin Greene

*A love of poetry begins
with hearing lullabies and
Mother Goose rhymes...*

Hush-a-bye, baby, on the tree top,
When the wind blows the cradle will rock;
When the bough breaks the cradle will fall,
Down will come baby, cradle, and all.

Hey diddle, diddle,
The cat and the fiddle,
The cow jumped over the moon;
The little dog laughed
To see such sport,
And the dish ran away with the spoon.

Hush-a-bye, baby is said to be "the first poem produced on American soil." According to folklore and nursery rhyme experts, Iona and Peter Opie, the author was a Pilgrim youth who came to America on the Mayflower. He was inspired by the Native American custom of placing baby in a birch-bark cradle hung on a branch of a tree. *Hey diddle diddle,* even older, is probably the best-known nonsense rhyme in the English language. What makes these rhymes so memorable?

The appeal of poetry
Poetry's appeal to young children is the rhythm and lilt of language, the sound of words tripping merrily off the tongue, the vivid images evoked by the words. It may be, as some believe, that the child receives his first impression of rhythm in embryo rocking. During the last two or three months of life in the womb, the embryo not only hears the mother's heartbeat, but outside sounds as well — such as her voice. The newborn infant can distinguish pitch (high/low) and volume (loud/soft) and is already familiar with the rhythmic patterns of human speech.

A love of poetry begins with hearing lullabies and Mother Goose rhymes in early childhood. The infant responds to the rhythm of language while being rocked in the parent's (or caregiver's) arms. Babies amuse themselves with rhythmic jabbering, repeating again and again some favorite sound. The Russian poet Kornei Chukovsky remarked that there seems to be a connection between composing rhymes and rhythmic movement, from the infant's rocking himself to the toddler's and preschooler's clapping, stamping, and jumping.

Nurturing your child's love of poetry
We can help children develop their innate attraction to the musicality of words by surrounding them with poetry from birth on. Poetry includes lullabies for babies, Mother Goose and action rhymes for toddlers and preschoolers, nonsense verse, psalms (some of the most beautiful poetry

ever written), and poems that tell a story, relate everyday experiences in a child's life, or describe the world of nature. Poetry appeals first to feelings. A poem can tickle our funny bone or make us feel sad, tell a story, or evoke an experience that lies hidden in memory. The poet Robert Frost said, "A poem begins in delight and ends in wisdom."

The parents' role in using poetry with young children
Poetry begs to be spoken or read aloud. You can recite poetry to your children while helping them with routine tasks, such as eating, dressing, and getting ready for bed. I recall having breakfast with a cranky 2 year old who refused to eat. I don't know what inspired his father to recite Lewis Carroll's *Jabberwocky* (from *Through the Looking Glass*) as he spoon-fed his son, but it worked like a charm. The toddler was spellbound by Carroll's poem and his cereal bowl was empty long before the end of the recitation.

Poems can be comforting. They can relieve boredom. At the sight of daffodils, half a century later, I can still recall the pleasure of hearing, for the very first time, Wordsworth's poem:

> *I wandered lonely as a cloud*
> *That floats on high o'er vales and hills,*
> *When all at once I saw a crowd,*
> *A host, of golden daffodils;*
> *Beside the lake, beneath the trees,*
> *Fluttering and dancing in the breeze.*

as my step-grandmother recited it on a long and, to me, boring Sunday drive.

The value of nonsense rhymes
Chukovsky believes that it is by means of fantasy as well as everyday experiences that children learn about reality. "The eagerness to play with topsy-turvies is natural to nearly every child at a certain stage of his mental growth," writes Chukovsky, "...his main purpose, as in all play, is to exercise his newly acquired skill of verifying his knowledge of things." The infant and toddler enjoy the rhythm and beat of "Hey diddle diddle," but the preschooler is amused by the absurdity of the situation. Mother Goose leads the way to a later appreciation of Lewis Carroll, Edward Lear, and modern masters of nonsense, such as John Ciardi and Eve Merriam.

How to choose poetry for young children
In selecting poetry to share with young children, look for poems that have child appeal. Very young children like repetition and rhythm. Poet Karla Kuskin says that rhythm gives a poem shape the way a skeleton holds a body together. Choose poems that delight the ear and that even have a

sense of mystery. It isn't necessary for the young child to understand the meaning of all the words, but there should be clear images and a musicality to which the child can respond.

Expose your child to a wide variety of poetry. "Don't be polite, bite in," invites Eve Merriam in *How to Eat a Poem* from her collection *A Sky Full of Poems* (Dell, 1986). Children respond to poems that appeal to the senses like *April Rain Song* by Langston Hughes (see *Sing a Song of Popcorn* in Resources, page 158) and *in Just-spring* by e.e. cummings, Resources, page 158. They appreciate the humor in poems about everyday events, such as *Mommy Slept Late and Daddy Fixed Breakfast,* by John Ciardi . Read them poems written by children (see *From Two to Five,* page 152, and *Miracles,* page 153). Chukovsky calls poems made by children "pictures in poetry" because they are so full of imagery.

Activities to use with poetry
• Make a game of a question and answer rhyme, such as *Brown Bear, Brown Bear, What Do You See?* (page 160).
• Give children an opportunity to write their own poems. It has been said that children are natural poets. This refers to their love of rhythm and their fresh outlook, not to their mastery of the forms of poetry.
• Introduce them to the poems of Eve Merriam to let them know that a poem "doesn't always have to rhyme."

• Even very young children readily recite jingles heard on television. You can encourage this "natural" memorization by repeating their favorite poems often, but do not demand memorization.

• Introduce children to pantomime (acting without speaking). Fingerplays are often the child's first conscious participation in pantomime. Toddlers enjoy pantomiming Mother Goose rhymes. Preschoolers are eager to act them out as mini-dramas, often substituting their own language for that of the rhyme.

• Invite your preschoolers to paint or draw a picture after hearing a poem. You might play background music in the mood of the poem.

• "Eat-a-Poem." Most preschoolers like to help in the kitchen. Before, during, or after preparing a recipe, share an appropriate poem, such as *Sunday Morning Toast* and *Peanut Butter Batter Bread* from Arnold Adoff's *Eats: Poems,* (Lothrop, 1979).

Suggestions for sharing poetry

• Read poetry aloud *often*. Keep a poetry anthology on your family bookshelf. See Resources (page 157) for suggestions.

• Before reading a poem to a child, read it aloud by yourself to become familiar with its rhythm, mood, and meaning. If you keep the poem's meaning in mind you will avoid the pitfall of "singsong" reading. As you read the poem aloud, see the images in your "mind's eye," hear the rhythmic patterns in your "mind's ear."

• Never share a poem you don't like yourself. Children are quick to sense an adult's insincerity. There are lots of poems to choose from. Pick those you enjoy.

• During the reading, or afterwards, share any pictures that accompany the poem.

• Repeat the poem. Welcome your child's desire to say it with you.

When you read to your child at bedtime include one or two favorite poems. You, as a parent, caught up in our culture's hectic pace, will appreciate a quiet time to unwind as much as your child.

Chapter 19
Through the Days
with Mother Goose

Laura Robb

*As youngsters hear these
magical verses, they develop
unique pictures with
their imagination.*

Three-year-old Sam watches his mom stir the pancake batter and pour it onto the hot griddle. "I've got a pancake song," says Sam. And he promptly begins to sing.

> *This is the way we make pancakes*
> *Make pancakes, make pancakes.*
> *This is the way we make pancakes*
> *Early in the morning.*

Because Sam's mother, Kate, has made Mother Goose rhymes an important part of her son's life, he can compose an original poem about making pancakes patterned after *Here We Go Round the Mulberry Bush.*

When Sam was an infant, Kate snuggled him in her arms as both sat in the rocking chair. During these shared moments, Kate sang some of her favorite rhymes. Then, at night Sam's mother and father always tucked Sam in by singing *Hush-a-bye-baby.* Bath times were accompanied by *Rub-a-Dub, Dub, Three Men in the Tub,* and after-bath play always included *This Little Piggy Went to Market.* Sam would giggle gleefully as Kate wiggled his fingers or toes repeating the rhyme again and again. Within a few months, Sam loved to be bounced on his daddy's knee to the rhythm of *Ride Baby Ride;* he soon began to clap hands to the sound of *Pat-a-Cake.*

Rhymes fit a child's daily life.
Mother Goose and Sam have become good friends because the rhymes and verses are a part of Sam's daily life. On a warm clear evening, Sam and his parents look for the first star and say the poem, *Twinkle, Twinkle, Little Star.* They greet the moon with:

> *The Man in the Moon looked out of the moon,*
> *Looked out of the moon and said,*
> *"'Tis time for all children on the earth*
> *To think about getting to bed!"*

Sam learned many animal sounds repeating *Bow-wow, Says the Dog,* and he's learning to count with, *One, Two, Buckle My Shoe; One, Two, Three, I Love Coffee;* and *One, Two, Three, Four, Five, Once I Caught a Fish Alive.* On rainy days, Sam and his mom look out the kitchen window and first recite, "It's raining, it's pouring/ The old man is snoring," and follow that by repeating many times, "Rain, rain go away/ Come again another day."

Rhymes help children learn language.
By hearing his parents recite the same rhymes again and again, Sam soon memorizes the rhymes and can chime in. Early on, Sam is learning rich

language that will become a unique part of his own language patterns. His parents help Sam find even more pleasure in daily occurrences with these Mother Goose language games, rhymes and jingles. Such early, rich language play enlarges children's vocabulary, stimulates their imagination, and offers language experiences that prepare them for reading.

The musical quality, the rollicking rhythms, the rhymes and varied language patterns of Mother Goose all delight young children. Preschool children learn to speak by experimenting with language. When parents chant these verses all day long, they interact with their children and offer countless opportunities to enjoy the verses in a lighthearted, creative way.

Children like to hear favorite rhymes at bedtime.
Many Mother Goose verses tell stories that you can read to your child before nap time and bedtime: *The Three Little Kittens, Mary Had a Little Lamb, Old Mother Hubbard,* and *This is the House That Jack Built* will entertain your preschooler. Your child will ask you to read these tales many times. Reread them frequently for young children love repetition. Not only will repeated readings continue to entertain, but your youngster may soon memorize the verses and begin saying them along with you.

Rhymes help develop a sense of humor.
Sam always laughs when he hears *Georgie, Porgie, Pudding and Pie.* Lips pursed, Sam mimes a huge kiss and then runs out of the room. "That's silly; say it again," he asks. And Sam repeats his mini-drama as his mother recites the rhyme. Children laugh at the surprise ending of *I Am a Gold Lock,* and the absurdities of *Heigh, Diddle, Diddle* and *Fiddle-De-Dee.* The swiftly moving action in all the verses hold young children's interest and develop their sense of humor.

Mother Goose is ageless, and her flights of fantasy, her wisdom, and her quickly-paced tales have entertained and fascinated children for hundreds of years. When parents weave nursery rhymes into everyday life they send their children a powerful message: *poetry is entertaining and meaningful.*

Children learn to listen to fine literature in natural and playful situations. As youngsters hear these magical verses and make them their own, they *become careful listeners, expand their vocabulary, and develop unique pictures within their imagination.*

Laura Robb

Cooking with Mother Goose
So many of the nursery rhymes talk about food. Plan a Mother Goose menu with your child. Here are some suggestions:

• Porridge (Pease Porridge Hot)
• Ham (To Market, To Market)
• Bread and honey (Sing a Song of Sixpence)
• Eggs (There Was an Old Woman as I've Heard Tell)
• Rolls (Blow, Wind, Blow! *and* Go Mill, Go!)
• Muffins (Oh Do You Know the Muffin Man?)
• Plum Pie (Little Jack Horner)
• Tarts (The Queen of Hearts)
• Pumpkin Bread/Pie (Peter, Peter Pumpkin Eater)
• Apple pie (An Apple Pie, When It Looks Nice)
• White Cake (Ride a Cock Horse to Banbury Cross to See What Tommy Can Buy)

Tongue Twister Fun
Help your child learn "Peter Piper picked a peck of pickled peppers." Try to see how quickly she can say the rhyme.

Games to Play

Invite the whole family and/or some of your child's friends to play *Ring a Ring o' Roses*, *The Farmer in the Dell*, *Here We Go Round the Mulberry Bush*, and *London Bridge is Falling Down*.

Here are suggested directions for these games. After you play them many times, ask your preschooler to add some original verses and play those, too!

Ring a Ring o' Roses

Two or more players join hands. Circle to the left or right. Fall down on the last line, "We all fall down."

The Farmer in the Dell

Play this game with 4 or more persons. Form a circle and select the 'farmer' to stand in the middle. As the group circles around the farmer chanting the verses, the farmer chooses a "wife" from the group, the wife chooses a "child" and the game continues until the 'cheese' the last person, is left.

Here We Go Round the Mulberry Bush

Circle left or right, and stop to pantomime the washing of hands and clothes, going to school and leaving school.

London Bridge is Falling Down

Two people face each other, join hands and hold hands above their heads, forming a bridge. As the group chants the verses, they continuously march in and out of the bridge. When they chant, "Take the key and lock him (or her) up," the arms of the bridge fall around the caught child.

Movement Activities

Your child can learn to skip with *To Market, To Market;* he can trot or gallop to *Ride a Cock Horse;* walk slowly to *A Dillar a Dollar;* sway to *I Saw a Ship A-Sailing;* or pretend to fly with *Ladybird! Ladybird! Fly Away Home.*

Mother Goose for Two Voices

Many of the rhymes use the question-answer format. Have your child answer the questions you ask in such verses as, *Baa, Baa, Black Sheep; Pussy Cat, Pussy Cat, Where have you been?* and *Mistress Mary Quite Contrary.* When your child knows the entire poem, reverse roles and have your preschooler ask the questions and you respond.

Fingerplays

Young children love to be actively involved in poetry with their bodies as well as with words. Use *Dance, Thumbkin, Dance* to teach your child names for his fingers. Make your youngster aware of his forehead, eyes, cheeks, mouth, and chin with *Here Sits the Lord Mayor,* and *Brow Brinky.*

Create a fingerplay for *Hickory Dickory Dock* or other rhymes by reciting the poem and using your fingers, hands and arms to act them out.

Sewing Cards

Select favorite animals from Mother Goose rhymes such as a cat, dog, pig, or lamb. Draw the animal on a piece of cardboard and have your child color it. Punch holes, one inch apart, around the outline of the animal.

Use a long shoelace or stiffen the ends of yarn by wrapping them with cellophane tape. Help your child sew in and out of the holes. Display the card and say the rhyme often.

Mother Goose Rhythm Band

Make simple rhythm instruments to use with your preschooler while chanting nursery rhymes. Fill a coffee can with dried beans, cover the can and shake. Use two small sticks to beat out rhythms. Pots and spoons make wonderful, percussive sounds. An empty, cylindrical oatmeal box makes a fine drum.

Poems such as *A Farmer When Trotting Upon His Gray Mare,* and *This is the Way the Ladies Ride* are perfect for musical accompaniments. Look in your Mother Goose book for many other rhythmic poems.

Creative Drama

Let your child dramatize such nursery rhymes as *Polly Put the Kettle On, Little Miss Muffet, The North Wind Doth Blow,* and *Little Boy Blue.*

Mother Goose Activity Calendar
31 activities to share with your preschooler during any month.
Laura Robb

SUNDAY	MONDAY	TUESDAY	WEDNESDAY	THURSDAY	FRIDAY	SATURDAY
				1 Read *The House that Jack Built* — a Mother Goose tale that adds new lines as the story grows.	**2** As you prepare to take your child marketing sing *To Market, To Market.*	**3** As you help your child wash hands clean recite *There's a Neat Little Clock.*
4 Make paper crowns for a King and a Queen. Have children wear the crowns and act out *Sing a Song of Sixpence.*	**5** Teach your child to gallop and trot to *Ride a Cock Horse to Banbury Cross,* and *Ride Away, Ride Away, Johnny Shall Ride.*	**6** Teach your child to march with *The Old Grand Duke of York.*	**7** On a trip to the shoe repair shop sing *Cobbler, Cobbler Mend My Shoe.*	**8** Learn how many days in each month with *Thirty Days Hath September.*	**9** Read nursery rhymes about cats and dogs such as *Pussy Cat, Pussy Cat, Where Have You Been?* — and then go to a pet shop.	**10** Help your youngster dress up as a favorite Mother Goose character. Then recite and dramatize the rhyme.
11 As you tie your child's shoelace recite *One, Two, Buckle my Shoe.*	**12** Have a tea party one afternoon and substitute your child's name as you chant *Polly, Put the Kettle On.*	**13** Make paper boats to sail in the sink or bathtub and sing *I Saw Three Ships A Sailing.*	**14** Help your child learn the months of the year with *January Brings the Snow.*	**15** Feed the hungry birds some bread or bird seed as you recite *The North Wind Doth Blow.*	**16** Play riddle games with Mother Goose verses, such as *I Have a Little Sister* or *Thirty White Horses.*	**17** Announce, "It's bedtime!" to your child with *The Man in the Moon Looked Out of the Moon.*

18	19	20	21	22	23	24
Make bread with your child and chant *Pat-a-Cake* as you knead the dough. Or chant the rhyme as you go to the bakery.	Have a Mother Goose snack of bread and honey and recite *Sing a Song of Sixpence* as you help your child spread honey on the bread.	Dramatize *The Three Little Kittens* with your child. Then read other books about mittens, such as Jan Brett's *The Mitten*. (Putnam, 1989)	Practice skipping to the barber shop — or any place else — by saying *Hippity Hop to the Barber Shop*.	Read the text and enjoy the illustrations in Maurice Sendak's interpretation of these favorite Mother Goose rhymes: *Hector Protector* and *As I Went Over the Water* (Harper & Row, 1965).	Play the *Jack Be Nimble* game by placing a small block (as a candlestick) on the floor. Have your preschooler jump over the "candlestick" while reciting the rhyme with you.	Use Mother Goose verses to talk about the weather with your child. Here are a few to share: *Rain, Rain, Go Away* ; *It's Raining, It's Pouring;* and *Blow, Wind, Blow.*

25	26	27	28	29	30	31
Ask your preschooler to help you water plants and wash their leaves as you recite *Mistress Mary, Quite Contrary.*	Teach your child some Mother Goose tunes using Nancy Larrick's *Songs from Mother Goose,* or *Sharon, Lois & Bram's Mother Goose.*	Practice learning the days of the week with *Monday Alone, Tuesday Together* and *Monday's Child is Fair of Face.*	Dramatize all the verses of *Jack and Jill,* and let your youngster's imagination direct the activity.	Read Mother Goose rhymes about pets to your child, such as *Old Mother Hubbard.* Then read Steven Kellog's *The Mysterious Tadpole* (Dial, 1977) to introduce your child to a most unusual pet.	Use buttons, colored markers, felt and glue to make Punch and Judy sock puppets. Then put your hand into the sock and use the puppets to dramatize *Punch and Judy Fought for a Pie.*	Help your youngster understand how Important it is treat pets gently by reading and talking about *I Love Little Pussy.*

Chapter 20
A Multicultural Celebration Through Literature

Ellin Greene

*...multicultural stories and poems
can give children positive images
of themselves and of people
different from them.*

Human beings are more alike than different

In spite of differences in color of skin, language, and customs, human beings share the same emotions and needs. We may speak in different languages, but we all use language to express feelings, to tell stories, to share information. All children have the same needs — to love and to be loved, to have enough food to eat and clothing to keep them warm, to feel they belong, to achieve, to have beauty in their lives, to learn, and to grow.

How can we help our children to grow up with pride in their own heritage and respect and appreciation for people from other racial and ethnic groups?

Role of literature

(All books with a superscript number (^{25}) are listed on page 142 with author, publisher, and date of publication.)

Well-written, well-illustrated multicultural stories and poems can give children positive images of themselves and of people different from them. When you read *The Snowy Day*[31] to a white child, that child sees that a black child enjoys making angels in the snow and building a snowman as much as he does. Peter, the book child, and the child (of whatever color) hearing the story, share the same feelings of exhilaration and joy at playing in the snow.

How to select multicultural books

Multicultural literature includes stories about everyday life, poetry, folk tales, and information books. See the list of outstanding books in this chapter to help you choose books for your child that are authentic in the setting, characterization, and values of the people presented. In addition, ask your librarian for recommendations.

Stories about everyday life should have a main character that stands out as an individual, not just as a symbol of a particular racial or ethnic group. *Uncle Jed's Barbershop*[41] gives African American children a sense of history and pride in achievement. In the segregated South of the 1920s, Sarah Jean's Uncle Jed is the only black barber in the county. His dream is to own his own shop, but when five-year-old Sarah Jean needs an operation, he uses his savings to pay for it. He saves again, only to lose everything when the bank fails in the Great Depression. But Uncle Jed keeps hold of his dream, and on his 79th birthday Sarah Jean is present to celebrate the opening of Uncle Jed's barbershop and to honor the man who taught her to dream, too. In another book, *Amazing Grace*[25], a modern little black girl breaks stereotypes and achieves her dream to act the part of Peter Pan in her school play.

Asian American respect for the elderly is evident in *Grandfather's Journey*[49]. The author, a Japanese American, honors the memory of his grandfather in his bittersweet account of three generations of a family torn by its love for two different cultures. In *Dumpling Soup*[48], a talented new writer and illustrator team draw on their different ethnic backgrounds to introduce young children to the food, games, language and customs of an extended Asian American family living on the Hawaiian island of Oahu. Seven-year old Marisa finally gets to help make <u>mandoo</u> (dumplings) for the family's New Year Celebration. Marisa's grandmother calls the family "chop suey" which means "all-mixed up." The family members include Korean, Japanese, Chinese, Hawaiian, and <u>haole</u> (Hawaiian for white people). Young children will identify with Marisa's pride in her first dumplings (and her initial fear that no one will eat them), and relish the warmth of family love that surrounds her. Unfamiliar Hawaiian, Japanese, and Korean words are explained in a glossary as well as within the text.

In *Music, Music for Everyone*[52], Rosa and her friends, Leora, Mae, and Jenny live in an integrated city neighborhood. They form the Oak Street Band, and their first performance is at a party celebrating Leora's great-grand-parents' fiftieth anniversary of the opening of their neighborhood market. The exuberant illustrations convey the warm caring of neighbors, young and old. In *Halmoni and the Picnic*[12] Halmoni (which means grandmother in Korea), has recently arrived in New York City from Korea and is finding it hard to adjust to American life. When her granddaughter, Yunmi, and her third-grade classmates invite Halmoni to chaperone them at their picnic in Central Park, Halmoni and her kimbap (a Korean dish made of rice, carrots, eggs, and green vegetables wrapped in seaweed) are received gladly. Other books that explore the special relationship between grand-parents and grandchildren, the need to love and to be loved, include *Grand-father and I*[10], *Grandmother and I*[11], and *Abuela*[16].

Wade Hudson, compiler of *Pass It On: African-American Poetry for Children*[27], believes that **poetry** holds a special place within the African American culture. His book introduces children to the works of some of the outstand-ing African American writers, including Langston Hughes, Nikki Giovanni, and Lucille Clifton. In *The Trees Stand Shining*[28], the close relationship that Native Americans feel for the earth is reflected in lullabies, short stories, and prayers. *The Tamarindo Puppy and Other Poems*[47], a bilingual book with bright childlike paintings, introduces children to a sprinkling of Spanish words. *Talking Like the Rain: A First Book of Poems*[32] contains over 100 poems about the important moments in a child's life, from dressing up and birthday parties to splashing in puddles and discovering the lovely whiteness of snow. The bright watercolor paintings accompanying the po-ems show people of different races and ages.

Preschoolers enjoy simple **folktales and legends**. There are many attractive anthologies with traditional tales from around the world, such as *The Fairy Tale Treasury*[23]. Pura Belpre remembers stories from her childhood in Puerto Rico in *The Tiger and the Rabbit and Other Tales*[7]. "The Bed," one of these tales, is a repetitive story that invites children to participate actively in the telling. Another fine collection of tales to share with your preschooler is *The Knee-High Man and Other Tales*[34].

You will find many beautiful picture book editions of single folktales at your library or book store, such as *Borreguita and the Coyote*[1], *Who's in Rabbit's House?*[2] and *The Eye of the Needle*[50].

Ask your librarian to suggest other titles appropriate for sharing with your preschooler. Preschoolers who are familiar with *Little Red Riding Hood* will be intrigued by *Lon Po Po*[53], the Chinese Red Riding Hood. The tale of *Cinderella* has been found all over the world. *Yeh-Shen: A Cinderella Story from China*[35], *The Korean Cinderella*[13], and *The Rough-Face Girl*[36] (Native American) are just a few that have been published in recent years.

Young children enjoy "why" stories. Try *Why the Sun and Moon Live in the Sky*[14], *Why Mosquitoes Buzz in People's Ears*[3], and *The Legend of the Cranberry*[21] which tells what may have happened to the mastodons (extinct elephant-like animals) and how cranberries came into our lives.

Information Books
Come Home with Me: A Multicultural Treasure Hunt[29] is a wonderful book with colorful photographs of things kids can find in African American, Irish American, Cambodian, and Latino communities in America. The book is based on the <u>Kids</u> <u>Bridge</u> exhibit that originally opened at The Children's Museum in Boston and then toured the country through the Smithsonian Sites Program. Museums are terrific places to introduce children to the arts and crafts of people from diverse backgrounds. If you don't live near a museum, borrow some art books from your public library, such as *A Child's Book of Art: Great Pictures/First Words*[40]. *The Goat in the Rug*[8] is an informative and amusing story of the making of a Navajo rug, as told by the goat, Geraldine. At your library you can also find books about ethnic holidays, folk songs and dances. Simple biographies like *Happy Birthday, Martin Luther King*[37] relate the life of an inspiring leader.

Multicultural Book Activities
• Croon lullabies and recite nursery rhymes to your baby. Sing spirituals and folk songs to your little ones. Books: *Baby's Book of Lullabies and Cradle Songs*[20]; *Tortillitas Para Mama: And Other Nursery Rhymes*[22]; *All Night, All Day: A Child's First Book of African-American Spirituals*[9].

• Take your child to the public library storytime where she will hear stories from around the world. Borrow picture book editions of folktales and read them to your preschooler.

• A fun way to help your child appreciate the contributions of ethnic groups to American life is to serve favorite ethnic foods, such as *tostones* (fried plantains) or *latkes* (potato pancakes). Books: *Come Home with Me: A Multicultural Treasure Hunt*[29]; *Holiday Treats* [24] and *The Multicultural Cookbook for Students*[4].

• Bake bread from another country. Book: *Bread, Bread, Bread*[42] has large photographs that show children the many types of bread enjoyed by people around the world.

• Prepare a Japanese meal and serve it with chopsticks. Book: *How My Parents Learned to Eat*[18].

• After reading *When Clay Sings*[5] to your child, let him make a simple clay pot and decorate it with paint.   ▨

Group Storytelling Activities

Ellin Greene

These storytelling activities are appropriate to use with a group of children. Many of these activities can be adapted for use with an individual child.

• When you tell a story from a major ethnic minority, introduce it in a way that is traditional to that culture. For example, Haitian storytellers begin with the call "Crick" and the audience responds "Crack" to show that they are ready to listen. West African storytellers wear a story hat, a hat with various objects attached to it and begin by having the audience choose an object and telling a story in which that object appears. Books: *Through the Eyes of a Child*[43]; *The World of Storytelling*[46].

• Become familiar with the various styles of storytelling associated with the major ethnic minorities. If you feel comfortable, use the appropriate style as you tell. In many African cultures, storytelling includes mimicry, voice changes for the various characters, movement, music and rhythm, and audience participation. On the other hand, in many Native American tribes, the listeners are expected to listen closely and not to interrupt the storyteller. Books: *Through the Eyes of a Child*[43]; *The World of Storytelling*[46].

•Introduce the children to folk characters from different cultures, such as Raven in the Pacific Northwest Indian tales and Anansi from West Africa. Point out that some of the characters move from one culture to another; for example, Anansi became Anancy in Jamaica, and the African rabbit Zomo became Brer Rabbit in the Americas. Books: *Raven: A Trickster Tale from the Pacific Northwest*[39]; *Anansi the Spider*[38]; *The Knee-High Man*[34].

•If the children want to talk about the story after hearing it, ask open-ended questions. For example, you might talk about the way the main character behaved and ask the children how they would have acted in the situation.

•Tell the children variants of familiar folk tales. Do not let them know what you are doing. Give them the pleasure of discovering old friends in new dress. Books: *The Korean Cinderella*[13], *Yeh-Shen*[35], *The Rough-Face Girl*[36].

•Tell stories using string and yarn, nesting dolls, or chalk. Book: *The Story Vine: A Source Book of Unusual and Easy-to-Tell Stories from Around the World*[45].

•In old Japan storytellers used a series of picture cards to tell their stories. You can make a Japanese "kamishibai" theatre out of a heavy cardboard box. (See directions on page 552 in the book *Through the Eyes of a Child*[43]). Have the children make picture cards after hearing a Japanese tale. Book: *The Two Foolish Cats*[51].

•Many stories lend themselves to flannel board telling. Make the flannel board figures and let the children retell the story using the figures. Books: *Why Mosquitoes Buzz in People's Ears*[3]; *Perez and Martina*[6].

•After telling a story, invite the children to act it out. Book: *Who's in Rabbit's House?*[2]. This story also lends itself to telling with puppets. Simple puppets can be made from paper bags or paper plates. Books: *Through the Eyes of a Child*[43], pages 304-305; *Tell and Draw Paper Bag Puppet Book*[44].

•Tell a pourquoi (why) story, then ask the children to create their own "why" story. Books: *Why the Sun and Moon Live in the Sky*[14]; *Why the Sky Is Far Away*[19]; *Why Mosquitoes Buzz in People's Ears*[3]; *The Legend of the Cranberry*[21]; *The Legend of the Bluebonnet*[15].

•Seek out persons in your community who still practice folk arts, such as pisanki (Polish egg decorating using a wax resist process) or origami (Japanese paper folding). Perhaps there are Hmong weavers, African American gospel singers, or Native American basket makers who would be willing to demonstrate their art to the children.

•Encourage the children to ask their parents and grandparents about family customs. If you practice ethnic traditions yourself, be generous about sharing information about customs, foods, etc. with the children.

•Read *Nine Days to Christmas*[17] to the children. Bring in a piñata (you can make one) and let the children play the piñata game. Book: *Through the Eyes of a Child*[43], page 549.

•Read aloud stories of ethnic holidays — Chanukkah, Christmas, and Kwanzaa. Ask the children how they celebrate their special holidays. Books: *The Chanukkah Guest*[33]; *An Island Christmas*[30]; *Celebrating Kwanzaa*[26].

•Plan a party using an ethnic theme. Play games, sing songs, dance traditional dances and serve traditional foods.   ▓

Books Discussed in Chapter 20

Ellin Greene

1 **Borreguita and the Coyote: A Tale from Ayutla, Mexico**, trans. and retold by Verna Aardema. Illus. by Petra Mathers. Knopf, 1991.

2 **Who's in Rabbit's House?**, retold by Verna Aardema. Illus. by Leo and Diane Dillon. Dial, 1977.

3 **Why Mosquitoes Buzz in People's Ears: A West African Tale**, retold by Verna Aardema. Illus. by Leo and Diane Dillon. Dial, 1975.

4 **The Multicultural Cookbook for Students**, by Carole Lisa Albyn and Lois Sinaiko Webb. Orynx Press, 1993.

5 **When Clay Sings**, by Byrd Baylor. Illus. by Tom Bahti. Scribners, 1987.

6 **Perez and Martina**, by Pura Belpré. Illus. by Carlos Sánchez M. Available in Spanish, **Perez y Martina**. Warne, 1966.

7 **The Tiger and the Rabbit and Other Tales**, by Pura Belpré. Illus. by Tomie de Paola. Lippincott, 1965.

8 **The Goat in the Rug**, by Charles L. Blood and Martin Link. Illus. by Nancy Winslow Parker. Four Winds, 1976.

9 **All Night, All Day: A Child's First Book of African-American Spirituals**, sel. and illus. by Ashley Bryan. Atheneum, 1991.

10 **Grandfather and I**, by Helen E. Buckley. Illus. by Jan Ormerod. Lothrop, 1994.

11 **Grandmother and I**, by Helen E. Buckley. Illus. by Jan Ormerod. Lothrop, 1994.

12 **Halmoni and the Picnic**, by Sook Nyul Choi. Illus. by Karen M. Dugan. Houghton Mifflin, 1993.

13 **The Korean Cinderella**, by Shirley Climo. Illus. by Ruth Heller. HarperCollins, 1993.

14 **Why the Sun and Moon Live in the Sky: An African Folktale**, by Elphinstone Dayrell. Illus. by Blair Lent. Houghton Mifflin, 1968.

15 **The Legend of the Bluebonnet**, by Tomie de Paola. Putnam, 1983.

16 **Abuela**, by Arthur Dorros. Illus. by Elisa Kleven. Dutton, 1991.

17 **Nine Days to Christmas: A Story of Mexico**, by Marie Hall Ets and Aurora Labastida. Viking, 1959.

18 **How My Parents Learned to Eat,** by Ina R. Friedman. Illus. by Allen Say. Houghton Mifflin, 1987.

19 **Why the Sky Is Far Away: A Nigerian Folktale**, retold by Mary-Joan Gerson. Illus. by Carla Golembe. Little, Brown, 1992.

20 **Baby's Book of Lullabies and Cradle Songs**, sel. and illus. by Yvonne Gilbert. Dial, 1990.

21 **The Legend of the Cranberry: A Paleo-Indian Tale**, by Ellin Greene. Illus. by Brad Sneed. Simon & Schuster, 1993.

22 **Tortillitas Para Mama: And Other Nursery Rhymes. Spanish and English**, sel. and trans. by Margot C. Griego, et al. Illus. by Barbara Cooney. Holt, 1981.

23 **The Fairy Tale Treasury**, sel. by Virginia Hamilton. Illus. by Raymond Briggs. Dell, 1986.

24 **Holiday Treats**, by Esther Hautzig. Illus. by Yaroslava. Macmillan, 1983.

25 **Amazing Grace**, by Mary Hoffman. Illus. by Caroline Binch. Dial, 1991.

26 **Celebrating Kwanzaa**, by Diane Hoyt-Goldsmith. Photographs by Lawrence Migdale. Holiday House, 1993.

27 **Pass It On: African-American Poetry for Children**, sel. by Wade Hudson. Illus. by Floyd Cooper. Scholastic, 1993.

28 **The Trees Stand Shining: Poetry of the North American Indians**, sel. by Hettie Jones. Illus. by Robert Andrew Parker. Dial, 1971. Reissued 1993.

29 **Come Home with Me: A Multicultural Treasure Hunt**, by Aylette Jenness. Photographs by Max Belcher. The New Press, 1993.

30 **An Island Christmas**, by Lynn Joseph. Illus. by Catherine Stock. Clarion, 1992.

31 **The Snowy Day**, by Ezra Jack Keats. Viking, 1962. Available in Spanish, **Un Día de Nieve**.

32 **Talking Like the Rain: A First Book of Poems**, sel. by X. J. Kennedy and Dorothy M. Kennedy. Illus. by Jane Dyer. Little, Brown, 1992.

33 **The Chanukkah Guest**, by Eric A. Kimmel. Illus. by Giora Carmi. Holiday House, 1990.

34 **The Knee-High Man and Other Tales**, by Julius Lester. Illus. by Ralph Pinto. Dial, 1992.

35 **Yeh-Shen: A Cinderella Story from China**, by Ai-Ling Louie. Illus. by Ed Young. Philomel, 1990.

36 **The Rough-Face Girl**, by Rafe Martin. Illus. by David Shannon. Putnam, 1992.

37 **Happy Birthday, Martin Luther King**, by Jean Marzollo. Illus. by J. Brian Pinkney. Scholastic, 1993.

38 **Anansi the Spider: A Tale from the Ashanti**, adapted and illus. by Gerald McDermott. Holt, 1972.

39 **Raven: A Trickster Tale from the Pacific Northwest**, by Gerald McDermott. Harcourt, 1993.

40 **A Child's Book of Art: Great Pictures/First Words**, sel. by Lucy Micklethwait. Dorling Kindersley, 1993.

41 **Uncle Jed's Barbershop**, by Margaree King Mitchell. Illus. by James Ransome. Simon & Schuster, 1993.

42 **Bread, Bread, Bread**, by Ann Morris. Photographs by Ken Heyman. Lothrop, 1989.

43 **Through the Eyes of a Child: An Introduction to Children's Literature**, by Donna E. Norton. Second edition. Merrill, 1987.

44 **Tell and Draw Paper Bag Puppet Book**, by Margaret J. Oldfield. Second edition. Creative Storytime, 1981.

45 **The Story Vine: A Source Book of Unusual and Easy-to-Tell Stories from Around the World**, by Anne Pellowski. Illus. by Lynn Sweat. Macmillan, 1984.

46 **The World of Storytelling**, by Anne Pellowski. Wilson, 1990.

47 **The Tamarindo Puppy and Other Poems**, by Charlotte Pomerantz. Illus. by Byron Barton. Greenwillow, 1980. Reissued 1993.

48 **Dumpling Soup**, by Jama Kim Rattigan. Illus. by Lillian Hsu-Flanders. Little, Brown, 1993.

49 **Grandfather's Journey**, by Allen Say. Houghton Mifflin, 1993.

50 **The Eye of the Needle**, retold and Illus. by Teri Sloat. Dutton, 1990.

51 **The Two Foolish Cats**, by Yoshiko Uchida. Illus. by Margot Zemach. Macmillan/McElderry Books, 1987.

52 **Music, Music for Everyone**, by Vera B. Williams. Greenwillow, 1984.

53 **Lon Po Po: A Red-Riding Hood Story from China**, trans. and illus. by Ed Young. Philomel, 1989.

Chapter 21
Information Books...
Educational and Fun

Laura Robb

From birth , a world
of information
surrounds your child.

(All books with a superscript number ([25]) are listed on page 150 with author, publisher and date of publication.)

Three-year-old Jeremy cuddles next to me on a bright blue bean bag. He starts the book *Color Zoo*[16]. "Look, this means STOP," and he points to the red square at the back of the book. "And green means GO." Jeremy tosses the book in my lap and jogs around me, shouting, "I'm going!" Once he's snuggled into the chair, I point to the yellow square and ask, "What does the yellow mean?" "Wait your turn, silly!" he answers. Jeremy's obvious connection between color and the meaning of traffic lights demonstrates a complex linkage between the colors in a book and his own experiences.

Why Information Books?
From birth, a world of information surrounds your child. And like Jeremy, your child makes sense of this world and develops language by doing, observing, conversing, and listening. Information books enhance and expand young children's experiences. Their rich illustrations, photographs, and simple texts offer many examples of the concepts children can learn in their everyday activities.

A Wide and Varied Selection
Information books come in different shapes, sizes and formats. The ones discussed here, I believe, are especially beneficial to preschoolers. Talk and questions will flow as you and your child enter the world of informational books and discover many ways to view an idea. The detailed illustrations or photographs, alone, invite youngsters to return to these books again and again.

Counting Books help children expand developing concepts about mathematics. Actively involve your preschooler in the book by playing counting games with the illustrations and telling stories inspired by the pictures. Then talk about the numbers you see in your everyday surroundings, such as in stores, street signs, and advertisements. Sharing a book this way helps bridge abstract concepts with everyday applications of numbers. As a parent you can introduce numerals and play matching games with *My Very First Book of Numbers*[13]. You can practice counting and tell stories about the colorful pictures in *How Many?* [29] or enthrall youngsters with counting the sights and sounds of a Caribbean spring in *One Smiling Grandma*[25].

ABC Books teach letter names and their corresponding sounds. They can also stir children's interest in their world. *The Folks In The Valley* [8] introduces preschoolers to life on Pennsylvania Dutch farms while *the alphabet tree* [26] shows children how letters become words.

Geography Books use colorful illustrations to introduce youngsters to the fascinating features of our earth. Together you can explore the vast world of the planet in *Geography From A to Z: A Picture Glossary*[24] .

Self-Awareness Books foster confidence-building and self-esteem by increasing children's understanding of their own identities. *My Hands*[6], *My Feet*[4] *My Five Senses*[5] and *I'm Growing*[1] help children recognize similarities between themselves and people of different cultures.

Animal Books, an all time favorite, can focus children on the fascinating parts of animals as in *Breathtaking Noses*[27] and *What Neat Feet!*[28] You can introduce your child to the birth and growth of a chick, puppy or rabbit through the *See How They Grow series*[41,42,43] or cultivate an interest in observing and preserving nature through books such as *Deer at the Brook*[7].

Other Cultures and Places come to life as you and your child journey to distant locales through books like *Tools*[35]; *Houses and Homes*[34], and *Hats Hats Hats*[33] or *People*[46], which celebrates similarities and differences of people all over the world. Such books offer insights into the common bonds that unite everyone, yet encourage youngsters to appreciate their own unique qualities.

Explore Colors in books that also challenge your child's language development and understanding of several concepts. *Planting a Rainbow*[17] introduces colors with themes of gardening, flowers, and seasons. In *Mary Wore Her Red Dress*[37] children will enjoy identifying colors, animals, settings, and will also learn a delightful song.

Science Books encourage children to think about the world and the universe while investigating subjects like astronomy, geology, pet care, ecology, plant and insect life. Acquaint your youngster with how milk arrives in a carton by reading *Milk: From Cow to Carton*[3] or conduct scientificexperiments using *Science Toys & Tricks*[48].

Books Instead Of Experiences?

Parents should remember that books are not a substitute for experiences; young children learn best by doing. Informational books help broaden a child's daily experiences as well as enhance new experiences. They also kindle the imagination and enlarge preschoolers' thinking and speaking vocabulary.

Information Book Activities

Laura Robb

Take a color tour of the supermarket and name the colors of the fruits and vegetables you see. Book: *Growing Colors*[32].

• Use water color or tempera paints to mix primary colors and obtain orange, green, purple, browns and grays. Book: *Color Dance*[22].

• Talk about opposites such as up-down, happy-sad, under-over. Book: *Opposites*[23].

• Count and learn the names of all the animals that board the train in Eric Carle's book *1,2,3, To The Zoo*[12]. Have fun counting backwards from 10 to 1. Book: *Moon Jump: A Cow Cowntdown*[11].

• Visit a pizzeria and learn how pizza is made. Talk about the ingredients and nutrition. Book: *Pizza Man*[38].

• Introduce fractions and have fun with wholes, halves and fourths by eating your way to understanding. Book. *Eating Fractions*[31].

• In your neighborhood, look for airplanes during the day and evening. Visit an airport. Talk about the inside of a plane, the types of planes, and what you discovered at the airport. Book: *Let's Fly from A to Z*[30].

• Thinking about purchasing a pet? Chat with a veterinarian, visit a pet shop, and read about different pets and their care. Book: *Let's Get A Pet*[49].

• Take listening walks in the park, through your neighborhood, the zoo, or a department store. Don't rush; don't talk. Just listen and discover the soft and loud sounds that surround you. After the walk, talk about the various sounds you heard. Book: *The Listening Walk*[44].

• Make traffic light stick or bag puppets. It's easy to do. Color, cut out, and tape a red, green, and yellow circle on a small brown paper bag or attach each circle to a wooden popsicle stick or stiff, cardboard strip. Now you're ready to play STOP, GO and WAIT games. Book: *Red Light. Green Light*[10].

• Draw a square, circle, triangle, rectangle, heart, oval, diamond, octagon and hexagon. Locate these shapes in your house and neighborhood. Book: *Color Zoo*[16].

• Bake cookies with your child. Discuss the ingredients, mix the dough, cut and decorate the cookies. Then eat and enjoy! Book: *Mr. Cookie Baker*[47].

• Feel the wind by holding out your hand on a breezy and windy day. Talk about things the wind can do like fly a kite, make noise, dry laundry on a line, and sail a boat. Book: *Feel the Wind*[15].

• Learn about the different kinds of trucks by watching trucks in your neighborhood and on the highway during car trips. Discuss the different things trucks are used for such as collecting garbage, delivering, and moving. Book: *Trucks*[18].

• Have you wondered why water rolls off a duck's back? Watch ducks swim and dive. Then read the book: *Ducks Don't Get Wet*[19].

• Listen to weather forecasts on TV. Watch the weather every day and discuss the clouds, color of the sky, temperature, whether it's rainy, sunny, cloudy, stormy or snowing. Book: *What Will the Weather Be?*[14].

• Introduce the idea of size by identifying large, small, wide, narrow objects. Compare people and objects in your home and neighborhood. Book: *Is It Larger? Is It Smaller?*[20].

• Tour your community fire house. You might even get to sit in a truck! Book: *Fire Engines*[40].

• Use a magnifying glass to look at a strand of hair, a blade of grass, or a piece of wool. What happens when you enlarge objects? Book. *Magnification: A Pop-Up Lift-The-Flap Book*[36].

• Talk about recycling and conservation and what your family and community do to protect and preserve our earth. Visit a local recycling plant. Book: *The Berenstain Bears DON'T POLLUTE*[9].

• Tour your town or community. Identify the school, library, supermarket and office buildings. Talk about the people who visit and use those places as well as the people who work there. Book: *Come to Town*[39].

• Understand what manners are and learn to practice good manners. Find out how to greet, interrupt, apologize, help, or talk on the telephone. Book: *Manners*[2].

• Talk about all the wonderful things skin does. For example: protect, perspire and keep out harmful germs. Look at your fingertips under a magnifying glass. Rub your fingers in fingerpaint and press tips on white paper, then talk about the loops and lines. Book: *Your Skin and Mine*[45].

• Experience "rough, smooth, and shiny" by feeling and looking at different textures such as a penny, tree trunks, silk, a wooden bowl, books, spoons, or pots. Book: *Is It Rough? Is It Smooth? Is It Shiny?*[21].

Books Discussed
in Chapter 21

Laura Robb

[1] *I'm Growing!* by Aliki. HarperCollins,1992.

[2] *Manners* by Aliki. Greenwillow, 1990.

[3] *Milk: From Cow to Carton* by Aliki. HarperCollins, 1992.

[4] *My Feet* by Aliki. Crowell, 1990.

[5] *My Five Senses* by Aliki. Crowell, 1989.

[6] *My Hands* by Aliki. Crowell, 1990.

[7] *Deer at the Brook* by Jim Arnofsky. Mulberry, 1986.

[8] *The Folks In The Valley* by Jim Aylesworth. HarperCollins, 1992.

[9] *The Berenstain Bears DON'T POLLUTE* by Stan and Jan Berenstain. Random House, 1991.

[10] *Red Light. Green Light* by Margaret Wise Brown. Scholastic, 1992.

11 *Moon Jump: A Cow Cowntdown* by Paula Brown. Viking, 1993.

12 *1,2,3, To The Zoo: a counting book* by Eric Carle. Putnam, 1991.

13 *My Very First Book of Numbers* by Eric Carle. HarperCollins, 1974.

14 *What Will the Weather Be?* by Linda DeWitt. HarperCollins, 1991.

15 *Feel the Wind* by Arthur Dorros. Crowell, 1989.

16 *Color Zoo* by Lois Ehlert. Lippincott, 1990.

17 *Planting a Rainbow* by Lois Ehlert. Harcourt Brace Jovanovich, 1989.

18 *Trucks* by Gail Gibbons. HarperCollins 1981.

19 *Ducks Don't Get Wet* by Augusta Goldin. Crowell, 1989.

20 *Is It Larger? Is It Smaller?* by Tana Hoban. Greenwillow, 1985.

21 *Is It Rough? Is it Smooth? Is It Shiny?* by Tana Hoban. Greenwilow, 1984.

22 *Color Dance* by Ann Jonas. Greenwillow, 1989.

23 *Opposites* by Rosalinda Kightly. Little, Brown, 1986.

24 *Geography From A to Z: A Picture Glossary* by Jack Knowlton. Crowell, 1988.

25 *One Smiling Grandma* by Anne Marie Linden. Dial, 1992.

26 *the alphabet tree* by Leo Lionni. Knopf, 1968.

27 *Breathtaking Noses* by Hana Machotka. Morrow, 1992.

28 *What Neat Feet!* by Hana Machotka. Morrow, 1991.

29 *How Many?* by Debbie MacKinnon. Dial, 1993.

30 *Let's Fly from A to Z* by Doug Magee and Robert Newman. Cobblehill, 1992.

31 *Eating Fractions* by Bruce McMillan. Scholastic, 1991.

32 *Growing Colors* by Bruce McMillan. Lothrop, 1988.

33 *Hats Hats Hats* by Ann Morris. Lothrop, 1989.

34 *Houses and Homes* by Ann Morris. Lothrop, 1992.

35 *Tools* by Ann Morris. Lothrop, '92.

36 *Magnification: A Pop-Up Lift-The-Flap Book* by Beth B. Norden and Lynette Ruschak. Lodestar, 1993.

37 *Mary Wore Her Red Dress* by Merle Peek. Houghton Mifflin, 1985.

38 *Pizza Man* by Marjorie Pillar. Crowell, 1990.

39 *Come To Town* by Anne Rockwell. HarperCollins, 1987.

40 *Fire Engines* by Anne Rockwell. Dutton, 1986.

41 *See How They Grow: CHICK* by Angela Royston. Lodestar, 1991.

42 *See How They Grow: PUPPY* by Angela Royston. Lodestar, 1991.

43 *See How They Grow: RABBIT* by Angela Royston. Lodestar, 1991.

44 *The Listening Walk* by Paul Showers. HarperCollins, 1991.

45 *Your Skin and Mine* by Paul Showers. HarperCollins, 1989.

46 *People* by Peter Spier. Bantam Doubleday Dell, 1980.

47 *Mr. Cookie Baker* by Monica Wellington. Dutton, 1992.

48 *Science Toys & Tricks* by L.B. White, Jr. HarperCollins, 1975.

49 *Let's Get A Pet* by Harriet Ziefert. Viking, 1993.

Resources for Section Four: Sharing Literature

FOR ADULTS

The Uses of Enchantment: The Meaning and Importance of Fairy Tales, by Bruno Bettelheim. Knopf, 1976. In this scholarly book, the author discusses the importance of including fairy tales in every child's life.

From Two to Five, by Kornei Chukovsky. Translated and edited by Miriam Morton. Foreword by Frances Clarke Sayers. Revised edition. University of California Press, 1968. A pre-eminent Russian specialist in children's language and literature shares with the reader his observations of the young child's development in language and love of poetry and fairy tales.

Child and Tale: The Origins of Interest, by Andre F. Favat. National Council of Teachers of English, Urbana, IL, 1977.

The Preschool Resource Guide: Educating and Entertaining Children Aged Two through Five, by Harriet Friedes. Insight Books/Plenum Press, 1993. Parents and professionals will want to keep this valuable resource book handy to find descriptions of materials in areas such as audio recordings, children's books, computer software, toys, and videos, as well as resources for adults.

Books, Babies, and Libraries: Serving Infants, Toddlers, Their Parents and Caregivers, by Ellin Greene. American Library Association, 1991. Library professionals, early childhood teachers, day care staff, and parents will find useful information about the library's role in early learning and parent education, theoretical concepts of child development, and comprehensive lists of books and other materials for children, parents, and professionals.

Read Me A Story: Books & Techniques for Reading Aloud & Storytelling, by Ellin Greene. Preschool Publications, 1992 (1-800-726-1708). Dr. Greene, educator, librarian, writer, and storyteller, (and the author of 4 chapters in this book) talks about which books children enjoy at different ages, and offers helpful techniques for reading aloud and storytelling.

Let's Do Poetry! Introducing Poetry to Children Through Listening, Singing, Chanting, Impromptu Choral Reading, Body Movement, Dance and Dramatization, Including 98 Favorite Songs and Poems, by Nancy Larrick. Delacorte, 1991. The subtitle says it all! Here is the perfect handbook for parents and teachers who want to assure a place for poetry in every child's life.

When Thought Is Young: Reflections on Teaching and the Poetry of the Child, by Richard Lewis. New Rivers Press, 1992. A small but profound book about the poetic nature of the young child, illustrated with poems by children and drawings by the author's daughter.

Miracles: Poems by Children of the English Speaking World, collected by Richard Lewis. A collection that has become a classic, offering poems by children between the ages of 5 and 13 from a variety of countries. First published in 1966, it is now available only through The Touchstone Center, 141 East 88th St. New York, NY 10028.

The Parent's Guide to Storytelling: How to Make Up New Stories and Retell Old Favorites, by Margaret Read MacDonald. HarperCollins, 1995. A clear and simple guide to storytelling for parents and grandparents, including familiar nursery tales, folktales, and tales from one's own imagination.

The Oxford Dictionary of Nursery Rhymes, edited by Iona and Peter Opie. Oxford University Press, 1951. This scholarly work brings together 500 traditional rhymes and songs with their histories and nearly 100 illustrations that include "reproductions of early appearances of the rhymes in ballad sheets and music books."

Play Learn & Grow: An Annotated Guide to the Best Books and materials for Very Young Children, by James L. Thomas. R.R. Bowker, 1992. A comprehensive guide to print and nonprint materials, offering parents and professionals an excellent resource.

FAIRY TALES FOR CHILDREN

Collections
The Fairy Tale Treasury, illustrated by Raymond Briggs, selected by Virginia Haviland. Dell, 1986. Thirty-two favorites selected by the former head of the children's book section at the Library of Congress and profusely illustrated with humorous full-color pictures. The treasury includes nursery tales, folktales from Europe and Africa, fables, and three stories by Hans Christian Andersen.

The Child's Story Book, by Kay Chorao. Dutton, 1987. Six beloved tales: *Jack and the Beanstalk, The Wonderful Teakettle, Hansel and Gretel, The Lion and the Hare, The Pied Piper,* and *The Ugly Duckling* have been illuminated with jewel-like richly detailed pictures.

Favorite Fairy Tales, by Cooper Edens and Harold Darling. Chronicle Books, 1991. This collection of fourteen classic fairy tales, including *The Sleeping Beauty,* is illustrated with pictures by turn-of-the-century artists, such as Arthur Rackham, Walter Crane, and L. Leslie Brooke.

The Knee-High Man and Other Tales, by Julius Lester. Dial, 1972. Retold with vigor and humor by a master storyteller, these six tales introduce young children to Mr. Rabbit and Mr. Bear, Mrs. Wind and Mrs. Water, and other characters from black American folklore.

The Helen Oxenbury Nursery Story Book, by Helen Oxenbury. Knopf, 1985. These short retellings of ten familiar tales, including *The Three Billy Goats Gruff,* are especially appropriate for reading aloud to toddlers and young preschoolers. The action-packed pictures will surprise and delight.

The Three Bears and 15 Other Stories, by Anne Rockwell. Crowell, 1975. Clear, rhythmic language distinguishes these retellings of folk and fairy tales from European and American sources and fables from La Fontaine and Aesop. Illustrated in bright watercolor paintings on every page.

Read Me a Story: A Child's Book of Favorite Tales, Scholastic, 1991. Fifteen familiar nursery tales, including *The Gingerbread Boy, The Little Porridge Pot,* and *The Turnip,* have been retold with gentle humor.

Single Tales
Borreguita and the Coyote, by Verne Aardema. Knopf, 1991. A little lamb outwits the coyote who means to eat her. A Mexican folktale illustrated with bold colorful paintings by Petra Mathers.

Why Mosquitoes Buzz in People's Ears, by Verna Aardema. Dial, 1975. When mosquito tells a tall tale to iguana it sets off a chain reaction that causes the death of an owlet. Mother Owl reacts by refusing to waken the sun so the day can come. To this day mosquito goes about buzzing in people's ears to find out if everyone is still angry at her. For their striking, imaginative art in this West African folktale, the husband-wife team of Leo and Diane Dillon received the 1976 Caldecott Medal.

The Three Bears, by Byron Barton. HarperCollins, 1991. The simple retelling and bold, childlike paintings will appeal to toddlers and young preschoolers.

Strega Nona, retold and illustrated by Tomie de Paola. Prentice-Hall, 1975. Like the Sorcerer's Apprentice, Big Anthony cannot stop Grandmother Witch's magic pot once it starts making pasta. When the town is overrun with pasta, Big Anthony's punishment is to eat up all the pasta! An amusing Italian folktale retold and illustrated in de Paola's inimitable style. A 1976 Caldecott Honor Book.

Little Red Riding Hood, by the Brothers Grimm. Retold and illustrated by Trina Schart Hyman. Holiday House, 1983. Storytelling details in the bordered frames and cozy domestic scenes characterize this version of a childhood favorite. A 1984 Caldecott Honor Book.

Snow White and Rose Red, by the Brothers Grimm. Delacorte, 1991. Two kind sisters befriend a huge black bear who is really a king's son bewitched by a wicked dwarf. In time, the bear-prince kills the dwarf, regains his natural form and fortune (stolen by the dwarf), and marries Snow White. Illustrated by Barbara Cooney in delicate black and white drawings and rose watercolor.

A Story - A Story, retold and illustrated by Gail E. Haley. Atheneum, 1970. A West African folktale that tells how Anansi the spider man earned the right to the Sky God's stories and how stories came into the world. The 1971 Caldecott Medal Book.

Anansi and the Moss-Covered Rock, retold by Eric Kimmel. Holiday House, 1990. Gentle little Bush Deer tricks the trickster Anansi in this humorous folktale from West Africa.

Tiddalick the Frog, by Susan Nunes. Atheneum, 1989. This unusual folktale from the Australian Aborigines tells what happened "long ago in the dreamtime" when a gigantic frog drank up all the water in the world and refused to release it. Only the little eel, Noyang, with his wonderful dance was able to restore Tiddalick's good humor and save the earth from becoming a desert.

Cinderella, by Charles Perrault. Translated and illustrated by Marcia Brown. Scribners, 1954. Delicate line drawings and watercolor capture the grace and elegance of the French version of Cinderella. The 1955 Caldecott Medal Book.

The Squeaky Door,   by Laura Simms. Crown, 1991. An amusing cumulative story about a little boy who is afraid of the sound of a squeaky door. The telling is loosely based on a Puerto Rican folktale, *The Bed,* in Pura Belpre's collection, *The Tiger and the Rabbit* (Lippincott, 1965).

Deep in the Forest, by Brinton Turkle. Dutton, 1976. Baby Bear takes a walk through the forest, discovers Goldilock's house, eats her porridge, rocks in her chair, and falls asleep in her bed before being discovered in this reversal of the classic tale. A wordless picture book.

The Two Foolish Cats, by Yoshiko Uchida. Macmillan, 1987. Cat friends Daizo and Suki quarrel over two rice cakes: each thinks he deserves the bigger rice cake. Wise old monkey settles their quarrel by eating up both cakes, leaving "nothing left for you to quarrel about." Caldecott medal winner Margot Zemach has captured the sly humor of this Japanese folktale in her full-color pictures suggestive of Japanese brush paintings.

Vasilissa the Beautiful: A Russian Folktale, adapted by Elizabeth Winthrop. HarperCollins, 1991. The Russian Cinderella has been illustrated with brilliantly colored paintings by the Russian artist Alexander Koshkin.

The True Story of the 3 Little Pigs, by A. Wolf as told to Jon Scieszka. Viking, 1989. Children who already know the traditional version will be amused to hear A. Wolf's side of the story. The droll illustrations by Lane Smith perfectly complement the telling.

Lon Po Po: A Red-Riding Hood Story from China, translated and illustrated by Ed Young. Philomel, 1989. In the Chinese version, three little girls outwit the fearsome wolf. This 1990 Caldecott Medal Book is recommended for older preschoolers.

Rumpelstiltskin, retold and illustrated by Paul O. Zelinsky. Dutton, 1986. To save her own life and that of her firstborn child, a miller's daughter must spin straw into gold and guess the name of the strange little man who helps her. Zelinsky's richly detailed oil paintings are set in the late medieval period. A 1987 Caldecott Honor Book.

The Three Wishes: An Old Story, retold and illustrated by Margot Zemach. Farrar, 1986. A woodcutter and his wife rescue an imp who gives them three wishes in return for their kindness. "Wish wisely," the imp advises. But when the man wishes for a pan of sausages and his wife wishes the sausages were hanging from his nose, there is only one way to use their last wish!

POETRY BOOKS FOR CHILDREN

In for Winter, Out for Spring, by Arnold Adoff. Illustrated by Jerry Pinkney. Harcourt, 1991. Soft watercolors and conversational poems reveal a young African-American girl's pleasure in the changing seasons and some important moments shared with members of her family.

A Treasury of Flower Fairies, by Cicely Mary Barker. Warne, 1992. An enlarged edition of sixty verses selected from a popular series that began in 1923. The poems are accompanied by delicate, botanically accurate watercolor illustrations of flowers and flower "fairies" (children with wings and pointed ears).

A Seed, A Flower, a Minute, an Hour, by Joan W. Blos. Illustrated by Hans Poppel. Simon & Schuster, 1992. In twelve short lines the Newbery medalist conveys to young minds the concept of change.

Ring o' Roses: A Nursery Rhyme Picture Book, with drawings by L. Leslie Brooke. Clarion, 1992. First published in 1922, this new edition contains the original twenty-one Mother Goose rhymes with new reproductions of Brooke's artwork. A modern classic.

The Baby's Lap Book, by Kay Chorao. Dutton, 1990. See also, *The Baby's Bedtime Book* (1984) and *The Baby's Good Morning Book* (1986). These first books for the youngest include, respectively, favorite nursery rhymes, lullabies and comforting poems, and cheerful verses to start the day. Illustrated with warm engaging pictures.

You Read to Me, I'll Read to You, by John Ciardi. Drawings by Edward Gorey. HarperCollins, 1987. Originally published in hard cover in 1962, this collection of humorous poems includes "Mummy Slept Late and Daddy Fixed Breakfast." Children reading on a first-grade level can read the poems printed in blue ink.

In My Mother's House, by Ann Nolan Clark. Illustrated by Velino Herrera.Viking, 1991. A reissue of a Caldecott Honor Book first published in 1941. The poems are based on stories written by Pueblo children.

I never saw a purple cow, and other nonsense rhymes, by Emma Chichester Clarke. Little, Brown, 1991. 117 nonsense rhymes about animals — real and imaginary, mostly from tradition but several by nonsense masters Hilaire Belloc, Gelett Burgess, Lewis Carroll, Samuel Goodrich, and Edward Lear, with sprightly illustrations in watercolor.

Pat-a-Cake and Other Play Rhymes, compiled by Joanne Cole and Stephanie Calmenson. Illustrated by Alan Tiegreen. Morrow, 1992. Thirty rhymes and games to play with babies and young toddlers. Clear directions and child-appealing illustrations.

The little dog laughed and other nursery rhymes, illustrated by Lucy sCousins. Dutton, 1990. Sixty-four traditional rhymes illustrated in bright childlike poster paintings.

in Just-spring, by e. e. cummings. Paintings by Heidi Goennel. Little, Brown, 1988. A joyous introduction to the celebrated word spinner and his "mud-luscious," "puddle wonderful" world.

Jamberry, by Bruce Degan. Harper, 1983. "Raspberry rabbits, Brassberry band, Elephants skating on raspberry jam"...a young boy and a friendly bear on an exuberant berry-gathering expedition.

Sing a Song of Popcorn: Every Child's Book of Poems, selected by Beatrice Schenk de Regniers, et al. Illustrated by nine Caldecott Medal artists. Scholastic, 1988. An attractive anthology of 128 poems by well-known poets from Robert Frost to Shel Silverstein, arranged under nine themes — Fun with Rhymes, Mostly People, and so forth. Each section has been illustrated by a different artist.

So Many Cats, by Beatrice Schenk de Regniers. Illustrated by Ellen Weiss. Clarion, 1988. A family with one "sad and lonely cat" acquires a dozen cats in this story told in rhyme. Preschoolers love counting and naming the cats.

The Glorious Mother Goose, selected by Cooper Edens. Atheneum, 1988. This book illustrates the 42 poems on its pages with illustrations by the best artists from the past such as Randolph Caldecott, Kate Greenaway, Arthur Rackham, and others.

Teddy Bear, Teddy Bear. Illustrated by Michael Hague. Morrow, 1993. Endearing bears dressed in bright warm colors illustrate this favorite action rhyme from childhood. Actions to accompany the words are given in "A Note to Parents."

Fathers, Mothers, Sisters, Brothers: A Collection of Family Poems, by Mary Ann Hoberman. Illustrated by Marylin Hafner. Little, Brown, 1991. Family life seen through the eyes of a child, this lively collection celebrates family members, from moms and dads to stepsiblings and babysitters.

Still as a Star: a Book of Nighttime Poems, selected by Lee Bennett Hopkins Illustrated by Karen Milone. Little, Brown, 1989. This anthology of fourteen nighttime poems and lullabies by Harry Behn, Eleanor Farjeon Rachael Field and other well-known poets is illustrated with dream-like paintings that perfectly reflect the mood of the poems.

Through Our Eyes: Poems and Pictures about Growing Up, selected by Lee Bennett Hopkins. Photographs by Jeffrey Dunn. Little, Brown, 1992. Poems by Nikki Giovanni, David McCord, Li-Young Lee, and others, with photographs that show children growing up in America's multi-cultural society of the 1990s.

Out and About, by Shirley Hughes. Lothrop, 1988. In rhyming text and realistically detailed pictures a little girl and her baby brother romp through the four seasons.

Coconut Kind of Day: Island Poems, by Lynn Joseph. Illustrated by Sandra Speidel. Lothrop, 1990. Sights and sounds of the Caribbean are evoked in poems and pictures depicting events in a day of a young girl in Trinidad.

Sharon, Lois & Bram's Mother Goose, illustrated by Maryann Kovalski. Joy Street/Little, Brown, 1985. This is a grand collection of nursery songs and rhymes, some traditional, some contemporary. Most include musical accompaniment for piano or guitar.

Dogs & Dragons Trees & Dreams: A Collection of Poems, by Karla Kuskin. HarperTrophy, 1992. Designed to introduce young children to poetry, this collection puts emphasis on the basic elements of simple poetry — rhythm, word sounds, rhyme and humor. Throughout the text Kuskin offers the adult helpful hints on how to read the poems aloud.

Talking Like the Rain: A First Book of Poems, selected by X. J. Kennedy and Dorothy M. Kennedy. Illustrated by Jane Dyer. Little, Brown, 1992. A splendid anthology of over 120 poems that appeal to very young children.

Ring-a Round-a Rosy: Nursery Rhymes, Action Rhymes, and Lullabies, illustrated by Priscilla Lamont. Little, Brown, 1990. Parents and other caregivers will appreciate this collection especially designed for infants and toddlers. Illustrated in soft pastels. Includes the music for nine favorite lullabies.

Songs from Mother Goose, compiled by Nancy Larrick. Illustrated by Robin Spowart. HarperCollins, 1989. Fifty-six Mother Goose rhymes with simple musical melodies.

When the Dark Comes Dancing: A Bedtime Poetry Book, compiled by Nancy Larrick. Illustrated by John Wallner. Philomel, 1983. Poems, lullabies, and lyrics of old folk songs to help children unwind and promote restful sleep, with notes for the parent reader and a short bibliography of books of poetry and songs for children.

Ring-a-Ring O'Roses & a Ding, Dong Bell: A Book of Nursery Rhymes, selected and illustrated by Alan Marks. Picture Book Studio, 1991. A collection of 76 classic nursery rhymes with vibrant paintings and playful black and white silhouettes by a young British illustrator.

Brown Bear, Brown Bear, What Do You See? by Bill Martin Jr. Illustrated by Eric Carle. Holt, 1992. a newly illustrated edition of a perennial favorite on the occasion of its 25th anniversary.

Sunflakes: Poems for Children, selected by Lilian Moore. Illustrated by Jan Ormerod. Clarion, 1992. Chosen with the older preschooler and young schoolchild in mind, this anthology includes verses by more than forty of America's best poets for children. Lively illustrations in soft water-colors.

Once: A Lullaby, by bp Nichol. Illustrated by Anita Lobel. Music by Arno Lobel. Greenwillow, 1986. In eighteen rhythmical stanzas a horse, a cow, a sheep, a pig, a dog, a cat and other animals fall asleep. Preschoolers will soon discover the pattern and join in singing and making the sound of each animal.

Tail Feathers from Mother Goose: The Opie Rhyme Book, by Iona and Peter Opie. Little, Brown, 1988. Selections from the Opie's vast collection of nursery rhymes, including unusual versions of known nursery rhymes as well as less known rhymes sent in by people who wanted to preserve them, are exuberantly illustrated by over sixty beloved artists.

The Animal's Lullaby, by Tom Paxton. Illustrated by Erick Ingraham. Morrow, 1993. A gentle bedtime ballad by the popular folksinger with stunning lifelike paintings of various animals about to go to sleep.

The Tamarindo Puppy and Other Poems, by Charlotte Pomerantz. Illustrated by Byron Barton. Greenwillow, 1993. "The Tamarindo puppy is a very nice puppy, is a muy lindo puppy whom we visit everyday." This reissue of a 1980 book includes thirteen childlike poems in English with a sprinkling of Spanish words.

Read-Aloud Rhymes for the Very Young, by Jack Prelutsky. Illustrated by Marc Brown. With an Introduction by Jim Trelease. Knopf, 1986. A treasury of over 200 poems about both everyday and imaginative events, with playful illustrations.

The Jessie Willcox Smith Mother Goose, illustrated by Jessie Willcox Smith. Derrydale Books (Crown), 1986. An illustrated collection of 750 Mother Goose rhymes, games, and riddles, including both the well-known and the less familiar.

A Child's Garden of Verses, by Robert Louis Stevenson. Illustrated by Jannat Messenger. Dutton, 1992. Twelve favorites by the beloved poet are presented in an engaging pop-up book.

Fiddle-I-Fee: A Farmyard Song for the Very Young, adapted and illustrated by Melissa Sweet. Little, Brown, 1992. The familiar cumulative nursery rhyme about a small boy, his cat, and other barnyard friends has been illustrated with whimsy and gentle humor. There is also a musical arrangement by Alain Mallet.

Taking Turns: Poetry to Share, collected by Bernice Wolman. Illustrated by Catherine Stock. Atheneum, 1992. Poems are paired, with a simpler poem on the right page for the child to read and on the opposite page a harder poem (in smaller typeface) for the adult reader. The twenty-six poems range in theme from books to ice skating.

The Lullaby Songbook, edited by Jane Yolen with musical arrangements by Adam Stemple. Illustrated by Charles Mikolaycak. Harcourt, 1986. Fifteen lullabies from around the world, with a simple arrangement for piano and guitar and a historical note about each.

MULTICULTURAL BOOKS FOR CHILDREN

Hoang Breaks the Lucky Teapot, by Rosemary K. Breckler. Illustrations by Adrian Frankel. Houghton Mifflin, 1992. (Vietnamese)

In My Mother's House, by Ann Nolan Clark. Illustrations by Velino Herrara. Puffin, 1992. (Native American/Tewa Indians)

Bigmama's, by Donald Crews. Greenwillow, 1991. (African American)

The Patchwork Quilt, by Valerie Flournoy. Illustrations by Jerry Pinkney. Dial, 1985. (African American)

Grandpa's Face, by Eloise Greenfield. Illustrations by Floyd Cooper. Putnam, 1988. (African American)

Aunt Flossie's Hats (and Crab Cakes Later), by Elizabeth Fitzgerald Howard. Illustrations by James Ransome. Clarion, 1991. (African American)

New Shoes for Silvia, by Johanna Hurwitz. Illustrations by Jerry Pinkney. Morrow, 1993. (Latino)

Mama, Do You Love Me? by Barbara M. Joosse.Illustrations by Barbara Lavallee. Chronicle Books, 1991. (Native American/Inuit)

Flossie and the Fox, by Patricia C. McKissack .Illustrations by Rachel Isadora. Dial, 1986. (African American)

Red Dancing Shoes, by Denise Lewis Patrick. Illustrations by James E. Ransome. Tambourine, 1993. (African American)

Back Home, by Gloria Jean Pinkney. Illustrations by Jerry Pinkney. Dial, 1992. (African American)

Chicken Sunday, by Patricia Polacco. Philomel, 1992. (Multiethnic)

Lion Dancer: Ernie Wan's Chinese New Year, by Kate Waters and Madeline Slovenz-Low. Photos by Martha Cooper. Scholastic, 1990. (Chinese)

Tap-Tap, by Karen Lynn Williams. Illustrations by Catherine Stock. Clarion, 1994. (Haitian)

A Chair for My Mother, by Vera B. Williams. Greenwillow, 1982. Available in Spanish, *Un Sillón Para Mama.* Mulberry, 1994. (Multiethnic)

"More More More," Said the Baby, by Vera B. Williams. Greenwillow, 1990 (Multiethnic)

Jenny, by Beth P. Wilson. Illustrations by Dolores Johnson. Macmillan, 1990. (African American)

Umbrella, by Taro Yashima. Viking, 1958. (Japanese)

MULTICULTURAL BOOKS: NURSERY RHYMES-POETRY AND SONG

Sing to the Sun: Poems and Pictures, by Ashley Bryan. HarperCollins, 1992. (African American)

Red Dragonfly on My Shoulder. Haiku translated by Sylvia Cassedy and Kunihiro Suetake. Illustrations by Molly Bang. HarperCollins, 1992. (Japanese)

Arroz con Leche: Popular Songs and Rhymes from Latin America, selections and illustrations by Lulu Delacre. Scholastic, 1992. (Latino)

Las Navidades: Popular Christmas Songs from Latin America, selections and illustrations by Lulu Delacre. Scholastic, 1990. (Latino)

Knoxville, Tennessee, by Nikki Giovanni. Illustrations by Larry Johnson. Scholastic, 1994. (African American)

Honey, I Love and Other Love Poems, by Eloise Greenfield. Illustrations by Leo and Diane Dillon. HarperTrophy, 1986. (African American)

Under the Sunday Tree, by Eloise Greenfield. Paintings by Mr. Amos Ferguson. HarperCollins, 1988. (African American)

Not a Copper Penny in Me House: Poems from the Caribbean, by Monica Gunning. Illustrated by Frané Lessac. Wordsong/Boyds Mill Press, 1993. (Caribbean)

Los pollitos dicen/The Baby Chicks Sing: Traditional Games, Nursery Rhymes, and Songs from Spanish-Speaking Countries, collected and adapted by Nancy Abraham Hall and Jill Syverson-Stork. Illustrations by Kay Chorao. Little, Brown, 1994. (Latino)

My Song Is Beautiful: Poems and Pictures In Many Voices, selections by Mary Ann Hoberman. Little Brown, 1994. (Multiethnic)

Coconut Kind of Day: Island Poems, by Lynn Joseph. Illustrations by Sandra Speidel. Lothrop, 1990. (Caribbean)

In a Spring Garden, edited by Richard Lewis. Illustrations by Ezra Jack Keats. Dial, 1989. (Japanese)

Dancing Teepees: Poems of American Indian Youth, selections by Virginia Driving Hawk Sneve. Illustrated by Stephen Gammell. Holiday House, 1989. (Native American)

Brown Honey in Broomwheat Tea, by Joyce Carol Thomas. Illustrations by Floyd Cooper. HarperCollins, 1993. (African American)

Golden Bear, by Ruth Young. Illustrations by Rachel Isadora. Viking, 1992/ Puffin, 1994. (African American)

MULTICULTURAL BOOKS: FOLKTALES AND LEGENDS

Ma'ii and Cousin Horned Toad: A Traditional Navajo Story, by Shonto Begay. Scholastic, 1992. (Native American/Navajo)

Star Boy, by Paul Goble. Bradbury, 1983. (Native American/Blackfeet)

The Bossy Gallito, retold by Lucia M. González. Illustrations by Lulu Delacre. Scholastic, 1994. (Cuban)

Two of Everything, by Lily Toy Hong. Albert Whitman, 1993. (Chinese)

John Henry: An American Legend, by Ezra Jack Keats. Pantheon, 1965. (African American)

The Funny Little Woman, by Arlene Mosel. Illustrations by Blair Lent. Dutton, 1972. (Japanese)

The Story of Jumping Mouse: A Native American Legend, retold and illustrations by John Steptoe. Lothrop, 1984. (Native American/Great Plains)

Section Five
Imagination
Creativity

Section Five
Imagination
Creativity

Introduction

The childhood sense of wonder "is found not only in the autobiographies and biographies of famous writers, artists, and scientists but also in the recollections of those ordinary people who are creative and imaginative — or who could be if they would get in touch with their earliest memories of play." (Dorothy G. Singer and Jerome L. Singer in *The House of Make-Believe: Children's Play and the Developing Imagination.* Harvard University Press, 1990.)

As an adult, you can reach back in your memory to think about the play you enjoyed as a child. You may recall the thrill of seeing the world from the height of a swing or the platform of a treehouse. You may remember how caring you were as you nursed your doll when she broke her arm. You may look back at yourself at the beach in the role of a brave prince protecting your sand castle from an onslaught of giants.

Adults can nurture imaginative experiences in the children they care about. The authors of the chapters in this section discuss the benefits of imagination and curiosity in young children and offer creative suggestions for promoting these attributes.

In addition, the chapter on humor tells us that it is not only fun to laugh, it is beneficial to physical and mental health. So read on and enjoy!

SECTION FIVE
IMAGINATION - CREATIVITY

Chapter 22
The Power
of
Imagination

Elizabeth J. Webster

"When I get as big as you, Dad,
I'm going to find me
a dinosaur to ride."

At age four Michael was fascinated by stories about dinosaurs, although he only vaguely understood the words "extinction" and "glacier." As his father put him to bed one evening, Michael confided, " When I get as big as you, Dad, I'm going to go find me a dinosaur to ride." When his father asked how he could do this, because dinosaurs disappeared long ago, Michael answered, "I'll walk around on a glacier and find an extinct old man who knows a dinosaur and then I'll go find it and ask it to put its head down so I can climb up. Don't worry, if he's slippery I'll have on my heavy tennis shoes."

Michael was exercising an extremely beneficial right brain function: imagination. (For a summary of both right and left brain functions, see pages 29-34.) Although some children will have more potential than others for rich imaginative activity, all can develop this ability.

Development of Imagination
It is clear that children's ability to pretend develops at least as early as their language permits them to make sentences. For example, when a day care group of two and three year olds became quite noisy, Sandra, age two, lay down on the floor, squeezed her eyes tightly shut and announced, "Shh, me, Sandy, sleeping." Even at this early age Sandy is pretending — evidence of imagination at work. Such imaginative behavior increases as children achieve greater language skills. It probably reaches its peak at about age four, when many children create imaginary playmates. Throughout these years preschoolers' play and conversation give further evidence that their imaginations serve important functions for them.

Becoming creatively self sufficient
The imaginative preschooler can use a common object such as a large cardboard box to create numerous entertaining playthings: a house in which he imagines furniture, a cave to be guarded, a boat from which he is   fishing, etc. This child may also want to take apart commercially built toys to try to make new toys from them. All such activity leads to future creative abilities such as those needed in the arts, architecture, creative writing, and teaching young children.

Planning ahead/visualizing consequences
In the early preschool years, the child can think only about the present, then later about the past. As she develops imagination she thinks about future possibilities and can then plan her future behavior. She thinks about potential consequences of her acts; that is, she can imagine that if she behaves in a certain way, certain consequences will follow. This means that adults will not need to teach her all she will know about how to

behave appropriately, even in situations that are new to her. For example, if she knows it is appropriate to express appreciation when someone does something nice for her, she will learn to do so in many situations.

Understanding others' feelings and points of view

A most important benefit of a child's growing imagination is being better able to see how other people might feel or think. For example, Jeremy told his preschool friend, Jenny, that his dog was "very sick." Jenny said, "Oh, aren't you sad and scared?" When Jeremy answered, "Mostly sad," she said, "I think I'd be sad, too."

Jenny, imagining how she would feel if her cat were sick, could then imagine how Jeremy might feel. She also had the language skills to discuss the matter. It seems evident that children who develop such empathy get along quite well with other children as well as with adults.

It also seems likely that children who have imaginary playmates benefit in social relationships from their attempts to interact with the playmate. For example, at age four, Robert, who had trouble sharing toys with other children, had an imaginary playmate named "Bossy." Robert told his mother that he sometimes got "so mad at Bossy; he doesn't know about sharing and he always wants to have his own way!" One afternoon Robert came in smiling broadly; when his mother asked why he was so pleased, he said, "I've finally taught Bossy to share his toys and now he's not so nasty and I like him more." This sounded to Robert's mother as though he had learned an important lesson in social relationships as he played it out in his imagination.

Learning new motor skills

In order to learn a motor skill, the child must not only be taught what to do, he must imagine himself able to do it and must then picture himself doing it. Perhaps four-year-old Jerry summed it up when he joyfully told his teacher he had learned to ride his new scooter. She asked how he learned it so quickly, and he said, "I saw it in my eyes." She asked what he meant and he patiently explained, "Oh, I planned where I'd put my feet and then I could see me riding *so* fast!"

Jerry's key words "saw me" and "planned" indicate the mental process of imagination. Suggestions for helping children develop more of this ability are listed on the following pages.

Activities for Promoting Imagination

Elizabeth J. Webster

Using crayons and paints

Coloring books can stifle imagination, particularly if the child thinks she must use certain colors or stay within the lines. More imaginative are such activities as letting the child put some drops of watercolor paint on a piece of paper and then arrange his "painting" by blowing gently through a straw until he says his picture is finished.

Children as young as three can enjoy this activity, with the caution that the adult should control the amount of paint used, make sure it is washable and nontoxic, and provide much newspaper or cloth to protect the area where the child is working. A similar caution pertains to the use of crayons: they, too, should be washable and nontoxic.

In these activities it is wise to encourage the child to create something the way he wants it to look, then if the adult wants to ask him to discuss it, to say, "Please tell me about that," rather than asking him what it is. (If the creation has come from his imagination, he may not be able to say what it is.)

Story telling followed by roleplaying

Reading and telling stories are activities most preschoolers enjoy. The stories that stir their imaginations are those in which they can create new ideas around the printed story, think of a different ending, etc. Children as young as four also enjoy playing roles, and some of the old nursery rhymes and tales lend themselves to this creative type of activity. For example, one group of four year olds acted out *The Three Little Pigs*. The three children playing pigs worked hard on their houses, piling imaginary straw,   pretending to nail boards and pile bricks. They took so long the "wolf" became bored, so he went off in a corner to practice his huffing and puffing. Finally, as he attempted to blow down each house, the "pigs" built them right back. Finally, the wolf decided to let all the houses stand, and he also decided to move in with the child in the brick house. This is but one example of the type of story children can create when permitted to do so.

Games of "What If" or "What Does"

A ride in the country or walk around the neighborhood can be used to foster imagination. The child can be entertained for quite a long time by being asked such questions as what a horse might be thinking as he nibbles grass, or what would happen if someone tried to ride a cow, or where birds go when it gets dark. Since there are no right or wrong answers here, the child is free to imagine anything, and sometimes in amusing fashion. For example, Roy lived in a rural area where white birds (egrets) were often seen sitting on the backs of grazing cattle. One afternoon his father asked him why he thought the egrets sat on the cattle. Roy thought for a moment, then said, "I think they get lonesome and need somebody to talk to, so they talk to the cows and then when they get hungry they're right close to the milk."

Using creative toys

As mentioned earlier, creative toys need not be expensive. It can be useful to parents to consider, besides providing paints, crayons, and modeling clay, items that the child can take apart and make into various objects such as blocks. Children who are developing active imaginations appreciate toys or objects they can manipulate; as one four year old confided, "I hate that car on the track that I have cause it just goes round and round and doesn't do anything."

Chapter 23
Nurturing Imagination and Creativity

Michael K. Meyerhoff

*The most beneficial role
that parents can play
is that of a good audience.*

A Batman suit can only be a Batman suit. But with a plain hat and a towel, a child can be many different characters... A doll house can only be a doll house. But a large cardboard box can be a house, store, spaceship, or almost anything.

Imagination and creativity blossom during early childhood. But it is not clear exactly where they come from. It may be that some children are simply born imaginative and creative, or it may be that certain environmental episodes instill imagination and creativity. The fact is that no one has been able accurately to predict the level of imagination and creativity a child will eventually exhibit, nor has anyone put together a program that will reliably increase a child's level of imagination and creativity.

On the other hand, it is evident that these qualities can be encouraged and enhanced during early childhood. Furthermore, it is critical to do so. Without adequate and appropriate nurturing, imagination and creativity will not only fail to blossom fully, they actually may be significantly diminished or destroyed.

Imagination and creativity have three requirements for growth.
• The first is *basic skill.* A child can only be as imaginative and creative as her ordinary mental and physical abilities will permit at each stage of development.
• Next is *opportunity.* Once a child is theoretically able to do a variety of imaginative and creative things with her mind and body, she must be given a chance to do so.
• And, finally there is *practice.* Like anything else, a child needs plenty of experience to become proficient at employing her mind and body in imaginative and creative ways.

This last requirement may be a problem if parents insist that there is only one "correct" way to do things. When a child is taught that there is one "right" way of doing things and all other ways are "wrong," she is not likely to get the sort of experience she needs to develop her imagination and creativity. Unfortunately, many parents and teachers do not realize the importance of nurturing these qualities. Since early childhood is a time when a lot of fundamental information must be absorbed and mastered, they often concentrate exclusively on transmitting "traditional" skills and knowledge. Consequently, they focus too closely on the content of their children's lessons, and they do not pay enough attention to how the children are learning or how they make use of what they have learned. At best, imagination and creativity are considered nice but not essential. At worst, they are considered annoying and distracting.

Therefore, it is a lucky child whose mother and father recognize the value of these qualities and then take the time and make the effort to nurture them during the early years. Fortunately, doing what needs to be done is not very difficult. And the results can be tremendously rewarding and fun for everyone.

Problem Solving

Imagination and creativity consist of two major components. One is *perception*. Several people may observe the same situation, but each individual will analyze it differently. Then there is *expression*. Several people may think the same thing, but each individual will convey the thought differently. Although imagination and creativity usually are associated with *expressive* activities, it is the *perceptual* or *analytic* component that a child develops initially.

The first signs of imagination and creativity surface rather subtly shortly after the first birthday during simple problem-solving. A child wants a toy that is on a high shelf, and she must figure out the best way to get it. Even at this age she goes through a process that involves perceiving and analyzing the situation. When she gets older she is able to express herself in words and other creative ways.

What is the parent's role in nurturing creative growth?

The key is to be patient and flexible right from the start. As a toddler begins to develop various skills, she should be allowed to use them as freely as possible (within safety limits) — even if what she does appears to be inefficient or inappropriate. For instance, once a child develops the ability to manipulate objects with her hands and the ability to classify them in her mind, she will enjoy playing with stacking rings, building blocks, puzzles, etc. If she is told that there is but one correct way of playing with these materials and her parents insist that specific pieces must be put in specific places, she will have little chance to exercise her emerging imagination and creativity. But if they let her try to put the square peg in the round hole, for example, she will be permitted to explore and investigate all sorts of possibilities. The feedback she gets from her own efforts will ultimately enable her to arrive at the solution that is obvious to her parents — and it might even enable her to come up with a better one.

Role-Play and Fantasy

As a child passes through toddlerhood and progresses into the preschool years, her basic mental skills improve dramatically, especially her memory and language capacities. Her basic physical skills advance as well. She becomes more adept at manipulating materials and fashioning them to suit her needs and desires. In addition, through ever-increasing experience, her knowledge of different people, places, items, and events expands enormously.

Now imagination and creativity are routinely manifested in role-play and fantasy behavior as the child can use her new skills and knowledge to put together all kinds of original structures, scenarios, relationships, and sequences. Consequently, at this point, she will engage in — and very much enjoy — a wide variety of "pretend" games and activities.

Many parents mistakenly assume that providing complex toys and detailed costumes will enhance their child's pretend projects. What they do not realize is that the "action" is taking place primarily inside the child's head, not in front of her. Therefore, such elaborate and expensive materials are not necessary, and they may actually inhibit the child's own imagination and creativity. A far better way to supply the "raw material" that will feed a child's role play and fantasy activities would be to provide her with plenty of "real world" experiences, such as neighborhood trips to the fire house, post office, construction sites, museums, and airports. Back home, with the child's imagination at work, towels become capes, cardboard boxes become boats or houses, and chairs in a row become trains or planes.

Books, too, can broaden a child's horizons and supply her with additional ideas for her role-play and fantasy activities. Keep literature appropriate to the child's level of development.

Movies and TV programs also expose a child to new ideas. Watch movies and television programs with your child and take the time to discuss them with her. But, caution is called for: when TV and movies take up too much of your child's playtime there isn't time left for creative expression.

As for the child's pretend projects themselves, as is the case with problem-solving, these can suffer from too much parental intrusion and instruction. On the other hand, parental participation is welcome *when the child directs the play and feels in control of what is happening.* And parental input also is appropriate on occasion, especially when role-play and fantasy behavior becomes intolerably outrageous, offensive, or violent.

Music, Art, Etc.
The basic mental and physical skills required to pursue other, perhaps more "classic" forms of imagination and creativity, such as music and art, ordinarily do not become well developed until the elementary school years and beyond. However, that does not mean that early exposure to these forms is not important. In fact, it is critical. But parents must recognize that

how a child is exposed is far more significant than *what* she is exposed to. Once more, patience and flexibility are essential. For example, a preschooler gradually will develop the abilities necessary to understand color schemes and perspective. Consequently, she will very much enjoy drawing and painting. Standard coloring books, where the child is instructed to stay within the lines and go by the numbers, do not encourage imagination or creativity. On the other hand, if the child is allowed to use art materials freely, she may discover that she has gifts and talents that someday will enable her to express her imagination and creativity in far more unique and impressive ways.

Of course, giving a child's imagination and creativity full support does not mean eliminating any and all restrictions on her behavior. She need not — and should not — be permitted to draw on the walls, paint the dog, or play the drums in the middle of the night. To avoid unnecessary problems, parents should recognize their child's developmental limitations and take proper precautions. Toddlers should be supplied with simple materials like fingerpaints and dough clay; be given a wide and washable work surface; and the materials should be nontoxic in case she decides to eat as well as paint or sculpt. Older preschoolers should also be supervised with an expensive musical instrument such as a piano.

Many children are pushed to learn proper techniques too hard or too soon. As a result, they experience a great deal of failure and very little enjoyment, and they quickly lose interest and enthusiasm. It is wiser for parents to wait until the child herself shows an eagerness to learn how to do it better — and then let her learn at her own pace. That way, proper technique will always support and expand her imaginative and creative capacity, rather than intrude upon or interfere with it.

The most beneficial role that parents can play is that of a good audience. A child's initial attempts probably will produce more "mess" than "art" and more "noise" than "music." Her first dances and stories probably will appear rather silly or even absurd by adult standards. Therefore, as always, it is critical to respect and appreciate the process, regardless of what the product looks or sounds like. A child whose parents scoff or laugh at her efforts will soon stop trying. But a child whose parents proudly display her crude pictures and applaud her less-than-perfect recitals will experience continuing enjoyment and show constant improvement.   ✻

Suggestions for helping a child engage in specific role play and fantasy activities

Michael K. Meyerhoff

As children get older, their pretend games and projects become more focused and complex. Through interesting and exciting "real world" experiences and exposure to books, movies and television, their minds become capable of generating increasingly specific role-play and fantasy activities. With just a little ingenuity, parents can help their child put together some very sophisticated setups. The following are examples of how common materials can be used for such purposes.

Doctor/Nurse
Adhesive bandages, tongue depressors, cotton balls, scratch pads (to write "prescription"), turkey baster (to use as a hypodermic needle).

Barber/Beautician
Hairbrush, comb, curlers, towel, old white shirt (for the uniform), plastic scissors (that can't really cut).

Grocery Store Clerk
Play money, calculator (to use as a cash register), paper bags, apron, empty food packages and containers.

Auto Mechanic
Visored cap, apron, flashlight, key ring with lots of keys, simple tools, "vehicles" (a tricycle or wagon will do just fine).

Teacher
Papers, pencils, erasers, paper clips, rulers, books, maps, gold stars or stickers.

Camper/Explorer
Canteen, plastic utensils, backpack, headband, flashlight, walking stick or cane.

Pirate
Eye patch, scarf or bandana, laundry basket (to use as a treasure chest), junk jewelry and coins (to use as treasure), large cardboard box (to use as a boat).

Post Office
Envelopes, gummed labels or Easter seals (to use as stamps), junk mail, small scale, shoulder bag, rubber stamp.

Truck Driver
Large chair, cap, maps, transistor radio (to use as a CB).

Circus Lion Tamer
Stuffed animals, cardboard cartons, hula hoops, small stool, broom handle.

Airline Pilot
Large chair, earmuffs (for use as headphones), plus a lot of clocks, outdoor thermometers and calculators (for use as "controls").

Chapter 24
Enhancing
Your Child's
Curiosity

Thomas Armstrong

*Preschoolers are naturally
curious and creative beings.*

"Think about times when your child said or did things that caused you to laugh, or think, or see things in a new way. The new words he made up. The machines he invented with odds and ends.... The drawings of strange worlds he created. The song he composed on the spur of the moment. These are the manifestations of your child's natural genius." (From <u>Awakening Your Child's Natural Genius</u>, by Thomas Armstrong, Ph.D. ©1991)

Preschoolers are naturally curious and creative beings. These marvelous individuals have so many questions, and so many novel ways of looking at things. How can you keep this sort of creativity and curiosity alive in your kids? Here are suggestions:

Keep Your Own Love of Learning Alive

Young children are powerfully affected by the modeling they receive from the significant adults around them (such as parents). If children can experience those adults as vital individuals who are wondering about things ("Wow! Look at that!"), taking in new experiences, learning new things and generally keeping their minds flexible and active, then they are likely to be favorably impressed and become more like their role models.

Honor Your Child's Uniqueness

Research from Harvard University suggests that children have at least 7 different kinds of intelligence:
- *linguistic:* uses language creatively
- *logical-mathematical:* thinks in terms of abstract relationships
- *spatial:* learns through visual input
- *bodily-kinesthetic:* earns through physical movements
- *intrapersonal:* learns best when left to himself
- *musical:* learns best through rhythm and melody
- *interpersonal:* learns through relationships with others

So look for your child to be creative or curious in any of these ways.

As adults, we're most often likely to praise or reward things that children say or do that we think are important. So, if you consider words and reading most important, you're likely to give the most strokes to your child when she says something original, writes something creative, or begins to read with flair. This same child, however, might not get the same reinforcement for drawing or athletic experiences if you don't value these as legitimate indicators of intelligent behavior. Each child has all seven intelligences but may be particularly creative in areas that haven't been emphasized in your family. It may be a stretch for you to validate these areas, but it's vitally important for your child's self-esteem that you do this.

Be Curious and Creative Together

One of the key elements that keeps coming up in studies of how children learn is the all important role that parental involvement has in activating inner genius. Children are geniuses. But that genius will not blossom unless the parent as gardener comes around to *sprinkle water, adjust sunlight, and provide other nutrients.* You need to get down on your hands and knees and play with your kids: paint pictures with them, play music with them on the drums or the piano, run with them, read with them, do simple math games with them. And out of these interactions, the qualities of genius (creativity, curiosity, and learning ability) begin to bubble up to the surface. Like a pump that's been primed, once the fountain gets started, it will be delightful to watch the creativity gush forth!

Don't Force Your Child to Be Creative

Creativity that needs to be forced isn't really creativity. We know from studies in creativity that there often is a long period when the child doesn't seem to be doing much. Yet it's often during these times that the child is really incubating her experiences and getting ready for a creative break-through. So if your child isn't interested in being creative today with the paints or reading or writing, don't force the issue.

Watch For Spontaneous Signs of Creative Involvement

These are precious and exciting moments when they occur. Maria Montessori referred to "the great work," when a child might sometimes spend hours engaged in a learning or creative activity, focused upon the task with total absorption and then coming out of the activity, as if from a meditation, feeling totally rested, alert, and happy. University of Chicago psychologist Mihaly Csikszentmihalyi refers to a similar phenomenon as a "flow" experience. This happens most often when a task is neither too hard for a person (this can create anxiety) nor too easy (this can cause boredom).

It's a paradox really. Creativity and curiosity are something that can't be forced and can't be taught, and yet as parents you are instrumental in *creating an environment* where creativity and curiosity can be activated. Similarly, having a rich collection of experiences and resources (such as those suggested in the following pages) are important for getting things started, but they are themselves not sufficient to begin the creative experi-ence. Creativity is a mystery really — a divine mystery perhaps. But though we don't totally understand it, we do know that our children have it, and so we owe it to them to honor it and allow it to grow and prosper in their lives.

Creative Experiences

Thomas Armstrong

Parents are the child's first teachers, and the home is his first learning center. Children learn best through enjoyable, hands-on activities that relate to their own lives. The following are a few suggestions:

Percussion Time
Get some simple percussion instruments (maracas, tambourines, rhythm sticks, drums etc.), and put on some music and play together rhythmically. Experiment with different kinds of rhythms. Turn off the music and have a percussion dialogue (you shake, they shake back). Have a great time.

Bubble Blowing
Put some dishwashing liquid in a kitchen or bathroom sink filled with a couple of inches of water. Outdoors, use a basin or pot. Provide bubble-blowing equipment, including straws, hollow cans, plastic tubing, or wire shapes made from paper clips or coat hangers. Then get creative about blowing bubbles. How large can you make the bubbles? What kinds of different shapes can be made? How can the bubbles be made to last longer by experimenting with different kinds of soap?

Nature Walk
Just taking a walk with your child is one of the simplest and best ways of activating curiosity and creativity in both of you. There are plenty of things to wonder about out there: Why is the sky blue? What makes the wind blow? What kind of animal is running over there? If these are questions you can't answer, jot them down. Later on you can both look for answers at

the library. Again, don't make this a lesson in science, but rather an opportunity to explore, experiment, and expand both of your worlds.

Weights and Measures
• Help young children use math by weighing family members on the bathroom scale. Compare each person's weight to household objects that can be placed on the scale: a dictionary, a toy truck.
• Measure items in your home using a ruler or tape measure. For example: the length of the living room couch, the width of your child's shoulders, the height of the kitchen table.

Dress-Up
Designate a hinged box or special drawer as a "costume shop" and put in it some old coats, dresses, shirts, shoes, hats and other clothes. Let your child play dress-up with his or her friends and provide a space for them to act out different roles wearing their favorite costumes.

Reading Sense
Look for picture books that intrigue young children. They enjoy touch-and-feel books, scratch-and-sniff books, books with flaps to lift or tabs to pull, books with colorful and creative illustrations. These books help to interest young children in reading, even before they can understand the words printed on the page.

Space Shifting
Using string or masking tape, mark off a circle of space ten or fifteen feet in diameter in an appropriate room of the house or outdoors. Let this space become an center of the earth, an asteroid, or any other place your child wishes. Once inside this space, your child's creativity (and the creativity of playmates) should determine the action that follows. Bring other props into the space to enhance the scene (for example, large cardboard box, blocks, etc.).

Wrapping Paper Dialogue
Get a large sheet of wrapping paper and some drawing/writing tools (pencils, marking pens, crayons etc.). Then have a written dialogue with your child on paper. He writes or draws something. You respond. Then you write or draw something. He responds. Repeat the sequence. For younger children, this conversation may consist of scribbles, for older kids, pictures and words. Most importantly, however, don't try to inhibit either what you write or draw or what your child does on the paper (for example, if your two year old scribbles and you feel like writing a sentence, that's fine; but don't use this as a writing exercise; be led by a sense of spontaneity and fun).

Chapter 25
Encouraging
Your Gifted
Preschooler

Marilyn Gilbert

*Gifts and talents
come in many packages —
intellectual, social,
emotional, creative,
athletic.*

At eighteen months old, Jacob is speaking in two or three word sentences... Sarah, at five years old, loves to play tunes on the piano... Jon, at age four, can read, and is always asking, "Why?"... Katy can climb trees and is learning to throw and catch a ball much better than most three-year-olds... Eileen, at age four, draws beautiful pictures, and combines colors and patterns in a very creative manner... Would these preschoolers be considered "gifted?"

What is meant by a "gifted" child?

Just what is *giftedness*?   Gifts and talents come in many packages — *intellectual, social, emotional, creative, athletic.*   Because of this variety, it is difficult to formulate one definition of giftedness appropriate for all.

In 1972, the U.S. Department of Health, Education and Welfare under the direction of Commissioner of Education, Sidney P. Marland, tried to fill the need, and issued guidelines for giftedness. The Marland Report said that gifted and talented children are those identified under these guidelines by professionally qualified persons. These children, by virtue of outstanding abilities, are capable of high performance in one or more of the following areas:

General intellectual ability; specific academic talent; creative or productive thinking; leadership ability; visual or performing arts; and **psychomotor ability** (the ability to translate ideas into actions).

This definition of giftedness is the one most generally accepted for the *school-age child* by experts. Translating the definition into recognizable characteristics appropriate for *preschoolers* may be helpful to you as parents.

<u>GIFTED</u> <u>PRESCHOOLERS</u> <u>FREQUENTLY</u> <u>DISPLAY</u>
<u>SOME</u> <u>COMBINATION</u> <u>OF</u> <u>THESE</u> <u>CHARACTERISTICS</u>

General Intellectual Ability

•*Good memory:* Beyond knowing how to count and recognize the letters of the alphabet, the child can frequently read with comprehension at a young age. The child is able to recall events that happened to him with appropriate names and words.

•*Vocabulary:* Learns new words easily, and uses them appropriately in the correct context.

•*Integrating ideas:* Can integrate new concepts and ideas into the frame-work of what she already knows.

•*Awareness:* The child "doesn't miss a trick." He can keep track of many things going on at once, in detail, is observant and alert.

•*Curiosity:* Asks "why" frequently, seeking to make sense of the world.

Creative or Productive Thinking
• *Creativity:* Thinks creatively, and asks "what if" questions.
• *Imagination:* Has a vivid imagination, makes up stories, plays let's pretend games, may even have an imaginary friend.
• *Energy:* The child is full of energy, needs less sleep and fewer naps.
• *Sense of humor:* Makes and appreciates jokes, can see humor in situations.

Leadership Ability
• *Social and Emotional:* Shows sensitivity, intuitiveness, empathy to the feelings of others.
• *Leadership:* Shows skill in helping children work together.

Visual or Performing Arts
• *Artistic:* Demonstrates proficiency in art forms such as drawing or music.

Athletic Ability
• *Athletic:* The child demonstrates skill and interest in athletic activities. She can, for example, throw and catch a ball, or perhaps swim proficiently at an early age.

Encouraging each child's special gifts
Each child has a gift or talent that makes that child special to those who love him. Often in order for giftedness to be demonstrated, your young child needs to be exposed to the types of activities in which giftedness can become apparent. Parents who foster a love of learning, love of reading, and the development of creativity in their children, gifted or not, give *them* a special gift that will encourage them to develop to their highest level of aptitude and that will last their whole lives.

Although, according to the above definition, few children may be deemed "gifted" the kind of help and encouragement given to gifted preschoolers, as described in this chapter, can be beneficial for the development of *all* children.

What is the point
of identifying giftedness
in your preschooler?

Marilyn Gilbert

Your questions about giftedness are a reflection of your concern about your child's welfare. You want to do your best for your child without pushing. You want to know what you can expect from your child and how you can best meet his needs.

Parents tend to be good judges of giftedness in their children, but many parents hesitate to evaluate their children for giftedness for fear of seeming boastful. If you suspect that your child is gifted, it is reassuring to be able to test your perceptions with your child's school psychologist. You may also want to get information by writing to ERIC Clearinghouse on Disabilities and Gifted Education (ERIC/EC), 1920 Association Drive, Reston, VA 20191-1589, or telephoning 1-800-328-0272.

*What are the needs
of gifted children?*

• To be with peers of like ability for stimulation, and to know that there are other children who are as quick and able as they are
• To have friends
• To have time to reflect and daydream so that they can "digest" what they are learning, to combine it with what they already know, make new connections, and use their new knowledge creatively and joyfully
• To have time for socialization and play
• To be loved for themselves, not just their special talent
• *Not* to have unrealistic expectations set for them
• *Not* to be overprogrammed into constant activities

Parent/preschooler Activities

Marilyn Gilbert

Parents frequently ask for activities for their gifted preschoolers. Very often, your child's interests can be your guide. Your child will express interest in certain kinds of information or materials, and you can try to fill the requests.

Visit the library

In working to fill those requests, the library is a wonderful resource. The children's librarian is specially trained in juvenile literature and can make recommendations as well as help you find what you need. Many libraries have a variety of programs to fit children's needs and interests, and frequently keep directories of local special interest activities for children. (The library is also a parent resource. Librarians can recommend books and periodicals, and names of local parent groups.)

Use conversation, poems, songs and stories

Talking to children from infancy stimulates language development. Recite nursery rhymes and poems, read stories and sing songs. (Many records and tapes now have the words included for just this purpose.) Before reading your child a story, you may want to read just the title, and then have your child tell you a story of his or her own that the book could be about.

Lita Linzer Schwartz, author of "Are You the Gifted Parent of a Gifted Child? in *Gifted Child Quarterly,* Winter 1981, suggests that "once language is established, exposure to other languages can also become part of the parent-child interaction... [for example] some of the *Babar the Elephant* books are available in bilingual editions, as are fairy tales and *Winnie the Pooh."*

Visit places of interest

Taking trips is a good way to broaden your preschooler's horizons and enhance language development. In addition to places like the local zoo and museum, a trip to a different neighborhood, hardware store, garden center, fire house or post office gives you and your child new areas to begin exploration, discussion and understanding of the world.

Provide your child with the opportunity for different types of imaginative play

Art and hobby materials will provide your child and her friends with hours of valuable learning experiences. A wide variety of materials, a place to use them, and the opportunity to choose how they will be used is the basis of the creative process. Putting the materials together in new and unusual ways is very satisfying. With no predicted conclusion, the youngster is free to capitalize on the characteristics of the materials and the spark of the moment. The process of creation is as important as the finished product. Encouragement of this type of creativity depends on parental support and acceptance of the child's work. It's better, for example, to say "How nicely you've used blue," than to say "What's that supposed to be?"

Provide props for imaginative play

"Make believe" is a form of thinking and learning, as well as a form of play. It requires concentration and inspiration to keep the illusion alive. Some good props to provide are ties, jackets, hats, aprons, slippers, purses, old kitchen utensils, plastic bowls, clean empty food containers, keys, and suit-cases. A toy phone is great for stimulating dramatic conversations. After a while your preschooler will also have ideas of what props to include. Adult participation in the scenarios your child creates fosters the spirit of pretending.

Encourage collecting

Collections of such things as coins, rocks, even labels from canned foods, can provide an interesting hobby. Grouping and regrouping the items in the collection gives the child a chance to develop different categories for classification. For example your child may group the labels in several ways — according to color, kind of food, style of lettering, and so on.

Measure and weigh things
Children love to use a two-pan balance-type scale. This doesn't give absolute weight, but can let your child experience "heavier" and "lighter." If your child shows interest, move on to a postage scale. Weigh a variety of things and have your child arrange them in some order according to their weights. Measuring spoons and cups used with sand or salt let your child experiment, beyond simple counting, to discover how many half cups equal a cup, how many teaspoons equal a tablespoon. This is a logical lead-in to cooking which introduces measuring, following directions, and reading with a purpose.

Provide toys that stimulate creativity
Blocks, simple figures of people or animals, dolls and large, empty cartons are good for imaginative play. A magnifying glass, although not a toy, is a wonderful tool for hours of exploration.

Needs of Parents
Parents of gifted children often find it useful to join parent groups in order to learn how others encourage their gifted children intellectually, socially and emotionally. Departments of education in local universities or colleges can be useful in helping you track down local organizations.

Chapter 26
Let's Pretend...
Creative Drama

Laura Robb

For most of the evening,
Sarah played in
our family room
which she transformed
into a beach.

When at home alone I sit
And am very tired of it,
I have just to shut my eyes
To go sailing through the skies—
To go sailing far away
To the pleasant Land of Play...

from *The Little Land*
in *A Child's Garden of Verses,*
by *Robert Louis Stevenson*

Recently three-year-old Sarah attended a dinner party at my house. For most of the evening, Sarah played in our family room which she transformed into a beach. Sarah knew where the waves crashed, the crabs sunned, and the location of her sand castle. Any adult who dared walk through that room had to enter Sarah's make-believe story world.

Your child, like Sarah, delights in dramatic play — a creative process that stimulates the imagination and builds self-esteem. A preschooler who develops his imagination usually is more resourceful, interacts well with his peers, and finds greater pleasure in moments of solitude.

You can help your child with creative play, by involving him in a variety of activities at an early age. These activities can also build the skills needed for success in school in the following ways:

Creative Drama Strengthens Motor (Muscle) Development
Even very young children love to move to music. Play some rhythmic music on the radio or phonograph, and allow your child to move freely and actively to the beat. Using room settings, pretend to sweep the floor and dust the furniture. Then visit a pretend park and ask your child what she would like to imagine that she will do there. Join her in the suggested imaginary activities (such as having a picnic, swinging, or going up and down on the seesaw.) Such activities develop a preschooler's muscle tone and physical coordination.

Creative Drama Builds Sensory Awareness
Children take in information about their world through their senses. Make your child aware of his eyes, ears, nose, mouth, and hands by asking him to point to each one. Help very young children by placing their fingers on each part. Design different experiences that activate each sense. See sensory awareness games described on pages 195-199.

Creative Drama Encourages Language Development

As you recite nursery rhymes and sing songs, you are expanding your child's vocabulary. Ask your child to be one of the animals in the poems (for example, one of the three little kittens who lost their mittens) and imitate its sounds and actions. By three, your child has become a great mimic who delights in imitating behaviors. Now he can create the sound effects for stories and poems. Read favorites such as *The Three Bears*, encouraging your child to act out different roles. Let your child speak the words of his character. Older preschoolers can tell the story and dramatize it. When your child's friends visit, suggest they create and perform original plays or plays based on stories.

Creative Drama Enhances Social Skills

As you dramatize ways to behave in different settings, you will increase your child's vocabulary and social skills. You and your child can pretend to speak on the telephone, to have dinner at a restaurant, or to meet somebody for the first time. You can take on the role of the child, and your youngster will be learning from you how to speak and behave in these social situations.

Creative Drama Allows Children to Express Emotions Safely

When your child expresses the feelings of pretend characters, he learns to understand and deal with his own strong feelings. For example, when he pretends to be Max in *Where the Wild Things Are*, he can act out his own anger and his loneliness. Or when pretending to be Gretel in *Hansel and Gretel*, she can show her own fears of being lost or hurt.

Creative Drama Develops Cooperation

When children are involved in dramatic play the participants must take turns *to listen* and *to speak*. Youngsters have to cooperate in order to decide what the story is about, who the characters will be, and how the play will continue. Learning to get along with others is an important skill for your preschooler. By involving friends and brothers and sisters in dramatic play, you provide enjoyable experiences that naturally build on the need to cooperate.

When you as a parent take part in your child's dramatic play, the activity brings you closer to your child and the play is enriched by your presence.⬚

Creative Drama Activities

Laura Robb

Remember, there is no "right" or "wrong" way to do these activities. By celebrating your children's interpretations, you help them find joy and satisfaction in imaginative play.

CAR ACTIVITIES

• Let your preschooler pretend to start the car, steer the car, toot the horn, stop the car.

• Have your preschooler use words to play "What do you see?" at stop lights.

• Have your child do a fingerplay to a poem you recite together.

• Ask your preschooler to use his face to dramatize: happy, sad, angry, disappointed, proud. Then let him tell you in words what those emotions feel like.

• Have your child pretend he is eating different foods such as a pretzel, a sour lemon, an ice cream cone.

• Let your child talk about a scene, using words to describe: the forest, the city, a grocery store, a library, the park, or what he sees as you drive along.

• Bring along a blank audio cassette tape, and let your preschooler sing, tell stories, or recite poems into the tape recorder. Play it back afterwards.

IMPROVISATIONS

Play with your child to create characters spontaneously. Let your child's imagination direct the activity.

• **Family Members** — *Your preschooler chooses the character he wants to be after observing family members and repeatedly participating in family activities. Your child can continue with the role play and expand upon it as he wishes. Examples of characters and activities are:* Mother washes the car; father barbecues; older brother or sister delivers newspapers; grandmother works in the garden.

• **Community Helpers** — *Your preschooler may have had a recent visit to the doctor for a checkup, or to the barber for a haircut. Examples of characters and activities are:* The doctor gives a baby a checkup; a policeman directs traffic; a teacher reads a story; a nurse fixes a cut finger; a salesman helps you buy shoes; a truck driver rolls along the highway; an attendant pumps gasoline into your car; the mailman delivers a package; a baker shapes rolls; a barber or hairdresser cuts your hair.

• **Entertainers and Athletes** — *Your preschooler may have been to an ice-skating rink, seen gymnasts on television, or read a story about a clown. Examples of characters are:* An ice skater; a gymnast; a dancer; a singer; a drummer; a violinist; a juggler; a clown, a high wire walker, a swimmer, a baseball pitcher.

• **Animals** — *A visit to a zoo, farm or pet store may evoke the desire to act out the behavior of:* Zoo animals such a monkey, a tiger, an elephant, a bear, or a snake; pets and farm animals such as a dog, cat, cow, pig, lamb, horse, mouse, hamster, and rooster.

• **Fairy Tale Characters** — *After reading many stories, your child may want to act out his own idea of how certain characters behave such as a:* King, queen, prince, princess; witch, beggar, soldier, giant, fairy, or *Favorite Storybook Characters such as:* Cinderella, one of the three bears or pigs, the wolf, the gingerbread man, the woodsman, Snow White, the wicked stepmother, Hansel, Gretel, the witch.

NURSERY RHYME FUN

• Create a finger play for *Hickory Dickory Dock* by reciting the poem and using your fingers, hands and arms to act it out.
• Act out *Humpty Dumpty.*
• Pantomime *Little Jack Horner.*
• Dramatize *This is the House That Jack Built* as a party activity with each child taking a different role.

• Dramatize *The Three Little Kittens, Sing a Song of Sixpence, Little Robin Redbreast, Little Miss Muffet,* and *Pussy Cat, Pussy Cat Where Have You Been?* (See Resources, pages 157-161, for suggested books of nursery rhymes.)

PROPS

Help your child use simple objects as props for dramatizations. Hold up a wooden spoon and help your youngster "stretch her imagination" by saying the spoon can become something else like oars for a rowboat or a magic wand. Use simple items such as a shoe, a pot, a leaf, or a stone. When you play this game you help your youngster make something familiar into something strange and wonderful.

MASKS

Use paper grocery bags or paper plates to make masks. Cut holes for eyes, nose, mouth. Decorate with crayons, yarn, or fabric.

PANTOMIME GAMES: WHAT CAN I SAY WITHOUT TALKING?

Which activities would your child like to pantomime?
• Rake leaves.
• Twirl to the ground like an autumn leaf.
• Walk through deep snow.
• Sweep the kitchen.
• Swim, run, hop, skip, jump.
• Fly like a bird; like an airplane.
• Be a gentle breeze; a furious wind.
• Walk a circle, a square, straight and crooked lines.
• Open a door or a window — then close them.
• Wrap a birthday present.
• Take your pet for a walk.
• Wash hands at the sink.
• Hammer a nail into a piece of wood.

PUPPET ACTIVITIES

• Your child can "write" puppet plays by telling them to you and having you write them down. Then she can perform the plays as you help narrate them.
• You and your preschooler can dramatize favorite stories and poems using easy-to-make puppets:

Sock Puppets
1) Stuff the "foot" part of a sock with scraps of fabric or foam rubber, or cotton. Paint a face on "toe" of sock, or use buttons, yarn, and fabric to create a character's face. Insert hand in sock to manipulate puppet.

2) Sew button eyes and yarn for hair near the toe of the sock. Insert your hand and make the mouth "talk" by moving your fingers and thumb.

Popsicle-Stick Puppets
Draw and cut out shapes for characters. Decorate shapes with yarn, felt, crayons, or fabric. Paste shapes to popsicle-sticks.

Kitchen-Utensil Puppets
1) Paint a face on a wooden spoon. Use yarn and glue for the hair. Attach a costume to the handle.
2) Tape face parts to a plastic spatula. Attach a costume to the handle.

GAMES THAT DEVELOP SENSORY AWARENESS

Touch Games
These activities help your child understand that he can use his sense of touch with his hands and the entire body. Have your preschooler pantomime (pretend without words) touching a hot stove, planting and picking flowers, and walking on sharp pebbles. Then ask your child to verbally express what is happening and how it feels.

You can blindfold older preschoolers and have them pull an object (spoon, crayon, ball, stuffed animal, book, etc.) from a large bag. By feeling the object, see if your youngster can decide what it's made of, if it's heavy or light, and finally, what it is.

Hearing Games
Have your child listen to and dramatize a variety of sounds right in your home. Start by asking your child to listen to and imitate the washing machine churning, the refrigerator humming, and the vacuum cleaner gobbling up the dirt. Make your child aware of all kinds of sounds such as the rain falling on the roof and trucks driving up your street. Produce these sounds on walks and in the car. As you read books stop and ask your youngster to imitate the sounds of characters and happenings in the story.

Seeing Games
Sharpen your child's powers of observation as you watch snow fall, a butterfly dance, and a cloud race across a windy sky. Encourage your child to be the snow, the butterfly, the cloud, and then to use words to describe what he sees.

Try playing *The Reflection Game.* Begin by making a happy face. Your child imitates you. Then move your arms up high, and your head to one side.

Your child does the same as if she were a mirror. Try taking turns with your child being the "mirror" or the "doer." This game can include miming emotions, animals, different movements, and fingerplays.
(See Fingerplays, page 75.)

Smelling and Tasting Games

Have a pretend smelling and tasting party using different foods. Give your preschooler a "rose" to smell and a "lemon" to taste. Let your child set the table for a pretend party and act out smelling and tasting the food.

You can do a similar activity with real food by blindfolding your child and offering him some foods, one at a time. He feels and smells the food and predicts what it will taste like. He will want to eat these foods, so select items that are tasty and nutritious.

Chapter 27
Importance
of Humor

Barbara Baskin

...facilitating the growth of
a sense of humor
is one of the easier
and more pleasurable ways
parents can contribute
to the mental health
and cognitive growth
of their offspring.

Humor contributes to mental and physical health

Emotional well-being is a goal all parents hope their children will achieve and, to that end, they actively promote activities which will enhance feelings of confidence and self-esteem. Strangely absent in books of advice to parents is mention of the development and encouragement of a sense of humor. Psychologists are currently examining the role of humor as a contributor to mental health, but also suggest its importance as a tool in combating physical disorders!

Humor is connected with thinking skills

Not only is humor associated with these important life components, but humor in children (as well as in adults) is closely connected with advanced thinking skills. Investigators report that creative children are seen by their peers as having a good sense of humor. Chapter 25 in this section (page 185) describes *gifted* preschoolers as those who make and appreciate jokes and can see humor in many situations. Parents can facilitate the growth of a sense of humor by capitalizing on many naturally arising or devised opportunities as well as through books.

Parents can nurture a sense of humor

Virtually all children have the potential for a good sense of humor but, as in any developmental attribute, it needs nurturing. And like most aspects of personality, its roots lie in the early years.

One enthusiastic mother and father reported that they began their children's exposure to humor by modeling jokes in front of them. The father would ask his wife, "Did you take a bath?" She'd reply, "Why, is one missing?" and they would laugh together. At first, the youngsters would laugh at such exchanges without recognition of them as jokes. Soon the older child began asking, "Is that a joke?" when he heard people laugh. He began to join in the family hobby. At first he only told the last line of the joke, then moved on to recalling and retelling jokes and funny stories. At the library, he often requested riddle and joke books, and began to teach his younger brother how to tell jokes. The question: "What kind of ears does a train have?" gets the response: "Engin<u>ears</u>!" and they both collapse in laughter.

A sense of humor may even be present during infancy

Researchers are still not clear exactly how or when a sense of humor begins to develop, but some claim that it is present during infancy. They suggest that the smiles, gurgles, or laughter at *peek-a-boo* or similar games are evidence that babies derive pleasure and display it when confronting events which puzzle them. Indeed, McGhee, the investigator who has examined humor in children most extensively, has concluded that when genuine laughter does occur, it comes about when children become aware of ideas or events that are *unexpected or different from what the child has experienced before*. Further, he claims that pleasure results when some thought is involved.

He also believes that the ability to notice incongruities begins to emerge at the beginning of the second year when children are able to note things that don't "make sense" — or hear the mislabeling of objects and events. When children are about three, they can detect absurdity and find it funny. For example, a child will laugh at a story when a chicken says, "Moo."

Parents may be uncertain either about how to encourage their child's sense of humor or may feel that their own is perhaps not up to the task. Fortunately, facilitating the growth of a sense of humor is one of the easier and more pleasurable ways parents can contribute to the mental health and cognitive growth of their offspring.

Suggestions for Encouraging the Growth of a Sense of Humor in a Preschooler

Barbara Baskin

After you are certain your child knows animal names, obtain a new book and begin to examine it together. Look at an elephant, and state decisively, "What a funny looking camel." Your child will look at the picture and then at a broadly smiling adult. (Your smile gives "permission" to contradict!) "That's not a camel, that's an elephant," the child says. You smile and say, "Oh, I think you're right." Again, you, the adult, make an error, your child corrects, and you respond, "Right again, I guess I made a mistake." Soon your child feels confident (emotional safety is a necessity to experiencing and expressing humor) and rises to the fun of the situation, enjoying the absurdity of his parent making such obvious errors. Soon, your child will want to turn the tables by intentionally mislabeling other things.

Draw attention to amusing aspects of your child's world.

For example, your three-year-old child is riding her tricycle and Grandpa says, "Now it's my turn to ride!" Or, after reading *A Chocolate Moose for Dinner* (Fred Gwynne, Prentice-Hall, 1976), serve chocolate pudding (mousse) for dinner, and comment that the girl in the book is having another kind of chocolate "moose." Your smile or laughter may (or may not yet) alert your child that such events are sources of amusement.

Since children model adult behavior,
tell and enjoy simple jokes, riddles, and stories in your home.
Q. Why did the man throw a clock out the window?
A. Because he wanted to see time fly.
If you're not already doing it, label the jokes and stories, commenting, "that's a funny joke" or "that was really silly" (a quality, by the way, not to be discounted). Obviously, such materials or behavior should not contain cruel or biased content.

Segal and Adcock (Your Child at Play, Newmarket, 1985) suggest revising nursery rhymes — for example, "Mary had a little elephant" and giving a child a funny name for an embrace — a *hugarooni!* Children may not "get the point" early on, but they will retain the idea that loved adults find such behavior entertaining, and ultimately seek to emulate them.

Read humorous books to your preschooler.

Even though books on the development of preschoolers typically do not address the development of humor (or many other critical aspects of intellectual growth for that matter!), it is clear that writers for preschoolers believe that such children have a sense of humor: Books of riddles, jokes, silly pictures and funny stories abound which are directed to these 4 and 5 year olds. Which ones tickle the funny bones of preschoolers?

To answer that question, many children's librarians in Suffolk County, New York, were asked to identify books which had amused preschoolers in the story hour. Further, they were asked: when storytelling to children, did they do anything to enhance the likelihood of laughter?

The following conditions brought the most humorous response from their young listeners:
• Librarians selected books *they* felt were amusing.
• They "got into" the absurdity of the story by speaking in funny voices to fit the characters in the story.
• They put themselves into a playful mood and were able to communicate that to the group.
• They told the story with expectations that children would laugh.

The storytellers also reported that when children with advanced language skills recognized the humor in a story, their laughter was often contagious. Sometimes listeners would be uncertain why they were laughing but, over time and with added story exposure and language maturation, they too came to a stronger awareness and appreciation of comedy.

Librarians confirmed that incongruity often generated laughter. Another very common one in the laughter-generating books was the frequency of rule-breaking: when words were said in nonstandard ways, when the main character did things children had been warned against, when characters violated their role or stereotype (a grandmother riding a motorcycle), children tended to find these hilarious.

Should parents be alarmed at the idea of children responding to nonsense or rule-breaking by laughter? Not at all. Research tells us that a sense of humor is a stimulant to problem solving and is closely connected to fantasy play and to creativity. Isn't it delightful to be able to share something so good for your child that is also such wonderful fun?

Resources for Section Five: Imagination Creativity

BOOKS FOR ADULTS

Awakening Your Child's Natural Genius: Enhancing Curiosity, Creativity, and Learning Ability, by Thomas Armstrong. Jeremy P. Tarcher/Putnam, 1991. With creative suggestions on innovative approaches to academics, how children grow through the arts, and ways to preserve each child's uniqueness, this important book (written by the author of chapter 3 in this section) helps parents understand how to encourage their children to develop their true gifts.

What's So Funny? Wit and Humor in American Children's Literature, by Michael Cart. HarperCollins, 1995. In this study of humorous books written for children since 1920, the author explores three basic types of humorous stories: talking animal books, tall tales, and family comedy, sharing his enthusiasm for children's books with his readers.

It's O.K. to be Gifted or Talented! by Joel Engel. Tor Books/St. Martins Press, 1988. A useful and practical guide for parents, this book includes stories that parents and children can read together to help youngsters communicate their feelings.

Look at Me, by Carolyn Buhai Haas. Chicago Review Press, 1987. A book that is chock full of creative learning activities for babies and toddlers. For creative drama activities, see the section on *Imaginative Play,* with activities for pretending, puppets, and dramatic play.

Humor and Children's Development: A Guide to Practical Applications, edited by Paul McGhee. Haworth Press, 1989

"Play Incongruity and Humor," by Paul McGhee in *Children's Play: Applied and Developmental,* edited by Thomas D. Yawkey and Anthony D. Pellegrini. .

A Parents' Guide to Encouraging Imagination and Creativity during Early Childhood, by Michael K. Meyerhoff. William Gladden Foundation (Dept. B, 7 Bridge Street, Cameron, WV 26033), 1992. One of a series of booklets published by the William Gladden Foundation about issues that affect children and their families. Written by the author of several chapters in this book, the booklet also includes a summary of developmental steps in the growth of imagination and creativity, equipment for encouraging fantasy play, and materials for enhancing artistic activities.

The House of Make-Believe: Children's Play and the Developing Imagination, by Dorothy G. Singer and Jerome L. Singer. Harvard University Press paperback edition, 1992. In this inspiring and thoughtful book, the authors, who are authorities in the field, explore childhood play looking at "the special mystery of how we develop our human capacity for mental travel through time and space."

Enjoy Your Gifted Child, by Carol Addison Takacs. Syracuse University Press, 1986. A down-to-earth guide for raising and enjoying your gifted child.

For additional information and resources contact: *ERIC Clearinghouse on Disabilities and Gifted Education (ERIC/EC),* 1920 Association Drive, Reston, VA 20191-1589, (1-800-328-0272).

BOOKS FOR CHILDREN

Willy and the Cardboard Boxes, by Lizi Boyd. Viking Penguin, 1991. Willy's Dad takes him to the office for the day. With some markers, scissors and string, and Willy's imagination, large empty boxes in Dad's office become an airplane, boat, fire engine, and finally a house where Willy falls asleep until it's time to go home.

Arthur's Nose, by Marc Brown. Little, Brown, 1986. Arthur the aardvark is discontented with the shape of his nose and goes to the doctor for a more attractive replacement. He tries on many models but the noses all look ludicrous and he finally happily realizes that his own is actually the best.

Why Did the Chicken Cross the Road? And Other Riddles Old and New, by Joanna Cole & Stephanie Calmenson. Morrow Junior Books, 1994. There are an assortment of over 200 riddles: number riddles, letter riddles, geography riddles, and on and on. Enjoy.

For Sand Castles or Seashells, by Gail Hartman. Bradbury, 1990. There is no limit to what a little girl can create, and does, at the beach and in other familiar places such as her backyard or a puddle on the sidewalk.

The Front Hall Carpet, by Nicholas Heller. Greenwillow, 1990. For an imaginative child, all the carpets and rugs in her house can be used to pretend that she is rowing a boat on a lake, ruling as a queen, or sitting beside a bear in the forest.

Where's Spot? by Eric Hill. Putnam, 1980. An adult dog wants its pup to know dinner is ready. It looks in reasonable places like under the bed or behind the stairs and discovers unlikely animals are occupying those premises. The dog accepts their presence, like the hippo in the piano, as perfectly reasonable in this entertaining book.

Amazing Grace, by Mary Hoffman. Dial, 1991. Grace loves to act, and when her class is preparing to put on a play of *Peter Pan,* she wants to play the part of Peter. One classmate says, "You can't be Peter — that's a boy's name." Another says, "You can't be Peter Pan. He isn't black." Grace's family tells her she can be anything she wants, if she puts her mind to it. The play is a big success with Grace as a marvelous Peter Pan.

I'm a Jolly Famer, by Julie Lacome. Candlewick Press, 1994. With the help of her dog, a little girl can become a farmer, a princess, little Red Riding Hood, or anything she wants.

Imagine, by Alison Lester. Houghton Mifflin, 1990. This book invites the reader to imagine what it would be like to live in the ocean, a jungle, and an icecap — and meet the creatures that live there.

Once Upon a Golden Apple, by Jean Little & Maggie De Vries. Viking Penguin, 1991. Daddy is reading to his two youngsters. But what kind of story is he telling? "Once upon a golden apple..." "No!" say the children. "Once upon a magic pebble..." "No! No!" Finally, Daddy gets it right, "Once upon a time..." "Yes!" This funny fairy tale can encourage children to make up their own plots to familiar stories.

What Do You Hear When Cows Sing? And Other Silly Riddles, by Marco and Giulio Maestro. (An I Can Read Book®) HarperCollins, 1996. As the author of the chapter on the *Importance of Humor* points out, silliness is a quality not to be discounted. These silly riddles are just the thing for young children to try out on their friends and unsuspecting adults. (The answer to the question in the title, by the way, is, "Moosic.")

If Dinosaurs Came to Town, by Dom Mansell. Little, Brown, 1991. Dinosaur fans can use their imaginations to think about what might happen if dinosaurs actually hadn't all become extinct — and a whole lot of them came into town. Illustrations show the traffic tie-ups caused by Diplodocus, the havoc on the farm when Stegosaurus visits the country-side, and the airplanes watching out for Pteranodon.

Let's Pretend, by Dessie & Chevelle Moore. HarperFestival, 1994. A board book for very young children who are asked to pretend to: drive a car, bake a cake, and to act like grownups.

Play Ball, Amelia Bedelia, by Peggy Parish. (An I Can Read Book®) HarperTrophy, 1995. Amelia Bedelia knows nothing about baseball, but she is willing to help out the neighborhood team when one player is sick — with hilarious results.

Where the Wild Things Are, by Maurice Sendak. Harper & Row, 1963. In this classic book, a young boy misbehaves and his mother sends him to bed without his supper. He imagines that a forest grows in his room and many large and scary wild things try to frighten him. But he tames them all and finally sails home in a magic boat.

That's Exactly the Way It Wasn't, by James Stevenson. Greenwillow, 1991. Mary Ann and Louie have been arguing, so Grandpa tells them a story about how he and his brother Wainey argued when they were children. According to Grandpa, he and Wainey got caught in a landslide, were saved by an armadillo, and finally were swallowed by a giant iguana. Wainey listens to Grandpa's story too, disputing various points, but they finally stop arguing and all eat ice cream together.

Time to Get Out, by Fulvio Testa. Tambourine, 1993. A young boy explores a tropical island. He imagines large waves and toy animals that come to life. At the end of the book, we discover that he is in his bathtub.

Never Mail An Elephant, by Mike Thaler. WhistleStop/Troll, 1994. A little boy has great difficulty in mailing an elephant to his cousin as a present for her birthday in this humorous story.

The Polar Express, by Chris Van Allsburg. Houghton Mifflin, 1985. A young boy dreams he travels by train, along with other children, to visit Santa Claus in a story that has become a Christmas classic about the special gift that comes to those who truly believe.

Do You See a Mouse? by Bernard Waber. Houghton Mifflin, 1995. While everyone in the very fancy Park Snoot Hotel insists that there is no mouse in the hotel, the reader can find a mouse in every illustration in this warm and funny book.

Free Fall, by David Wiesner. Mulberry Books edition, 1991. In this wordless Caldecott Honor book, a boy dreams that he falls through the skies—meeting chess pieces that come alive, visiting a castle, slaying a dragon, and changing size as he visits strange places—until he finally lands back in his own bed.

Hurricane, by David Wiesner. Clarion, 1992. The morning after a hurricane, two brothers find an uprooted tree which becomes a magical place transporting them on imaginative adventures.

And Then What? by Jake Wolf. Greenwillow, 1993. Willy asks his mother what they are going to do that day. As she lists each activity Willy asks, "And then what?" His mother uses humor and imagination to describe fanciful adventures.

King Bidgood's in the Bathtub, by Audrey Wood. Harcourt, Brace Jovanovich, 1993. His royal highness loves playing in the bathtub and won't get out for lunch, for a fishing trip, or even for a party. No one knows what to do until his page pulls the plug and the king has to get out.

Stories, by Philip Yenawine. The Museum of Modern Art, New York/ Delacorte Press, 1991. Using reproductions of paintings by Chagall, Matisse, Rousseau, and others, this book encourages children to imagine what is happening in a painting, and to make up stories about the pictures.

Section Six
Music
Movement
Art

Section Six
Music - Movement - Art

Introduction

• *Imitating the way animals move, a preschooler walks with heavy tread like an elephant, to slow and stately music.*

• *A lively rendition of "Old MacDonald" on the radio has a toddler singing "E - I - E - I - O," while bouncing and and clapping to the rhythm.*

• *A kindergartener steps back from her easel, admires the brilliant colors she has just painted, and tells a nearby adult, "It's a butterfly!"*

There are many ways to express your thoughts and feelings. Youngsters are able to express themselves through music, movement, and art if they are given the opportunity.

The authors represented in this section offer valuable information about how the arts are important to a young child's development, with plentiful suggestions for activities and exercises.

SECTION SIX

MUSIC - MOVEMENT - ART

Chapter 28
Sounds Like Fun

Mitzie Collins

*... it is within the family
that children receive their
earliest and most valuable
musical instruction.*

Three-year-old Patrick plays by himself, building an edifice of blocks, scampering in and out of the room for additional toys, but always staying near the tape recorder, which is playing, for the fourth time, his favorite recording of children's songs and games. He occasionally sings a verse of one of the songs he hears. Six-month-old Louise quiets down as her mother sings her a lullaby, becoming restless when the singing stops. Five-year-old Stephen marches happily with his father to the car after listening to an outdoor concert given by a community band. All of these children are responding to music.

All Children Respond to Music
Parents sometimes think that musical training for children must consist of formalized lessons with a teacher, but it is within the family that children receive their earliest and most valuable musical instruction. The first instrument an infant responds to is the human voice. The simple, rhythmic tunes of *Mother Goose* have been introducing babies to music for centuries.

We sometimes label children as "musical" or "unmusical"; in fact, all children respond to music and can learn to participate actively in music if they are given the opportunity. Children gain musical skills, just as they gain language and motor skills, in a gradual process influenced by their family and community environment. If parents enjoy and value music, and   provide, from infancy, a variety of musical experiences for their child, the child will be "musical."

Often, it is only the musically precocious child, one who sings well at age two, who is earmarked for musical training. However, the child who is moving through the developmental sequence at a slower pace has equally as much musical potential.

The Parents' Role in Nurturing an Appreciation of Music
What can you do to nurture your child's instinctive love of music at every stage of development?

Infants can be provided with the sensations of a variety of musical sounds. It is important for babies to hear rattles, music boxes, songs, chants and rhymes.

Toddlers need opportunities to listen to recorded music that is not just being played in the background. Beginning at this early age, in a very informal way, parents can help children acquire a vocabulary about instruments and music. Simple comments such as, "That's a piano," "Hear the flute," "Now the music is very slow," or "That sounds like a march," are important ways children learn words to describe sound. Having a musical instrument (such as a piano or guitar) in the house is one of the best ways to promote curiosity and interest in music.

Three year olds love to listen to songs and frequently make up their own. Folk songs are particularly appropriate for this age, because of their rhythm and frequent repetition of text. Parents who encourage singing at home or in the car provide an important building block for a love of music.

Four to six year olds love to play with language and delight in creating rhymes and learning choruses with nonsense syllables. Children of this age enjoy having their own tape recorder and parents would do well to invest in a selection of the many excellent children's records and tapes that are available, or to borrow them from their local library. (See Resources, page 245, and the chart on pages 218-219.)

Attending children's concerts and summer outdoor musical programs as a family are wonderful ways to build positive musical experiences. When choosing a day care or preschool program, look for one that includes musical activities as part of its curriculum.

At every stage of your preschooler's growth, your goal should be to nurture your child's lifetime enjoyment of music.   ▨

Tips for Parents

Mitzie Collins

•Listening is the most valuable "musical" skill a child can acquire. Make a game of listening to and repeating words, rhythms or sounds.

•Play all kinds of music: classical, folk music, jazz, and pop tunes. Your child needs to have a variety of musical listening experiences. Sing the themes or tunes with your child.

•Show your child different musical instruments. Help her recognize the instruments and understand the sounds they make. When watching TV concerts, point out the various instruments when they are shown. If possible, have instruments available for your child to play and experiment with.

•Play music for dancing. Remember, young children always respond rhythmically, but not necessarily in exact time with the music they are listening to.

•Play music you enjoy as background for family activities, but also take time with your child to listen to specific pieces.

•Develop a repertory of "family" songs: they might range from pop tunes to favorite folk songs. Teach your child songs you remember from your own childhood.

• Help your child to recognize when his own voice is low or high or loud or soft. Never criticize a child who is not singing in tune.

• Use singing to ease difficult transitions through the day: For example, children will respond more readily to cleanup time when the activity is accompanied by a familiar tune such as, "It's time to put the toys away," sung to "Here we go 'round the mulberry bush." And bedtime is more welcome when accompanied by a lullaby.

SOME FORMAL APPROACHES
TO TEACHING MUSIC TO YOUNG CHILDREN

Suzuki Method
One approach to music for young children is found in the Suzuki method, founded on Japanese educator Shinichi Suzuki's conviction that children should learn music the same way they learn their own language, by hearing and repeating. Suzuki instruction is now available for children as young as three and four on piano, violin, and harp. Suzuki instruction demands a very high level of participation from the parents. While this method is ideal for some three and four-year-olds, for others the technical demands are too great.

Orff and Kodaly Methods
While the home is the center of non-structured musical experiences, music programs for young children based on the Orff-Schulwerk or Kodaly philosophies are especially valuable. Famous composers Carl Orff and Zoltan Kodaly also lent their time and talent to the teaching of music to young children. While there are some differences between their methods, both are based on an understanding of the developmental sequence of musical growth, and both focus on physical movement, speech rhythms, guided listening, singing and the playing of percussion instruments (for example: drums and xylophones). These programs provide additional instruction that readies a child for formal lessons, if desired, at the elementary school age.

Chart of Musical Development with Suggested Activities and Songs
Mitzie Collins

AGE	MUSICAL DEVELOPMENT
2-9 months	Begins to listen attentively to musical sounds; is calmed by human voices. Starts vocalizations, appearing to imitate what he hears.
9 months to 2 years	Begins to respond to music with clear repetitive movements. Interested in every kind of sound; begins to discriminate among sounds and may begin to approximate pitches. Most attracted to music that is strongly rhythmic.
2 to 3 years	Creates spontaneous songs; sings parts of familiar songs; recognizes instruments and responds more enthusiastically to certain songs. Strong physical response to music.
3 to 4 years	Continues to gain voice control; likes songs that play with language; and enjoys making music in groups as well as alone. Concepts such as high and low, loud and soft are beginning to be formed. Likes physical activity with music.
4 to 6 years	Sings complete songs from memory, is gaining pitch control and rhythmic accuracy. Loves language play and rhyming words. Attention span increases for listening to records.

ACTIVITIES	*SONGS*
•Rock and sing to your baby. •Introduce a variety of rhythmic sounds, such as rattles, music boxes and rhymes.	*By 'm Bye*, and *Hush Little Baby*, (pages 71 and 147, respectively, in the book American Folk Songs for Children, Seeger.)
•Dance your baby up and down on your knee or in your arms while singing rhythmic chants and songs. • Give your child simple percussion instruments, such as drums, rattles, and jingle bells, for sound exploration. •Sing and chant nursery rhymes and repetitive folk songs during various daily activities.	*Loop De Loo*, Shake it to the One, Mattox. *Sally Go 'Round the Sun*, Sounds Like Fun, Collins.
•Let your child hear different musical instruments. •Lead your youngster in simple imitative musical games such as *Old MacDonald Had a Farm.* •Teach some simple fingerplays, for example, "The Eensie Weensie Spider." (See page 75 in this book.)	*Skip-to-my-Lou*, (page 166 American Folk Songs for Children, Seeger.) *Drop My Thumb*, Sounds Like Fun, Collins. *Jim-Along Josie*, Reach to the Sky, Ribaudo.
•Help your child hear and sing lots of songs. •Attend some informal musical programs with your preschooler. •Integrate music and songs with the day's activities.	*Bluebird, Bluebird*, Shake it to the One, Mattox. *Old John Braddledum*, Reach to the Sky, Ribaudo.
•Consider a developmentally based music program for your child. (See page 217 in this chapter, **Some formal approaches to teaching music to young children.**) •Provide a variety of taped music, as well as exposure to different instruments. •Teach songs that use word play, repetition, and nonsense syllables.	*The Opposite Song*, Sounds Like Fun, Collins. *Yo Te Amo*, Reach to the Sky, Ribaudo. *Bought me a Cat*, American Folk Songs for Children, Seeger.

Chapter 29
Music to Their Ears

Rae Pica

*Music is critical
to the development
of language
and listening skills.*

Plato wrote: *Music ... gives a soul to the universe, wings to the mind, flight to the imagination, a charm to sadness, gaiety and life to everything.*

The baby in her crib bounces up and down to the accompaniment of the radio. The toddler happily demonstrates how he can dance and clap to his favorite tune. The preschooler creates a rhythmic chant while pounding on clay, or suddenly sings an original verse about peanut butter while spreading it on a slice of bread.

Music is quite naturally a part of children's lives. Anyone who lives and works with preschoolers will tell you how much the children enjoy music. In addition to the pleasure that music gives, it offers many other benefits.

What music means to children's lives

• *Music exposes children to different cultures.* Music provides children with their first exposure to the existence and richness of their own culture, as well as the heritage and cultures of other people and regions. Perhaps it's because music is a nonverbal form of communication and so can bridge the gaps among people of differing backgrounds.

• *Music is critical to the development of language and listening skills.* Music and the language arts (listening, speaking, reading, and writing) consist of symbols — which are representations of actual things. For example, the word "cat" — whether spoken or written — immediately brings to mind a furry thing that purrs. When you *sing* or *act out* the words to a song, abstract concepts are made more real.

Music activities can also help expand vocabulary and improve attention span, concentration, and memory. For instance, *B-I-N-G-O* is a musical spelling activity that also follows a pattern and requires memory and concentration as hand claps replace the letters in each verse. The *Hokey Pokey* helps children differentiate between right and left while it also enhances their understanding of concepts such as *in, out,* and *around.*

• *Music is also mood-altering.* If parents are looking to make routine activities more enjoyable, bring peace to overstimulated children, or conversely, provide a little extra energy to a low point in the day, music can help! More and more research is being conducted on the power of music to alter moods and even restore and maintain health.

• *Music helps develop children's appreciation of beauty.* Music educators believe that the most important role of music in a child's life may well be what it offers aesthetically. By helping to develop their appreciation of beauty, parents can significantly enrich their children's lives.

The enjoyment of music is for every child

A child's musical experience should not be limited by an ability to sing, or play an instrument. Even if children possess such talent, their musical experience should not be limited to these two avenues. And what of the child who shows no interest in, or aptitude for, singing or playing an instrument? If all children are to fully experience music, they should explore it as a whole, being given opportunities to listen, sing, play, create, and move.

Though many will never become professional — or even amateur — musicians, if they've had many and varied musical experiences, they will know they can rely on music to offer peace, enjoyment, or a little extra energy. They can also turn to music when they wish to learn more about a region or a culture. If children receive a rich variety of musical experiences, music will continue to serve them into adulthood.

Suggestions for Parents

Rae Pica

Your preschoolers are exposed primarily to the music they hear on radio and television. To broaden your child's music education, choose from a wide variety of styles. Possibilities include jazz, folk, country, bluegrass, blues, rhythm and blues, rock and roll, disco, gospel, New Age, opera, swing, and Dixieland. Classical music alone offers an almost unlimited number of possibilities for use with children.

How do you go about offering your preschoolers worthwhile musical experiences? Your first objective is to make the music a natural part of the home environment. Realize, too, that you need not be an expert in the field of music— or sing or play an instrument —to help your child enjoy music.

Five types of musical encounters every child should have:
• *Listening* Children will sit and listen to music if it's fun. Because learning to listen is so important, you can make a game of listening for something specific in the music. For example in Prokofiev's *Peter and the Wolf,* each character is represented by a different instrument: Peter, the little boy, is depicted by a violin, while other characters are identified by the sounds of other instruments. Your child will enjoy identifying each character by the instrument being played. On a simpler level, you could ask your preschooler to tell you if the music is soft or loud, slow or fast.

"Statues" is an excellent activity that emphasizes both movement and listening. Suggest that the children move in any way they like while the music is playing. They have to listen carefully because when the music stops the children must freeze into statues and stay that way until the music begins again. (You, the parent, control the pause button on the tape player or the needle on the record player.) Each time you play *Statues*, use a song with a different "feel" (a march, a waltz, rock and roll) to expose your preschoolers to a variety of musical styles.

• *Singing* Most children love to sing and often break into spontaneous song. When that happens, encourage them by joining in. Adding hand motions and other actions also make a contribution, by enhancing listening and adding greater meaning to lyrics. *Where Is Thumbkin?* and *I'm a Little Teapot* are excellent examples. The car is a great place for singing activities. Whether it be songs that your child learned in preschool, or songs you remember from your own childhood, sing-alongs are a fun way to experience music and ensure a pleasant ride!

• *Playing* This category involves exploring all the different sounds that your child is exposed to daily: in the home, on the street, at a shopping mall, in the park. It also involves the playing of instruments: bells, toy drums and xylophones, even pots and pans. All contribute to the child's overall music education and provide an awareness of sound that can enrich daily living. So, if your child has the inclination to test the sounds made by pots and pans, or to pound the piano keys, try to wait it out. Or, better yet, join in the fun!

• *Creating*   Whether your children are inventing songs, experimenting with sounds, or making up dances, they are creating on a musical level. And, any time you offer your encouragement, you're promoting creativity. Ask your preschooler to contribute new actions feelings to the song *If You're Happy and You Know It.* Challenge her to respond musically by asking questions in a singsong voice. For example, you could sing "Would you like a snack now?" Occasionally when there's music playing in the house and there are no distractions, ask your child if the music reminds her of anything. Does it make her feel happy or sad? Does it remind her of a certain animal or character? If so, ask her to show you what that emotion, animal or character looks like — using her facing, hands or whole body.

• *Moving*   It is practically impossible to think of music and movement separately. Young children respond to music with their whole bodies. When children tiptoe to soft ballet music, stamp their feet to loud marching music, move in slow motion to Bach's *Air on the G String* or rapidly to Rimsky-Korsakov's *Flight of the Bumblebee,* they are experiencing the music on a variety of levels. Not only are they listening, but they are using their bodies, minds, and spirits to express and create. And, because they are using more than one sense, what they learn will make a lasting impression.⬛

MUSICAL VARIETIES

Ethnic/Cultural Music
Polish and Mexican polkas, German and Austrian waltzes, Irish jigs, Italian tarantellas, Scottish Highland flings, English folk songs, African chant and drum music, Caribbean calypso and reggae, South American Indian music, Latin rhythms, Greek and Middle Eastern dances, Native American songs, Spanish flamencos.

Musical Textures
Full orchestra, marching band, solo instruments: piano, drums, violin, trumpet, clarinet, small groups of instruments, voice alone (a capella), electronic instruments, acoustic guitar, to name a few.

Musical Styles
Jazz, folk, country, bluegrass, blues, rhythm and blues, rock and roll, disco, gospel, New Age, opera, swing, classical, and Dixieland.

Chapter 30
Creative Movement

Elizabeth Bernard Pettit

*Music and rhythm
are natural
to a
child's development.*

Music and rhythm are natural to a child's development.   Children love moving to music, stretching, jumping, rolling and sliding. Here are some ways you and your preschooler can enjoy these activities. By using some of these suggestions, you and your child will deepen and strengthen the creative bond at this special time in both your lives.

How to Begin

In bare feet and stretchy clothes, you both can roll and stretch on a thick carpet, an exercise mat, or a mattress placed on the floor. Music can be classical (Bach, Vivaldi, Mozart) jazz (Joplin, Ellington, Basie) or any music that makes you want to move. Use CDs, cassettes, (check them out of your local library, if available) or your favorite radio station.

You both stand tall while you jump and turn to each of the four corners of the room. You can hold hands and slide together with your feet. You can lift your child high and then low. (If your preschooler is too heavy, have her stretch up high; then bend down low.) You can run together fast, and then softly and slowly tiptoe around the room.

Using Props

You can use a prop, such as brightly colored yarn. Primary colors, red, yellow and blue, are best. With the yarn, you both can make the three most important shapes that are made by a dancer, artist and even a composer. *The first shape* is a circle or round shape. You and your child find round shapes on your own bodies (head, eyes, belly button) and round shapes in the room. Then you can make a round dance together. *The second shape* is a straight line with the yarn. You can find straight lines in the room and make straight lines with your arms and legs as well as stretching the whole body. *The third shape* with the yarn is called a curve.

The best way to make a curve is to pick the yarn up high in the air ("stretch to the sky") and let it drop as it will to the ground level ("the earth"). You can make curves with your arms, your legs, and your whole body as though you were a tree in the wind. Find curves in the room and see if you can copy them with your arms and legs and the whole body. You can expand upon these activities by adding other props such as scarfs, feathers, or rhythm instruments (see making musical instruments on the following page).

Listen

Then listen to the music, and hear how the sounds are either long and straight, very round, or curved and wiggly. Listen to some jazz by Joplin or others. This music is very clear about rhythm. We all have rhythm in our bodies, but many of us do not use it very well. Everything living has rhythm, and by listening to the strong rhythm beats in the music, you can transfer them to your own bodies. Start with clapping, first with your hands together and then on different parts of the body (knees, hips, shoulders). You can clap both on the "earth" and "sky" levels (stretching up high or low to the ground). You can jump, hop, run, fly and use many other movements in time to the beat of the music. You and your child can end with a rhythm dance together.

Goals

The goal of this kind of creative movement is not to perform in front of an audience, but to enjoy the process of moving your body to the music, and the fun of the interaction between you and your child. If you look for a creative movement program for your preschooler, search for one that places the emphasis on the *process* rather than on *performance*.

Making Your Own Musical Instruments

Lois Ross

Making musical instruments with your child is not only fun, but is also educational, creative and emotionally satisfying. Making something of his own gives your preschooler a feeling of pride. After you and your child have constructed the musical instruments, you can take the experience a step further and use what you have created to make music together.

You can teach your child to use her skills to complete an instrument by herself with just a little help. For example, a shaker could be made from an empty frozen orange juice container. (For safety be sure that the can's edges are smooth.) Add beans or rice to the can and close the cover with tape. With a round-edged scissor, your child can cut out a piece of paper to cover the can, decorate the paper with bright colors, and paste the paper on the container. You now have a lovely shaker.

Other materials around the house can be used for different kinds of instruments. To make a drum, use empty plastic food containers or oatmeal boxes (again, your preschooler may cut out a piece of paper to decorate the container and paste it on). Attach ribbon with brass paper fasteners to each side (see illustration on page 227). To make a tambourine, two aluminum pie tins can be used. Fill with bottle caps or large beans, attach colorful ribbon to wave as it is shaken, and tape the tins together. For a guitar, use a shoe box with a hole cut out of the cover and stretch some rubber bands across the top. Wooden spoons can be used as rhythm sticks by beating one against the other.

After these homemade instruments are completed, you can demonstrate to your child how the instruments are played: the drum is hit, the shakers and tambourine are hit or shaken, the strings of the guitar are plucked (pulling each string with nail or finger) or strummed (brushing all fingers back and forth across the strings). In this way your child is getting an education in the methods of playing instruments, and also learning how sound is produced.

Now the instruments can be used as an accompaniment to a song or recorded tune by keeping a steady beat or playing a rhythmic pattern. Or you and your child can use them in a marching band, parading through the house!

The next time your preschooler says, "there is nothing to do," try sharing a musical project like this with him. It may turn out to be a very special creative experience.

Chapter 31
Benefits of Movement
for Young Children

Rae Pica

Creative movement
offers children
frequent opportunities
to experience success.

Show me you can touch your toes
Then bring your hand up to your nose
Put a smile upon your face
Do it all in your own space!

Creative movement is important to preschoolers in great number of ways. But parents planning to enroll their children in programs offering creative movement — whether it be at a dance studio, gymnastics center, preschool, or child care center — should make sure that *creative* movement is what's actually being offered.

True creative movement is based on the fact that young children learn best by doing. So it uses a problem-solving approach to instruction that allows for exploration and discovery. With problem solving, there are usually *many* ways for the children to respond to the teacher's challenges (often presented with statements like "Show me you can..." or "How many ways can you find to...?"). And because there are no incorrect responses, children experience success again and again, and their confidence in their abilities soars.

**Following are just some of the benefits
— in addition to self-confidence —
derived from creative movement.**

Physical Fitness. Though we tend to think of preschoolers as being active all the time, the sad truth is that children today are not nearly active enough. Creative movement offers children frequent opportunities to experience success. And if a child's early encounters with movement are successful, confidence-building, and fun, that child is much more likely to want to keep active throughout his or her life. So the parents' most vital role in creating physically fit human beings may simply be ensuring that their children's natural love of movement does not fade.

Social Development. When children learn to adjust their movements to be part of the group's pattern, they learn about consideration and cooperation. These traits are further promoted when children move in pairs and can achieve success only by working together. An added bonus is that when children work together to meet a goal, they come to accept the ideas — as well as the similarities and differences — of others.

Creativity and Self-Expression. Can you imagine a world without creativity and self-expression—not just in the arts, but in science, business and industry, education, and life itself?

The ages between 3 and 5 are thought to be the best for developing the creativity that exists in every child. So movement activities emphasizing creativity and individuality are especially valuable. A child is required to use her or his creativity and to respond in her or his own way when asked:
• to demonstrate how slowly a turtle moves.
• to place weight on three body parts only (for example, having only two feet and a hand or two hands and a foot in contact with the floor).
• to discover the number of ways it's possible to balance at a low level in space (for instance, balancing on the knees only, or squatting low and balancing on the balls of the feet).
With each success, children grow more confident with their creativity, and discover that it's okay to be an individual.

Development of Thinking and Reasoning. Because the child's earliest learning is based on motor development (movement of all kinds), subsequent knowledge is, too. In order to fully grasp their meaning, young children need to physically experience concepts like *up and down, forward and backward,* and *big and small.* By moving in *straight, curving,* or *zigzag* pathways, or by creating *round, flat, wide,* and *narrow* shapes with their bodies, they explore the concepts of *space* and *shape.* These experiences help them to learn how to classify and categorize: balls and tires are *round,* elephants are *big,* squirrels are *small,* etc. This exploration of basic concepts through movement can become the foundation for later academic achievement.

But there's more: Creative movement activities that use a problem-solving approach enhance children's problem-solving abilities. They discover that there is always more than one way to solve any problem or meet any challenge.

And statistics show that the majority of us (not *just* young children) learn by doing. Or, as the well-known saying goes, "What I hear. I forget. What I see, I remember. What I do, I know." What your children do, as they explore movement possibilities, they will most likely know for the rest of their lives.

Another benefit for young children is the development of self-awareness. Self-awareness activities are explored on the following pages.

Creative
Movement Activities

Rae Pica

Self-awareness is a wonderful benefit derived from creative movement. These four activities that you can easily explore with your preschoolers at home place special emphasis on self-awareness.

My Face Can Say...

Background Information. Talk to the children about body language and how sometimes we can express what we're feeling or what we want to say with no words at all. And the face, being the most expressive body part we have, is very capable of doing just that!

Activity. Ask children to show you, with their faces only, how they would express the following:

"I'm tired."   "That smells awful."
"I'm sad."   "That tastes yummy."
"I'm mad."   "What a surprise!"
"That smells good."   "That tastes yucky."
"I'm afraid."   "I'm happy!"

My Hands Can Say...
Background Information. Explain that, like our faces, our hands can also "say" many things for us.

Activity. Using only their hands, ask them how they would express the following:

"Hello."	"I'm cold."
"Stop!"	"Naughty, naughty."
"Come here."	"Good-bye!"
"I'm mad."	"I'm scared."
"Go away."	"Yea!"

Feeling Sad
Background Information. Discuss sadness with the children, asking for examples of times they've felt sad. How did their faces and bodies look when they were feeling sad? How did they move? Did they move quickly or slowly? "Bouncy" or "dragging?" Assure the children that it's okay to feel sad sometimes — everybody does.

Activity. Put on a soft, slow (and, if possible, sad) piece of music for this activity. (Samuel Barber's *Adagio for Strings* is a perfect example, but there are many instrumental numbers—often found on recordings used for quiet times — that would also be appropriate.) As the music is playing, ask the children to show you how their faces look when they're sad. Continue with the following questions:
• How do you walk when you're sad?
• How could you show me with your hands and arms that you're sad?
• Can you make up a "sad dance" to this music?
• Can you show me you're sad in a sitting position? Lying down?
(Note: Parents can use a similar procedure to explore happy feelings, or any other emotion.)

The Body Poem
Background Information. Read the following poem to the children without any activity at first, so they know what to expect. Besides the parts mentioned in the poem, what other body parts do they have more than one of? How many of each? How many teeth and hairs do they think they have?

Activity. Explain to the children that you're going to read *The Body Poem* again, and this time they should touch or display the appropriate body parts as they're mentioned in the poem. For the last segment, they should shrug on "So why, do you suppose" and move their hands, from top to bottom, the length of their bodies on the next two lines. The poem is as follows:

I have two feet,
Two ears, two legs,
Ten fingers and ten toes;

I have two knees,
Two lips, two hands,
And even two elbows;

I have two eyes
And four eyelids.
So why, do you suppose,

With all these parts
On my body
I only have one nose?!

Note.: This activity should be performed slowly at first. But as the children become familiar with the poem (and are even reciting it themselves), they'll have lots of fun if you do it faster each time. Once they're thoroughly familiar with it, you might want to introduce them to the concept of *accelerando,* beginning the poem very slowly and gradually speaking faster and faster as you recite the lines — so it actually ends in a rush! (From *Special Themes for Moving & Learning* by Rae Pica. Human Kinetics, 1991, reprinted with permission.)

Creative movement activities can also help children become aware of the world around them. Pretending to be animals can promote empathy.

How They Move

Background Information. Discuss the animals and methods of locomotion mentioned in the following song lyrics before asking the children to portray these creatures.

Activity. After your discussion, have the children realistically act out the lines of the song.

> Animals move in different ways
> Depending on how they're made
> Birds were made so they could fly
> And a duck can swim and wade.
>
> An elephant walks with heavy tread
> And swings his trunk to and fro
> Dogs will run and wag their tails
> As they happ'ly come and go.
>
> A cat will stalk on silent paws
> To catch unsuspecting prey
> Like mice hiding in the grass
> Who quickly scurry away.
>
> A penguin waddles; an eagle soars
> Rabbits and kangaroos hop
> Snakes slither and turtles crawl
> Frogs leap and horses clip-clop!
>
> Gallop, hop, swim, or walk
> Slither, crawl, or stalk
> Run, fly, leap, soar
> Are there any more?

(From *Let's Move & Learn* by Rae Pica and Richard Gardzina. Human Kinetics, 1990, reprinted with permission.)

Chapter 32
Creative Art

Lila Lasky

...children frequently express their unique ideas and feelings through art.

Three-year-old Benjamin grabs a large lump of blue clay dough from the mixture his daddy had just prepared. Opening and closing his fist, he watches in fascination as the cool, damp substance oozes out between his fingers.

Fun and Learning

Young children are enticed by paint, markers, crayons, clay and shiny papers. The bright colors and interesting textures of these and other art materials invite children to explore and manipulate them.

Your preschooler can have many enjoyable experiences experimenting with art processes. While having fun, Benjamin or Kara will also be acquiring skills and knowledge necessary for later academic work. They may be learning **math** concepts as they count the number of crayons in the box, or match the number of brushes to the containers of paint. They may become aware of **science** concepts, as they observe that colors change when they are mixed together, that wet paint dries, or that the moist clay dries and hardens (evaporation). They will be practicing **language** while describing to you the symbols in their art work. In addition art experiences can improve your child's eye/hand coordination, and heighten his aesthetic awareness (sense of beauty and wonder).

Working Along with Your Child

You may enjoy working along with your child. The quality of your time together will be enriched if, while you are doing "your thing" your child feels free to create her own work. Your thoughtful comments about your child's creations during and after art time can further enhance the experience. Rather than saying, "I love it," you can qualify your statement by saying why: "You used some pretty colors," "Those lines are long and wiggly," or "You filled the page with all kinds of shapes."

With support and guidance, young scribblers begin to create delightful lines, colorful forms, and symbols that are their very own. In fact, given space to work, appropriate materials, plenty of time, and lots of encouragement, children frequently express their unique ideas and feelings through art.

Finding Spaces and Places

At home, the space you provide might be the kitchen table, a corner on the floor, or another well-lit area which is near a water source and free of too much traffic. Consider using a wall on which you tape a large sheet of paper for the art work. You can protect other surfaces with newspapers, a plastic tablecloth or drop cloth. Some parents place the drawing/painting paper inside the lid of a large, flat box. Others allow their youngsters to sprawl comfortably on the floor for art time. Try to arrange materials for art in a place your preschooler can reach. This will foster independence in choosing and cleaning up.

Out-of-doors, you can offer your child art experiences at the park, beach, yard and even the sidewalk when the weather is warm. These places are convenient for explorations with water, sand and chalk. If the outdoor space offers tables and benches, many of the same activities which you provide at home can be brought out-of-doors.

Attending Museums and Art Classes

Young children need a great deal of preparation before a museum visit. The visit should be brief and the museum chosen with care. The best kinds of museums are those which offer hands-on participation for children. Check newspapers and libraries for announcements of such opportunities.

You may want your preschooler to attend an art class. Having your child attend an art class can be an fine introduction to group experience and is an excellent bridge to full-time school attendance. However, art classes for children under three serve mainly to provide opportunities to socialize with others. Bear in mind that if this is to be a first experience away from home, having a parent along can be very supportive. Some classes offer such dual participation. It is a good idea to ask to observe before enrolling in a class. Be sure that participants are free to explore materials in their own ways — since formal instruction in drawing can inhibit creativity. 　　▓

Providing Appropriate
Art Materials

Lila Lasky

• Your child can make designs with moist sand at the beach and in the park or backyard sand box.
• Your child can "paint" with water on fences, building walls, and side-walks. (A wide house painter's brush and a bucket of water are all you need.)

If you plan to purchase art materials, bear in mind that preschoolers frequently place things in their mouths. Therefore, read labels to be sure that the contents are not toxic. Avoid containers with sharp edges and tools with pointed ends.

Select art materials that can be used in several ways and will encourage your child's inventiveness in using them. Choose large sheets of paper (at least 12" x 18 ") and tools that are easy to grasp.

The materials on the following list are basic for preschool art. They can be purchased at most art supply stores and some toy stores. Items with an asterisk* can also be made at home. (See Recipes for Homemade Materials, page 240.)
• crayons and markers (thick)
• tempera paint
• potters clay or dough clay*
• fingerpaint*
• school paste or glue
• blunt-end scissors
• colored chalk
• paint brushes (1/2" - 2" wide)
• assorted scraps of paper, fabric, yarn for collage
• shelving paper, newspaper, wallpaper, gift wrap and paper bags to use as work surfaces.

Allowing Time

If you introduce one type of material at a time, your preschooler will not be overwhelmed. When, after repeated explorations with the same material, she seems comfortable with the process of using it, you can show another material. Once two or three alternatives have been introduced, your child can begin to choose from among them, or combine them.

Offering Encouragement

Encourage all of your child's early artistic explorations. It is useful to remember that preschoolers cannot represent things. That is, their early drawings do not look like objects we can recognize. Nor do young children see things as adults do. To encourage your preschooler's art experiences, try to:

• accept your youngster's accomplishment, even if incomplete to your eyes
• provide blank paper, not coloring books for creative art
• avoid "showing how" or finishing your child's art
• explore an art process
• display your child's work proudly at home or at your workplace
• enjoy watching your child's development through art.

RECIPES FOR HOMEMADE
ART MATERIALS

Children will enjoy preparing these homemade clays, which can be colored or used in their natural state. Store them in the refrigerator to extend their life.

Self-hardening dough clay (baker's clay): 1 cup flour, 1/3 cup salt, 1/3 to 1/2 cup water.Mix the dry ingredients in a plastic bowl, then add the water gradually. When it forms a ball around the spoon, knead the dough well, adding water if too crumbly. **You may add a few drops of vegetable oil for soft dough clay.**

Adding Color: To add color to this recipe with the least mess, place the clay in a strong plastic bag. Drop in approximately three to four drops of food color or two teaspoons of tempera paint per cup of clay. Knead the color into the mixture by squeezing the bag until the color is evenly distributed.

Fingerpaint: A simple procedure for making finger paint is to mix two parts of liquid laundry starch with one part powdered tempera paint or a few drops of food color. Fingerpaint should be spread on a moist, slick surface (either paper or plastic). Add a little more liquid laundry starch to help it spread more easily.

Suggestions for Expanding Basic Art Processes

Lila Lasky

Once your preschooler has had opportunities to explore basic art materials, you may wish to enrich and extend the experiences by offering some of the following possibilities.

"Painting" and Color Mixing

Materials: Food colors, "Q tips," muffin tin or styrofoam egg carton, 10" paper plates, white paper napkins, plastic medicine dropper.

Provide a variety of colors of tinted water in the egg carton or muffin tin. Your child may wish to:
• use the colors to paint with the "Q tips" on the paper plates. While this can be done on flat paper, the plate's raised lip will contain any puddles that form.
• try mixing new colors by squeezing medicine droppers full of two or more colors into a new section of the divided container.
• dip folded corners of a paper napkin into different colors. When you open up the dried napkin and hang it on the window, it becomes a lovely translucent decoration.

Printmaking
Materials: fingerpaint, cut up sponges, wood scraps and spools, cardboard tubes, kitchen utensils, tongue depressors, and other found objects, paper, paper towels.

Your preschooler can make:
• a print from a fingerpainting. The painting should be done directly on a plastic or formica type surface. Place a clean sheet of paper on top of the wet finger painting. Help your youngster to press down carefully on the entire paper. Lift the paper, and admire the print.
• prints from a variety of objects, such as a potato masher or other household utensil. First place some fingerpaint on the surface or edge of the object. (Use a finger, brush, or sponge.) The child then presses the object onto a paper. This process is repeated many times, to create an allover design. You may find that prints from sponges are the easiest for your preschooler to handle. These printed papers make attractive gift wrapping.
• footprints, handprints and thumbprints, applying the paint as described above. Your older youngster may wish to add crayon lines to thumbprints to create fantastic creatures.

Assemblage and 3D Collage
Materials: found materials such as cardboard boxes, bottle caps, wood scraps, styrofoam bits used in packaging, small cardboard tubes, yarn, colored tape, pipe cleaners, colored markers, glue.

Does your child love to build things? This may be the perfect activity. By assembling some of the materials suggested above, a preschooler can create an attractive centerpiece, paperweight, or decoration for your mantel.

Your preschooler can:
• glue smaller things onto a larger wood or cardboard base.
• use markers to decorate the completed assemblage.
• make an assemblage that fits a theme, such as fall or spring things.
• decorate a carton or cartons with collage material. If you find a carton which fits over your child's head, cut out holes for eyes and nose and enjoy the masquerade.

Resources for Section Six: Music Movement Art

BOOKS FOR ADULTS

Music: A Way of Life for the Young Child, by Kathleen M. Bayless and Marjorie E. Ramsey. Merrill, 1991. In its fourth edition, this book includes songs, ideas, suggestions, and musical concepts tested and endorsed by parents, teachers, caregivers, and students. The text has three parts: Music in the Earliest Years, Music in the Preschool Years and Kindergarten, and Music for Every Child.

A Moving Experience: Dance for Lovers of Children and the Child Within, by Teresa Benzwie. Zephyr Press, 1988. This book stems from the author's belief that children "need to move, create, and value themselves..." The book is filled with ideas for activities that allow children to express themselves.

Learning Through Play: Music and Movement, by Ellen Booth Church. Scholastic, 1992. Written for early childhood professionals, this book offers numerous ideas for movement and music activities to use with infants and toddlers, young children, and special-needs children. Also included is a special message to families, which makes recommendations for nurturing creativity, self-expression, and self-esteem through music and movement.

Leading Young Children to Music, by B. Joan E. Haines and Linda L. Gerber. Merrill, 1992. The opening line of this book's preface states, "We believe that music is every child's birthright." In its fourth edition, the book is divided into two parts: The Rationale and Musical Experiences.

Movement Activities for Early Childhood, by Carol Totsky Hammett. Human Kinetics, 1992. This paperback includes a collection of classroom-tested activities for preschoolers that makes learning new skills fun. The author divides the book into four areas of movement, targeting a child's ability rather than age in the areas of 1) locomotor skills; 2) ball-handling skills; 3) gymnastic skills; and 4) rhythmic activities.

All Ears: How to Choose and Use Recorded Music for Children, by Jill Jarnow. Penguin Books, 1991. The title of this paperback, written by a parent, for parents, says it all. Chapters include: "Why Good Listening Makes Good Sense," "How to Develop the Great Family-Listening Habit," "Making Musical Selections," and "The *All Ears* Sampler of Music.

Art: Basic for Young Children, by Lila Lasky & Rose Mukerji. Order #106 NAEYC, 1980. This paperback is filled with colorful examples of how art benefits children, written by the author of a chapter in this book. Exciting project ideas for fostering creativity are helpful for teachers and parents.

Experiences in Movement, by Rae Pica. Delmar Publishers, 1995. This comprehensive text, by the author of two of the chapters in this book, explores the role of movement in the child's physical, social, emotional, and cognitive development — in both indoor and outdoor settings.

Special Themes for Moving & Learning, by Rae Pica. Human Kinetics, 1991. Appropriate for children ages 4 to 8, this book consists of 38 favorite themes, including occupations, holidays, animals, transportation, and seasons. Each theme has 5 movement-inspiring activities.

Growing Up With Music: A Guide to the Best Recorded Music for Children, by Laurie Sale. Avon Books, 1992. The author includes reviews for each recording and an index of song titles and performers. Music is listed by age group: (with separate chapters for ages 0 to 2, 2 1/2 to 4, and 4 to10). There are also chapters that focus on lullabies, holiday music, French and Spanish recordings, and classical music.

Where Is Thumbkin? by Pam Schiller and Thomas Moore. Gryphon House, 1993. This book offers 500 activities to use with songs you already know — like "Farmer in the Dell," "Hokey Pokey," and "If You're Happy and You Know It." Included under each song are Thematic Connections, Things to Talk About, Related Bibliography, and Related Records and Tapes, as well as activities.

Dance for Young Children: Finding the Magic in Movement, by Sue Stinson. American Alliance for Health, Physical Education, Recreation and Dance, 1988. Although aimed at the teachers of young children, this book has some wonderful information for parents about the importance of creative movement and dance. There are examples of activities and an appendix listing resource materials.

Encouraging the Artist in Your Child (*Even If You Can't Draw*), by Sally Warner. St. Martin's Press, 1989. This useful book is divided into two parts. The first half deals with ideas and projects for children aged 2 to 5 years; the second, for children aged 6 to 10 years. It promotes the author's relaxed and pressure-free approach, is enjoyable to read, and has clear, specific instructions. Sally Warner has also written, *Encouraging the Artist in Yourself* (*Even If It's Been A Long, Long Time*), St. Martin's Press, 1991.

AUDIO AND VIDEO TAPES FOR CHILDREN

Sounds Like Fun, by Mitzie Collins, #8204, available as a record (1982), a cassette (1983), and a song book (1994). Sampler Records Ltd., (PO Box 19270, Rochester NY 14619. 1-800-537-2755). A collection of traditional folk songs and singing games for preschoolers, written by the author of a chapter in this book.

Shake It to the One That You Love Best, by Cheryl Warren Mattox, available as a book and a cassette. Warren-Mattox Productions, 1989. (Distributed by JTG, 1024C 18th Ave. South, Nashville TN 37212, 1-615-329-3036.)

Let's Move & Learn, by Rae Pica and Richard Gardzina. Human Kinetics, 1990. Distributed by Moving & Learning, 346 N. Barnstead Rd., Center Barnstead, NH 03225, 1-603-776-7411. A 2-cassette set of 32 movement-motivating songs geared toward toddlers, preschoolers, as well as kinder-gartners through 3rd-graders, by the author of two of the chapters in this book. Parents may follow the easy movement suggestions in the accompa-nying booklet or let the song lyrics and music guide and inspire the chil-dren.

More Music for Moving & Learning, by Rae Pica and Richard Gardzina. Human Kinetics, 1990, 1-603-776-7411. This package comes with an instructional booklet and six cassettes featuring 62 songs and 5 favorite themes, including animals, holidays, relaxation (quiet times), exploring different cultures, and pretending. It's designed for preschoolers to children 8 years of age.

Reach to the Sky, by Sue Ribaudo, #8916: available as a cassette and a song book. Sampler Records Ltd., 1989 (PO Box 19270, Rochester NY 14619. 1-800-537-2755).

BOOKS FOR CHILDREN

Slither, Swoop, Swing, by Alex Ayliffe. Picture Puffins edition, 1996. Snakes slither, cats pounce, and frogs hop in this lively book, as a variety of energetic animals move in their own ways. Young children will probably join right in, imitating their movements.

Dancing Class, by Lucy Dickens. Viking, 1992. In Laura's dancing class, she joins the other toddlers in the fun — marching, stretching, sliding, and flying, ending with ring-around-the-rosy. The bouncy, colorful illustrations capture the humor and excitement of the activity.

Ding Dong! And Other Sounds, by Christine Salac Dubov.Tambourine Books, 1991. In this book with cardboard pages for the youngest preschoolers, toddlers will see photographs of children playing a variety of different instruments, along with a one-word description of the sound each makes. On the last double-page spread, all the children come together with their instruments for a final *ta-ra-ra-boom-dee-ay!*

A Baker's Portrait, by Michelle Edwards. Lothrop, Lee & Shepard, 1991. Michelin is a portrait painter who paints her subjects "warts and all," and therefore has very little business. When she is hired to paint her aunt and uncle, who are excellent bakers, but quite ugly, she is in a dilemma. She resolves it in a funny and touching portrait, finding a way to make a picture that goes beyond the way people look, to show instead the way they really are.

One Ballerina Two, by Vivian French. Lothrop, Lee & Shepard, 1991. An energetic little girl and a graceful older girl perform a variety of ballet steps, counting down from ten pliés to two final curtsies and one happy hug. The appealing illustrations are by Jan Ormerod.

The Nutcracker: A Pop-Up Book, illustrated by Phillida Gili. HarperCollins, 1992. In this magical book, the reader can open all the children's gifts, look behind every shuttered window in the doll house, pull a tab to allow the mice to emerge through the floor panels, and open a door for the sugar plum fairy to pirouette into the ballroom. This version of the story — famous as a ballet danced often in the Christmas season — is written by Jenni Fleetwood.

Georgia Music, by Helen V. Griffith. Mulberry Books edition, 1990. A little girl and her grandfather enjoy two different kinds of music together: the music of his mouth organ, and the music of the birds and insects near his cabin in Georgia.

Rosie's Ballet Slippers, by Susan Hampshire. HarperCollins, 1996. Join Rosie in her first ballet class and enjoy the excitement. The illustrations by Maria Teresa Meloni catch the joyous enthusiasm of the young dancers.

Angelina Ballerina, by Katharine Holabird. Clarkson N. Potter/Random House, 1983. Angelina is a mouse who wants to be a ballerina more than anything else in the world. She dances at suppertime, bedtime, and on the way to school. This has its difficulties, but a pleasing solution is found.

Rabbit Mooncakes, by Hoong Yee Lee Krakauer. Little, Brown, 1994. Hoong Wei is nervous about playing the piano for her aunties, uncles, and cousins at the Harvest Moon Festival. But a loving, supportive family makes the recital turn out just fine, with a treat of beautiful rabbit mooncakes at the end.

Going to My Ballet Class, by Susan Kuklin. Bradbury Press, 1989. What happens in a real-life ballet class? This book follows Jami and her first-year ballet class from their warm-ups through their floor work, to their final bow. The story is illustrated with color photographs and includes notes for parents on how to choose a ballet class for young children.

Can't Sit Still, by Karen E. Lotz. Dutton, 1993. Through every season of the year, a young girl skips, hops, bikes, and dances her way through her city neighborhood.

I Spy — An Alphabet in Art, devised & selected by Lucy Micklethwait. Greenwillow, 1992. In 26 beautiful paintings by such artists as Magritte, Renoir, and Chagall, children are challenged to find an object from A to Z.

Regina's Big Mistake, by Marissa Moss. Houghton Mifflin, 1990. The teacher asks the children in Regina's class to draw a jungle or a rain forest, but Regina is worried that she will make a mistake. Finally, she lets her creativity take over, and when her picture is hung with the others, each different, Regina thinks hers is perfect.

Making Music: 6 Instruments You Can Create, by Eddie Herschel Oates. HarperCollins, 1995. After introducing a variety of musical instruments, this book shows you how you can make your own instruments from items found around the house.

How Music Came to the World, retold by Hal Ober. Houghton Mifflin, 1994. In this centuries-old Mexican legend, the gods of wind and sky put aside their traditional rivalry to bring music to the world. Carol Ober's exciting illustrations reflect the motifs of many Mexican cultures.

My Mama Sings, by Jeanne Whitehouse Peterson. HarperCollins, 1994. Mama knows a song for every season and occasion. Her little boy loves to hear her sing on hot summer nights, or walking through piles of dry leaves, or when the slow rain drips from the windows. But one day everything goes wrong and Mama has no songs to sing. So her son makes up a special song for her in this warm and touching story.

Alvin Ailey, by Andrea Davis Pinkney. Hyperion, 1993. This inspiring biographical narrative history is based on actual events that occurred during the African-American dancer's lifetime.

I Have Another Language: The Language Is Dance, by Eleanor Schick. Macmillan, 1992. With poetic words a young girl expresses the excitement of anticipation as she prepares for dancing for the first time on a stage in front of an audience. During the performance, while she cannot say in words the things she is experiencing, she feels "the power of speaking another language: the language of dance."

It Looked Like Spilt Milk, by Charles G. Shaw. Harper & Row, 1988. This classic book presents an array of torn paper shapes which children can identify.

Boy, Can He Dance! by Eileen Spinelli. Four Winds Press, 1993. Tony's father wants his son to follow in his footsteps as a chef. But Tony only cares about dancing. Tony doesn't want to disappoint his father, so he tries to cook. However, squeezing lemons, chopping carrots, even peeling a mountain of potatoes all start him tapping — with disastrous consequences. But fate takes a hand in this lively, funny story, with happy results.

Sophie's Dance Class, by Ruth Tilden. Hyperion, 1996. "Sophie goes to dance class every week." And, by pulling a tab on each page, the reader will be able to help her perform pliés, arabesques, and pirouettes. Great fun for aspiring ballerinas.

Cherries and Cherry Pits, by Vera B. Williams. Greenwillow, 1986. In this beautiful book, Bidemmi is a little girl who draws pictures and tells stories about them. As she visits with her neighbor, we see the child as drawn by the book's author/illustrator in water color paintings, as well as Bidemmi's own magic marker drawings.

Section Seven
Science
Nature

Section Seven
Science - Nature

Introduction

As a child growing up in a city environment, I never knew the names of trees (maybe just a maple tree) or birds (except a robin) so it was a comfort to me to read the words of one of the authors of this section. She states that it isn't so important to be able to identify each tree, flower, or bird. "Many naturalists consider it more important to encourage the *questioning,* rather than just naming something and not learning any more about it."

Children are always questioning. That is one reason that another author in this section declares, "Your child is a natural scientist.... He is discovering. He is observing. He is questioning." And what should adults do about this powerful curiosity? *Help it and encourage it.*

Look over the gardening projects in this section, as well as the nature and environmental activities. Read your child the story about *Enjoying Birds.* Observe with your youngster! Experiment! Use the resources available to you both. *Learn about the world together.*

Chapter 33
Your Child is a
Natural Scientist

Michael Glaser

Your preschooler
is a curious child.
...He is discovering.
He is observing.
He is questioning.

Your preschooler is a curious child. He is a natural scientist. Long before he learns to talk, long before he learns to walk, he is thinking like a scientist. He is discovering. He is observing. He is questioning. From the moment your child is born, he is desperately trying to make some sense out of the bewildering world around him.

Encouraging Your Child's Curiosity
You, as a parent, have the good fortune to assist in this scientific discovery. It's up to you to provide a laboratory. Let her experiment with things that roll, things that bounce, things that bend. (Like it or not, she will also experiment with things that tear and things that break!) Help her to understand the things she sees. Encourage her curiosity.

Sometimes, it isn't easy. Your preschooler will rejoice in the discovery that a coffee can makes a wonderfully loud sound. She may deduce that a cookie tin will too. As a scientist, she has to test her deduction. Over and over again. The louder the better. Science sure is fun.

While you may need to control your youngster's curiosity a little, it is important that you don't discourage it entirely. Curiosity, and science, will take your child a long way toward learning about the world.

Observing, Organizing, and Comparing
Science is a way of looking at things. It is a way of organizing knowledge and reorganizing it again when the evidence demands it. Science requires careful observation and critical thinking. It demands, and encourages, an open mind.

Help your child to look closely at things. Help him to compare things. Look at plants. Look at animals. How are they the same? How are they different? Help him to sort things into groups. Give him the chance to sort things (like shells or leaves or blocks) his own way and to explain his criteria. Did he sort them by size, by shape, by color, or some other special way? Encourage him to try a different criteria. Help him to see that there is more than one "right" answer. Science encourages creativity.

Let your young child experiment with all sorts of things. Magnets are exciting. Water is fascinating. Flashlights and balloons, magnifiers and straws all invite inquiry.

Using Resources

Use the resources available in your town or city. A nearby nature center or science museum will surely be an enriching experience for your child. A park or a beach or a backyard should offer enough riddles to last a lifetime. Your local library, of course, is an invaluable resource. Many fine children's books will motivate your youngster to find out more about nature and science. (See Resources on page 291.) Many more books are available to help answer questions.

Don't be afraid of science. Don't be afraid to say, "I don't know." Say it, though, in a way that encourages further inquiry. Encourage your child to keep wondering. Your child was born with that sense of wonder. It is up to you to nurture it, to enjoy it, and to treasure it.   ▩

Science Toys

While some materials for science activities may be found around the house or outdoors, others may be purchased in a science or toy store. Also, toy catalogs can be a good resource when you want to buy science toys. Here is a sampling of science toys from recent catalogs:

• adventure kit for exploring: (adjustable belt includes compass, whistle, canteen, telescope and flashlight).
• ant farm
• baby's first mirror
• big binoculars
• bug study kit (with 2-way magnifier, screened-in bug house, and bug book)
• dinosaurs: authentically detailed vinyl dinosaurs, dinosaur puzzles, dinosaur kites
• flashlight that works without batteries
• luminous universe stickers to stick on your child's ceiling
• magnets: magnetic block set, magnetic marbles
• measuring tape with big numbers
• musical instruments
• redwood seedlings to plant indoors or out
• super ears to hear distant sounds
• wrist walkie-talkie
• young explorer backpack
• young naturalist guide to nature
• zoo animals, realistically colored vinyl figures

Chapter 34
Geography
&
Outer Space

Michael K. Meyerhoff

Over the river and through
the woods to grandmother's
house we go...
But how do we get there?

According to a recent survey, more than a third of United States citizens cannot locate Canada on a map. An Atlanta newspaper reported that a ticket agent at Olympic headquarters [for the 1996 Summer Olympics] refused a telephone order from someone in New Mexico because her office "does not handle requests from foreign countries." And when a prominent professional athlete who was traded to a Boston team was asked by a television interviewer how he felt about moving to New England, he replied, "I thought Boston was in Massachusetts."

The average person's lack of knowledge in the area of geography is appalling — but it is not surprising. After all, for most people, learning geography was strictly a matter of formal instruction involving nothing more than rote memorization. No wonder they failed to understand, much less appreciate, the subject fully.

It doesn't have to be that way. In fact, learning geography can be a lot of fun. As long as parents recognize and respect their child's developmental limitations and inclinations, they can easily put together a variety of play activities that make introducing this subject an enjoyable as well as enriching experience.

Furthermore, these activities can be initiated long before the subject of geography is introduced in school. Throughout the early years, there are plenty of opportunities to help children become familiar with general principles and even absorb some specific material.

What does an understanding and appreciation of geography entail?
Spatial relations, physical characteristics, landmarks, and labels are a few of the essential elements. How can these be transformed into meaningful and pleasurable experiences for a young child? As always, it is smart to start with something simple and familiar and then gradually move on to increasingly complex and far-reaching challenges.

For instance, by late infancy (18 months to 2 years) a child ordinarily is well-acquainted with her own home. Using cardboard and crayons, her parents can make little replicas of the major pieces of furniture found in each room; and then place the pieces appropriately on a large sheet of paper depicting the overall layout of the house. Depending on the size of your house, you can start with one section at a time, then gradually expand the activity to include the entire structure.

Of course, the child should be permitted to play with these materials at any time and in any way that she pleases. However, every once in a while, her parents can join her and play a special game. One version might be to have the child close her eyes while the parents remove a few pieces, and then ask the child to return the pieces to their original spots. Another version might be to tell a story about a little girl looking for a lost item in the house, and ask the child to act out the story on the paper using one of her favorite dolls as a prop.

As the child moves through toddlerhood the same type of games can be expanded to include not only the child's house, but her immediate neighborhood as well.

In addition, the parents can draw a rough map of the neighborhood; and then, while taking a walk through the real thing, the child can be encouraged periodically to stop and draw in pictures of the buildings, trees, and other major structures she sees. She also can be asked to "show how far we've gone" by using a bright red marker to trace a line between each starting and stopping point.

During the remainder of the preschool period, geography games can become infinitely more sophisticated. Maps can be prepared and the picture-and-line routine (described above) can be played in connection with anything from a short trip to the market to a long journey to visit Grandma and Grandpa in another state. And with each repetition of the event, greater detail can be added to the places pictured — possibly to the point of including the names of significant towns, streets, bridges, etc.

Once a route has been traveled repeatedly and these maps become reasonably complete, the parents can employ numbers to identify various areas. Then, instead of the child constantly inquiring "Are we there yet?" the parents and child can periodically discuss the question "Where are we now?" And instead of the child becoming impatient while waiting for the end of the journey, she can occupy herself by keeping track of "how many more numbers do we have to pass through before we get to Grandma's house?"

More advanced geography games

Meanwhile, the subject of geography can be extended to a national and even an international scale by employing a large map of the country and a world globe. Anytime an interesting location is mentioned in conversation, on television, or in a movie, the parents can use a sticker to show the child precisely where it is. Different stickers can be used to designate places where the child has been and places where she would like to go. And the child can be encouraged to attach small pictures or little toys to the stickers so she will be able to recall exactly what it was that initially motivated her to learn about that particular spot.

It is critical to keep in mind that these activities are "games" and not "drills." Parents should always be prepared to follow their child's lead rather than a pre-set agenda; and the child should never be "required" to do anything. Furthermore, it is important to remember that the goal is not to have the child recite a long list of state capitals, but merely to have her gain a good feeling for the essential elements of geography through concrete experiences that are directly meaningful to her.

And don't forget that these activities are just suggestions. In promoting developmentally appropriate play, there is no substitute for the right-on-target knowledge that a child's parents are uniquely qualified to provide; and there is nothing more wonderful than the remarkable ingenuity exhibited by mothers and fathers who have committed their creative talents to the task of bringing pleasure to their child.

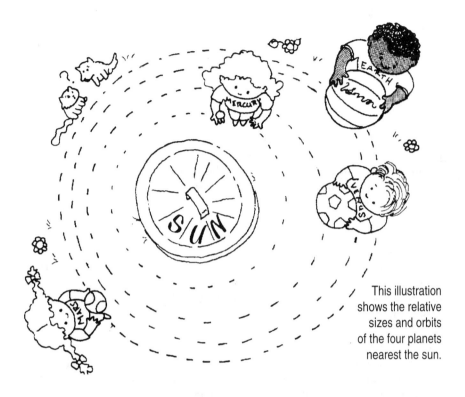

This illustration shows the relative sizes and orbits of the four planets nearest the sun.

Extending Geography Lessons to Outer Space

Michael K. Meyerhoff

There's the legendary example of the father who managed to take his preschool child's geography "lessons" far beyond the borders of the earth. When his four-year-old son became fascinated with "Star Trek" and outer space in general, the father decided to set up the solar system in the front yard. Using a beach ball, a basketball, a softball, a golf ball, etc., he collected nine "planets" that were of proportional size, and he laid them out in a way that approximated their relative distance from the "sun" (a huge aluminum garbage can cover).

His four-year-old was enthralled with the arrangement and continually asked questions about the objects and phenomena represented. For a while, given the fairly static nature of the display, the father had difficulty explaining certain concepts such as "orbit." He also noticed that despite a strong desire to do so, his son was having trouble keeping track of each planet's name as the discussion moved back and forth across the yard.

Suddenly, other kids from around the neighborhood began dropping by to take a look at the bizarre collection of balls in front of the house. The father gave each child a ball to hold and a "space name" like "Mercury" or "Venus" to use in a new game. Soon, he had the children moving their planets in big and small circles around the sun and calling out their special names as they passed each other.

Every weekend for the next several months, all the kids in the neighborhood would come over to the front yard to play "the planet game." And years later, when an elementary school science teacher started lecturing his class about the solar system, he was amazed to discover that some of his students already knew more about the subject than he would have expected.

As this story clearly illustrates, the easiest and most effective way to educate a young child is to teach her what she wants to learn when she wants to learn it, and to make sure the material is presented in a tangible and entertaining manner. And the most accurate way to measure a young child's educational progress is simply to note how much fun she is having.

Chapter 35
Becoming a "Nature Detective..."

Carol B. Hillman

Why do birds sing?
What makes a flower grow?
Where do squirrels
sleep at night?

Why do birds sing?
What makes a flower grow?
Where do squirrels sleep at night?

Young children are both natural learners and natural "scientists." By their very nature they have an innate zest for observing and questioning the world around them.

Because nature is all around them — even in a city neighborhood — parents can encourage and sustain that very attitude of interest and inquiry.

A child observes the behavior of the adults around her as a model for her own way of thinking and doing. Your own eagerness and enthusiasm to enjoy the out-of-doors is the primary factor in reinforcing your child's growth in that direction.

Answering children's questions
Learning does not take place only in the schoolroom. Questions should always be viewed as the workings of a mind eager to learn, and should be answered as soon as possible to the best of your ability. If you are unable to answer a question, let that be a perfect opportunity for you and your child to investigate the subject matter together.

How reference books help
It is helpful to have basic reference books at home or access to a library, so that identification of birds, flowers, or trees can be made. (Golden Press publishes paperback nature guides, science guides and field guides. See Resources, page 291). However, remember that the greatest pleasure could be just watching a sparrow drinking water or picking up a fallen red maple leaf.

Make a walk an "expedition"
Add a little fun and drama to an everyday walk. Bring along some simple, inexpensive "tools," such as a personal magnifying glass. From the very start let your preschooler know that caring properly for a magnifying glass is a position of responsibility. Preschoolers can also help make their own "binoculars." These are two matching cardboard toilet tissue rolls decorated with tempera paints and stapled together at both the top and bottom. Punch one hole on each side and use heavy colored yarn to make a "strap" that can go around the neck. Adding to the fun, your child can wear a special "nature detective" hat or cap. Also, if possible, take along a simple camera to document your findings.

Get to know one little area

Your preschool naturalist will become aware in noting the changes that take place in the same area over a period of time. For example, a simple walk in a wooded area or a park on the same path, taken once a week can bring forth surprising discoveries. This can be started at any time of the year. The primary factors are: the consistency of the actual walk, the sameness of the ground covered, the "scientific tools" described earlier, with the addition of a plastic bag for collecting. By looking for differences in this one small plot of land, the walk can heighten everyone's senses and make you more aware of the evolving patterns of nature.

See which birds visit "your land" — and keep a record of which times of the year they appear, and when they leave. What are the different colors of the male and female? What do their songs sound like? Look around and see what different trees, shrubs and flowers grow on "your land." What particular odors do the bark and flowers have? With a stick, do some digging in the earth and see what treasures may be found. Together, roll over a log or rock and see what critters may be living there. Be sure always to place the log or rock back to their original positions. You and your child may well have been looking at the homes of many small creatures.

To care deeply as a child for one small piece of land can carry over into later years to act responsibly about the world environment. ▓

Chapter 36
In Sharing Nature, Questions Mean More Than Answers

Laura Carey

*Take time to smell
the roses with your child.*

Because we don't know the names of more than a handful of trees or flowers or birds, we can't answer all of our children's questions that seem to come in an endless stream. The only insects we may recognize are an ant, a bee, and a butterfly.

Well, who says you have to be able to identify everything? Naturalists consider it more important to encourage the *questioning,* rather than just naming something and not learning any more about it. Isn't it more valuable to spot a bird flying with some grass in its beak and watch with amazement as it builds a sturdy nest out of grass and mud than say, "Oh, that's a robin," and never look again?

Sharing new experiences
The things that we retain the longest are our attitudes, values, the way we *feel* about something. The least remembered are the facts. What do you remember from your childhood? Does the feel of an approaching electrical storm still make you tingle with excitement? Does the smell of the ocean bring back happy memories of your first family trip to the shore?; the buzz of a bee your first picnic? Nature is all around us and provides memories that will be with us forever.

You and your child can enjoy learning together
Look at nature from your child's point of view. It's a sad but true fact that many of us have lost our ability to appreciate "just being." We don't know how to lose ourselves in the wonder of life. Your child is an expert at it!

Take your daughter or son outside to a park or field or your yard — wherever you can find a little green space. Now watch. Your child is experiencing many things for the first time. And so might you, if you look at things he or she is looking at. Being smaller and closer to the ground, your child will notice things crawling in the grass. He may be watching a lady bug walking delicately up a the stem of a flower. Look closely at it. How does it move its legs? What is it using its antennae for? What do the mouth parts look like? Does it stop to eat anything? Let it walk on your hand and then your child's (carefully). Does it tickle? Can you feel it?

Bring a small magnifying lens and together see what tiny things really look like. Can you see veins in a leaf or veins in the wing of a dragonfly or butterfly? What about the earth? Does it become beautiful when seen as something other than a stain to wash out? Now look at the sky, the clouds, or even the trail left by a jet plane.

Use all of your senses
Your child will automatically reach to touch. She is putting information into her little computer through *all* of her senses. Explore together the world around you. Touch the grass, a flower petal, a rock, tree bark — even a caterpillar, but be gentle.

Listen. All of the seasons have their own unique sounds, but spring and summer probably have the greatest variety. Together close your eyes and you'll be surprised at how much more you will hear without the distraction of sight. Have your child hold up his hand and put up a different finger each time he hears a new sound. Try to distinguish between different bird songs by listening and then looking for the songster.

Night sounds are fun to do this with also. There are many insect and other sounds to be heard on a spring or summer evening. Think of the excitement your youngster will feel as you search through the night with a flashlight for the source of the sounds you hear. You may find a cricket, or a katydid (sounds just like its name) or a peeper (tree frogs that sound like sleigh bells in the distance).

Don't forget your noses. Each different area you go to will have its own unique smell. Each season or type of weather also has an aroma all its own. Together breathe in the scent of the place or the day and some day in your child's adulthood, he will get a whiff of that particular scent and remember vividly the day you shared together. Take time to smell the roses with your child.

Nature Activities
for You
and Your Preschooler

Carol B. Hillman & Laura Carey

Here are some ideas on ways you and your child can share in exploring the world around you.

Color Search
Stop by your local hardware store's paint department and bring home a few color samples. Now choose a color and go on a search with your preschooler to find as many things in nature as you can that match your sample. Even if you live in the city, there are many mosses, molds, and fungi that grow on brick, cement, or concrete. Don't think you need to choose only "earth tones." You will be surprised at the variety of colors you and your child will find.

Shape Search

Try the same activity as the one above, using a variety of geometric shapes (circles, triangles, stars, squares, crescents). All of these shapes can be found hidden in a tree's bark or buds, insect coloration, cracks in the sidewalk, or frost on the window.

Name That Weed

Even the most enthusiastic scientist isn't able to identify *every* plant or bird or insect. Why don't you and your child make up your own system? When you're walking in the park, or playing in your yard and you come across an interesting weed, call it the first thing that pops into your mind or your child's mind. Look it over closely and find the words that describe it to you the best. For example: you might see goldenrod and call it "fireworks" or see the weed known as burdock and name it "sticker balls." Now you've identified it and the next time you come across it, you and your child will know it by name. It works with insects and birds and anything else you come across.

The Touch Bag

Collect some items from outside and put them in a bag. For example: acorn, walnut, small stone, twig, leaf, seed, feather. (For younger preschoolers, use only 3 or 4 things to start, and show them the items first.) Now have your child reach in and choose an object in his hand. Have him describe how it feels (smooth, rough, hard, soft, etc.). See if he can guess what it might be, and then have him take it out and see what it is. You might want to put in a small toy to add to the surprise. Your child will really giggle when he pulls that out. You could try making up a story with the help of your child about each item. Wonder about the weather the leaf lived through, or the places the seed may have traveled from, or towns the bird may have seen before one of its feathers dropped out.

Bark Rubbings

A fun art activity is the making of designs by doing rubbings of different textures. Each tree has its own unique bark that will produce a beautiful pattern on paper. Hold a piece of paper against the trunk of a tree and have your child rub lightly with a crayon or chalk until a print appears. Do this with several trees and compare. Have your child look at the rubbing, then feel the bark to see what kind of pattern rough bark makes as compared to smooth bark. You can also do leaf rubbing, rock rubbings, or even building rubbings (being careful not to get crayon or chalk on the object).

The Unnatural Trail
Choose an area in your yard or a nearby park and mark off a section about thirty (30) feet long that has some shrubs or plants tall enough to hide things in or under. Now hide 10 or 15 human-made objects there. Some should blend in and some should stand out brightly. You can use a marble, a toy car, a plastic dinosaur, a balloon, a birthday candle — anything that would be fun to hunt for . Now hunt with your child through the area and watch his delight as he discovers each item or maybe even a natural surprise like a frog, a bird's nest, or a preying mantis.

Natural Concentration
This game, for older preschoolers, is nature's version of the TV game show "Concentration.'" All you need to do is collect a variety of natural objects — some of the same things you collected for your Touch Bag as described above. (You can start with a few objects, and add more as your child becomes more experienced at playing the game.) Put them out on the ground or on a table and cover them up with a towel or handkerchief. Have your child pay close attention. Tell her you'll only uncover the things for a short time and it's her job to try and see and remember what is under the covering. Now lift the cover for about ten seconds while she carefully looks over the collection of objects. Now cover them up and ask your child to name all of the items she remembers seeing. Write them down as she says them. Together uncover the objects and compare what's there with what was remembered. Discuss each item and where it came from and what it is for. The acorn is from an oak tree and one day will grow into an oak tree if it gets enough water and sunlight. A leaf needs sunlight to make food for the tree. A feather grows on a bird and helps it fly. You can add different objects and really sharpen your child's observational skills — and your own!

Make a Flower and Leaf Press
Take two 6" x 6" pieces of 1/2" plywood or lumber and cut 2 pieces of blotting paper to 5" x 5". Buy four bolts (about 3" long), four washers and four wing nuts. Drill holes at each corner of the wood for the four bolts to go through. You and your preschooler can collect favorite flowers and leaves. Place one piece of wood flat on a table. Then place one sheet of blotting paper on it — being careful not to cover up the holes. Arrange your flowers and leaves on the layer of blotting paper. Place the remaining sheet of blotting paper over them. Match the remaining piece of wood to the four holes. Hold together and put the bolts through the holes. Place the washers over the bolts, and tighten with the wing nuts. This press will dry and preserve the flowers and leaves. You can then make a simple book to put them in.

Walk in the Rain
In the spring or summer when it rains you and your offspring put on your raincoats and boots and head for the out-of-doors. Splash in every puddle, tilt your heads back, open your mouths, stick out your tongues and see if you can catch some raindrops. Another time, put on your bathing suits, go outside in your backyard with a bar of soap, lather up, and take a shower in the rain.

Make a Simple Bird Feeder
This is for both city and country dwellers. Take either an 8"-10" log or 2" x 4" piece of wood. Drill about 8 one-inch holes around it. Put a large screw eye in the top. Go to your favorite supermarket and ask the butcher for a package of suet or beef fat. Now, cut off pieces and fill the holes. Hang this outside where you can watch the birds come for a morning or evening snack. Also, except when it's freezing, put a pie tin or shallow container filled with water, so that the birds can always have a cool fresh drink and sometimes even take a bath.

Sleep in a Tent Under the Stars
When possible, pitch a tent outside and spend a summer night with your young camper, each tucked into your own sleeping bag. There is nothing quite so wondrous as lying down on your back looking up at a star-studded sky, drinking in the cool night air and listening to the soft night sounds. It is not important to know the names of the stars or to identify the distant croak of the green frog. It is enough just to be there and feel the beauty that nature affords.

Chapter 37
Enjoying Birds

Lester Feldman

*To be read
to a young child
by an adult.*

Watching birds in Your neighborhood
Some of the most beautiful living things we share our planet with are the birds.

Because birds can fly, it's sometimes hard to get a good look at them. One way to get to see birds more easily is to feed them.

Feeding birds
By placing bird feeders right outside your window, you can watch them and get to recognize the different ones in your neighborhood. If birds know there is food for them, they usually will nest nearby.

Different kinds of birds eat different kinds of foods. Some eat seeds. You can buy sunflower seeds or a "wild bird" seed mixture at your supermarket or garden nursery. There are many kinds of bird feeders available. The simplest thing is to just sprinkle the seed on the ground.

CARDINAL

Other birds eat insects and worms. (In other words, they are meat eaters.) You can feed these birds suet. Your butcher trims this in his shop and he will usually give you some if you explain that it's food for the birds. You can buy a suet holder (it looks like a small cage) and hang it on a tree.

There are some kinds of birds that we don't have to feed. Their foods are the flying insect, live fish, even frogs and mice. They usually don't live around our houses — but in wild places like swamps or open farmlands. To see these species we have to go to where they live.

DOWNY
WOODPECKER

Parent birds feed their young, called fledglings, all day long! So you can look forward to very busy feeders.

Most fledglings leave the nest when they are a few weeks old and they are then are on their own forever. The parents will probably never see their young again. The following year, the parent birds will have a new nest full of young.

Very young birds do not get their parents' colors, or plumage, until they are able to fly or able to feed and take care of themselves.

Watching birds take a bath is quite a sight!
Another way to get a good look at birds is to watch them bathe. Birds love to bathe. This helps to keep them healthy and also provides water for them to drink.

Garden nurseries usually sell bird baths made of concrete or plastic. You can even use a shallow dish as a bird bath. It's a good idea to place it close to a shrub or tree because birds like to have a safe place to dry themselves.

R O B I N

Don't be surprised to find other wild creatures like squirrels or racoons drinking from your bird bath.

Learning more about birds
For some people, feeding and having water available for birds is enough enjoyment.

But if you want to know more, then you can learn about the different kinds of birds, each with their own names and their own ways.

Some birds are named for their color — like the blue jay, goldfinch, and red-wing blackbird.

Some birds are named for what they do — like the woodpecker, creeper, and flycatcher.

Some birds are named for their song — like the bobwhite quail, pewee, chickadee, mockingbird, warbler, and whip-poor-will.

Birds live in every part of our world. You can find them on the beaches and the seas, in high mountains, in deserts, even in the frozen Antarctic... as well as your neighborhood.

A good idea is to study pictures of the birds that live where you live or where you plan to visit. There now are picture books called *field guides* for almost every place on earth. (See Resources on page 291.)

No matter where you travel or vacation, you can look forward to the thrill of seeing and identifying birds that you've never seen before.

RED-WINGED BLACKBIRD

Author/illustrator Lester Feldman is an amateur ornithologist. He's been enjoying birds since he was a boy. He supports many conservation organizations and gets out to watch birds wherever he travels. At his home on the North Fork of Long Island, New York, he and his wife have counted over 125 species that they can see from their house in their garden, in the sky, and in the adjacent water and woods .

Chapter 38
Gardening with Your Preschooler

Laura Robb

*Growing things
helps your
preschooler to learn
about the world.*

Learning how living things change and grow
Three-year-old Douglas uses a sponge and gently washes the leaves of his flowering plants. "I'm a gardener," he proudly announces, and he takes me on a tour of his garden which grows in the sunny windows of his parents' apartment.

"I grow vegetables," he tells me. "Mommy helps." I follow my nephew to the kitchen window, crowded with milk cartons and a plastic dishpan. Douglas climbs up his stepping stool. "Hi radishes," he says, and his small hand lovingly strokes the plants. "Mommy...hurry!" And Douglas points to the new bean shoots. "They just peeped through."

"Feel the soil." Carefully, Douglas places my fingers on the brown earth. "Wet or dry?" he asks. "Dry," I answer.

"They need a drink," he announces. Then he tells me that his plants need food and water and sun and lots of love. And I say, "Just like you."

By gardening with his parents, Douglas is learning that growing plants is like "growing" a child. You can help your child become a gardener like Douglas, and offer ways to learn about what makes living things change and grow.

Start involving your child with gardening chores when he begins to toddle around the house. Ask questions and encourage talk about these new experiences of sowing seeds, watering, and talking to plants. Talk about why plants need water, sunshine, and care. Listen to your child's responses, and use "gardening talk" to help him see that plants, like children, start small, and with proper nurturing, grow tall and strong.

Begin with neighborhood plant walks
Point out flowers, plants, and trees as you take walks with your preschooler. Use plant and tree guidebooks to identify the great variety you both discover. (See Resources on page 291.) Watch trees bud and shoots arrive. Use your child's fingers to measure seedlings as they grow. Feel the bark of trees. Enjoy the sights, smells, and sounds of spring on your neighborhood excursions. Pull up some weeds and look at their root systems. Explain that roots hold plants in the ground and supply them with water and food.

Discover the magic of planting seeds
Help your preschooler become involved with gardening right from the start! You can get advice from your local nursery, the instructions that are right on the seed packets, and materials at the library. Shop for seeds together and let your youngster choose some things to grow. Make sure

you select plants that germinate quickly, like radishes, and satisfy your preschooler's need for fast results. Find a sunny window or patch of land. Indoor plants will thrive in milk cartons, plastic dishpans, or wooden boxes. Punch drainage holes in the bottom of each container and set on a tray, bowl, or aluminum pie plate. Put the appropriate plant food in the soil you use either indoors or outside. Give small hands the larger seeds to plant such as beans, squash, peas, pumpkin, marigolds, or nasturtiums. Identify different plants with markers. Water, weed, and thin plants together.

Growing things helps your preschooler to learn about the world
Spend time every day with your preschooler watching your plants, talking to them, and sharing gardening chores. Stop frequently for a hug and to answer questions. This way you build an awareness that seedlings, like your child, need nourishment, sunshine, and constant loving care. Teach him not to taste plants or berries unless an adult says, "OK." When garden failures occur, help your preschooler see these as natural parts of the life cycle.

Gardening brings children closer to nature, and they develop a sense of wonder about the world. Through active involvement, young gardeners learn about seeds, flowers, vegetables, fruits, and nutrition. They develop pride in growing plants and the knowledge that plants need nurturing to grow. The following activities will encourage your child to become a keen observer of nature, find satisfaction in helping things grow, and experience the joy of eating the produce that he grew himself.

Gardening Projects

Laura Robb

Help your preschooler understand why plants and people grow by discussing what they both need to develop. Begin with an experiment that shows how plants, like people, get thirsty. Don't water a plant for a few days. Observe and talk about what happens to the plant's leaves. Let your child touch the droopy leaves. Ask him to predict what will happen when you water the plant. After watering the plant, talk about the changes you observe, and ask, "Why must we care for plants?" Such thought-provoking questions start your child thinking about nurturing and responsibility.

rinse twice a day & drain

EAT!

1/3 full

Sprouting Beans
Materials: Alfalfa or mung bean seeds, a quart jar, cheesecloth, water, and a strainer.

Directions
1. Soak beans in water overnight; drain.
2. Place beans in jar until 1/3 full; cover with cheesecloth and rubber band.
3. Keep jar at room temperature; rinse twice each day, draining off all water through the cheesecloth.
4. Sprouts are ready to harvest and eat in 4-5 days.

Carrot-Beet Dish Garden
Materials: beets, carrots, knife, cutting board, a shallow dish, sand or small pebbles, water.

Directions
1. Cut 1 inch off the top of each beet and carrot.
2. Fill the dish with sand or pebbles.
3. Stick the cut carrot or beet tops into the sand or pebbles.
4. Add enough water to cover the cut surfaces. Keep the crowns of the veggies above water.
5. Place the dish in good light — not direct sun.
6. Keep enough water in dish to cover bottoms of veggies.
7. In about 1 week new leaves begin to sprout. Plants last 3-4 weeks.

Grow Lima Bean Seedlings

Materials: A tall, clear plastic glass, 4 large, dried Lima beans, paper towels, dark construction or blotter paper.

Directions

1. Line the inside of glass with construction paper; trim top so it meets rim of glass.
2. Fill lined glass with crumpled paper towels.
3. Place the beans between the tumbler and construction paper. Add enough water to moisten toweling and construction paper.

4. Cover outside of glass by wrapping it with dark construction paper. Tape edges together.
5. Place on a sunny window sill, and lift covering the same time each day to observe what is happening.
6. Draw a picture of how the beans look each day to see how they change. Help your preschooler understand that he is watching how seeds develop under the ground.
7. In two weeks your seedlings will be ready to plant.
8. They will be ready to harvest in approximately 8 weeks.

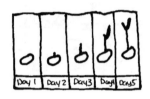

Indoor-Outdoor Activities

Containers for indoor planting: use plastic tubs, milk cartons, plastic cups, or wooden crates. Make sure you punch holes in the bottom for drainage. Place containers on an aluminum pie plate, a tray, or in a bowl.

Growing Chart

Vegetable	Days to Germinate	Days to Harvest
Radishes	7 to 14	25 to 60
Carrots	7 to 14	65 to 75
Leaf Lettuce	7 to 14	40 to 50
Summer Squash	7 to 14	50 to 60
Pumpkin	7 to 14	95 to 120
Tomato	7 to 14	50 to 85

Fun with Seeds & Plants

Seed Mosaics
• Collect and dry seeds from different fruits in egg cartons. You can also use a variety of colorful, dried beans and corn.
• Help your preschooler arrange seeds in a design on cardboard or thick construction paper. Glue the seeds in place.

Percussion Instruments
• Place a mixture of large seeds (such as pumpkin, sunflower, or corn) and beans in a coffee can with a plastic lid.
• Shake the container and use for marching, dancing, and creative drama.

Grassy-Haired Faces
• Use red, blue, or black marker pens and help your preschooler draw a face on a clear plastic cup.
• Fill cup with absorbent cotton, sprinkle grass seed on the top, and moisten.
• Enclose in a plastic bag. Remove bag when grassy hair begins to grow. Keep the cotton moist.
• Style the grassy hair when it becomes too long.

Radish Seeds
Hand Rhyme by Laura Robb

(Start on knees.)
10 tiny radish seeds
Planted in a row.
(Pretend you are planting.)
Grow, little seeds grow.

10 tiny radish seeds
Drink water and warm sun.
(Flutter fingers like rain.)
(Make a big circle
with arms for sun.)
Grow, little seeds grow.

10 tiny radish shoots
Now begin to push.
(Push fingers upward.)
Slowly, slowly,
Up, up, up.
Push, little shoots push.
(Stand up.)

10 tiny radish plants
Standing in a row.
Grow little plants grow.
(Hold up 10 fingers.)

Calendar of Gardening Activities
31 activities to do with your preschooler
Laura Robb

SUNDAY	MONDAY	TUESDAY	WEDNESDAY	THURSDAY	FRIDAY	SATURDAY
				1 Make popcorn and tell your child that this food comes from special corn seeds.	**2** Cut out pictures of things that grow from seeds and put in your child's picture book.	**3** Make a display of edible seeds by pasting them on cardboard for identification.
4 Help your child act out the story of *The Carrot Seed* (See Resources, page 294).	**5** Take your child on a trip to a farm or orchard.	**6** Teach your child the finger rhyme about radish seeds growing, as printed on page 281.	**7** Let your child dictate a story to you about growing things.	**8** Pick berries and let your child help make a pie, or eat them as a snack.	**9** Select some flowering bulbs and help your child plant and care for them.	**10** Observe how house plants lean towards the sun. Turn the plants and note what happens by the next day.
11 Visit a shop that sells gardener's tools. Discuss what you've seen and learned.	**12** At the library find children's books about gardens. (See Resources, page 292.)	**13** At a local nursery look at the plants and find out which flowers will grow well at your house.	**14** Plan a menu with your child that uses things grown in a garden.	**15** Grow sprouts and make a sandwich with lettuce, tomato, sprouts, and mayonnaise.	**16** Buy a variety of nuts (seeds) in shells. Open them, study the nutmeats, and eat.	**17** With your child's help gather different kinds of tree leaves for a book with the name of each tree on a page.

18	19	20	21	22	23	24
Talk about all of the different ways a fruit or vegetable can be prepared: corn on the cob, corn fritters, creamed corn, popcorn. What about apples? peanuts?	Show how water travels from a plant's roots through its stem to the leaves —put food coloring and a celery stalk in a glass of water. See it travel up the celery's tiny tubes.	Help your child plant seedlings in 2 different cups. Place one in the dark and one in the sun. Water both. Watch what happens and talk about why plants need sun.	Walk in woody and grassy areas and tell your child to use her eyes, ears, nose, and hands. Later talk about all the things you saw, heard, smelled, and touched.	Soak orange seeds in water for 2 days. Place pebbles in a small flower pot, Fll with potting soil to 1" from the top. Plant 2-3 seeds 1/2" deep. Water well. (Tree will not bear fruit.)	Make a garden book with your child. Cut out pictures of fruits, trees, and vegetables and paste in a scrapbook. Encourage your child to talk about the pictures.	Take a neighborhood tree walk. Help your child identify different trees by their leaves and bark. (See Resources page 292: *Peterson Field Guides: Trees and Shrubs.*)

25	26	27	28	29	30	31
To find out what's inside a seed, soak lima beans overnight in water. Remove seed coats gently; pull the halves apart. In soil, tiny leaves and root would develop into a bean plant.	Have a seed party. Slice an orange, grapefruit, apple, banana, and cantaloupe. Discuss how the seeds are alike and different. Make a fruit salad and enjoy a healthy snack.	Make a food face with grated carrots as the shape of a face, cucumber round eyes, a celery nose, a sliced radish mouth, eyebrows from raisins and apple slices for ears.	Study a tree by feeling the bark and looking for insects, bird's nests, and woodpecker holes. Talk about the changes that occur during each season.		Play a color game with fruits and vegetables in the supermarket. Ask your child which ones are red, orange, green, brown, yellow, or purple.	Discuss scarecrows (like the one in The Wizard of Oz) with your child. Explain that a farmer uses them to keep crows and other birds from eating the seeds that he's planted.

Watch Seeds Germinate

Materials: A plate, absorbent cotton, water, a plastic bag, and seeds such as marigold, radish, lettuce, or cress.

Directions
1. Put a layer of cotton on the plate.
2. Sprinkle seeds over the cotton. If you use more than one type of seed, put each on a different plate.
3. Moisten cotton and seeds.
4. Cover with plastic bag; keep out of direct sun.
5. Remove bag daily and watch the seeds.
6. Discuss what you see and mark on a calendar the progress of the seeds as they sprout.
7. Use a magnifying glass to study the root system.
8. In a few days seedlings will be ready to plant.
9. See growing chart on page 280 for harvesting time.

Chapter 39
Teaching Preschoolers Environmental Awareness

Janet Dengel

*Preschoolers can best learn
about their environment
through the five senses.*

Will you teach your children what we have taught our children, that the earth is our mother? What befalls the earth befalls all the sons of the earth. This we know, (Believed to be from a speech in 1855 by Chief Seattle of the Duwamish Tribe, for whom the city of Seattle, Washington, was named.)

Across the country, preschoolers are learning about the environment, pollution, ecology, recycling, and saving wildlife. They are also learning that even their seemingly small efforts can make a difference.

Environment
"While it's important to learn about whales and tropical rain forests," says Ruth Buirkle, a naturalist who teaches three and four year olds, "it's more important for preschoolers to learn about their backyard. You have to start on their level so they'll know the importance of every insect and every flower."

Preschoolers can best learn about their environment through the five senses. Encourage your youngster to become a watcher, a listener, and an explorer. Go on a "silent hike" with your child and listen for the noise of birds, crickets, and dogs barking. Relate the sounds to experiences from his own life. For example: the birds are calling to each other—how does his mother call him?

Tactile discovery is the primary way preschoolers explore and evaluate their world. Let them touch soft petals, feel rough bark, or prickly pine needles. Along with teaching awareness, this is an opportune time for young children to learn not to pick flowers, break off branches, or disturb animals' homes.

Ecology
Preschoolers can better understand ecology —the relationship between living things and their environment— through everyday happenings. Tell them that, just as they go to the refrigerator or mommy goes to the store to get food, a bird must peck for worms for her baby birds and bring the food to her nest.

When your child eats his vegetables, ask him what that plant needed to live. Point out that soil, water, sunshine and clean air are necessary for plant life.

Recycling
"Everything old can become new again," is the message that storytellers, puppet shows, and museums have been conveying to young audiences.

By becoming the first generation to grow up recycling, your preschooler can be taught that his actions can have a positive effect on the environment.

This age group seems to have a natural interest in trash. They enjoy playing with empty cereal boxes as much as expensive toys, and go running to the window when the trash collectors come. Throwaways can easily be used with this age group to make craft projects. Keep a box in a closet for your preschooler to save empty plastic bottles, cardboard, and scrap paper for a rainy day.

Your industrious preschooler can also help sort plastic and aluminum cans into containers they have colorfully decorated. (Watch for sharp edges on cans.) He'll gladly help you bring the materials to the local recycling center or to the curb for pickup.

Conservation
Another area where an enthusiastic preschooler can take an active part in environmental matters is through energy conservation. Put your youngster in charge of checking to make sure lights and television sets are turned off when they are not being used. Tell him that keeping the refrigerator door closed and turning off faucets can help ensure that there will be enough electricity and water for everyone. A chart with stars awarded for good conservation behavior will reward your preschooler.

Family conservation projects, such as riding bikes to the store instead of driving or wearing sweaters so the heat can be lowered, will be readily embraced by a preschooler. If you have a garden, a compost heap is a great way to reduce solid waste, and your preschooler will enjoy throwing banana peels and watermelon rinds onto the pile.

Wildlife
Children love to visit zoos to see exotic animals and hear stories about whales, bald eagles, and tigers.

Although preschoolers usually love soft, cuddly animals, some children may dislike insects and reptiles. By learning about wildlife right in her neighborhood, your child is more likely to gain a respect for all animals. Go for walks to discover spider webs and anthills as well as bird's nests and doghouses. Teach your preschooler not to step on bugs outdoors or disturb animals' habitats. Explain the difference between wild animals and domestic ones. Let your youngster crawl on the grass to experience the world from an animal's point of view.

Pollution

Experts recommend avoiding complex subjects such as global warming or the greenhouse effect with a child of this age.

Instead, use activities that she can understand. For example, make a happy face and a sad face out of paper plates. Attach each one to a stick. Look at newspaper or magazine pictures of litter, dirty beaches, smoke stacks, a beautiful park, clear skies. Ask your child to hold up the face that shows how the picture makes her feel.

Tell your child that April 22 is the anniversary of Earth Day, which was first celebrated in 1970. By teaching your children an awareness of, respect for, and positive action toward our environment, every day in the future can be Earth Day for them.   ▓

Activities to Help Develop Environmental Awareness

Janet Dengel

Preschoolers have an inborn love for the outdoors and animals. With a little guidance and a lot of fun, that love can be nurtured into a lifelong respect for the ecology and wildlife. The following suggestions encourage activities that teach preschoolers about the environment, ecology, pollution, recycling, conservation, and wildlife.

An *ecology hunt* allows a preschooler to romp outdoors while looking for animal footprints, moss, a feather, a smooth rock, a spider web, or a dandelion. The longer your list of "finds," the prouder your preschooler will be.

Color is important in nature, and a preschooler can have fun with a *forest color search* by finding three things that are green or four that are yellow. As an example of its importance, just as the yellow traffic light signals caution to your preschooler, the bright yellow of a bumblebee warns predators to beware.

Study a *mini-environment*. Give your preschooler a piece of string about three feet long to lay down in a circle, or mark an area with a hula hoop. Then, kneel down together to investigate your mini-environment with a magnifying glass. What color is the soil? Are there any rocks? How does the grass feel? Do you see any insects?

Plant a tree or adopt one to fight air pollution. Water the tree; draw pictures of it, and have your child dictate a story or poem about the tree. See how it changes each season. Explain that the tree uses the air we breathe out and gives us the oxygen we need in return.

Discover what's below the surface of a local stream or brook with a home-made *water periscope*. Using an empty milk carton, cut off the bottom. Cover the opening with clear plastic wrap and hold it on with a rubber band. Immerse in the water and look through the plastic to view rocks, particles in the water, maybe even a tadpole.

To learn about *water pollution*, take a large pail and let your preschooler collect sand, pebbles, and leaves. Add clean water. Ask your preschooler, "If you were a fish would you like to live in this type of environment?" Then add soap bubbles. "If you were a fish, could you live in this water now? Could a fish breathe in this environment?"

Discuss *noise pollution* by telling your preschooler to close her eyes and listen. Play soft music, slam a door, hum quietly, and bang a pot. Which sounds did your child like? Which were too loud? Switch places and let her have some noisy fun.

Make an *antipollution mobile*. Cut out pictures of blue skies and clean lakes and untouched forests. Glue them onto cardboard circles and squares, punch a hole at the top of each one, and tie with string onto a wire hanger, and hang from the ceiling.

Make a *recycled draft snake* to conserve heat. Use leftover pieces of material and sew a long patchwork tube. Have your preschooler stuff it with old stockings and holey socks. Use it at the bottom of doors and windows to keep out the cold.

See how many times your preschooler can *recycle a paper bag.* After bringing home groceries in the bag, use it to carry books to the library, collect pine cones, make a puppet out of it, and then line the bottom of the garbage with it. Put a star on the bag for every reuse.

Find a recipe for *homemade recycled paper.* All that's needed is old newspaper, starch, a pan and a small screen. One source for the recipe is *The Brownie Girl Scout Handbook,* 1986, Girl Scouts of the U.S.A., 830 Third Ave. New York, NY 10022. This book is available in libraries.

Design an *ecology jigsaw puzzle* by drawing and coloring a lake, mountains, and trees. Cut out pictures of animals, plants, people and insects, and paste them on. Glue the picture onto cardboard and cut out pieces for a jigsaw puzzle. This will show your preschooler the interconnection between all life in a graphic way.

The movement and imagination involved in *body acting* will catch on fast with preschoolers as they act out things found in the environment. They can pretend to be a seed growing, a leaf falling, or a tree swaying in the wind.

Make your own tree by using *fallen* branches, leaves, bark, and berries. Let your youngster create an art design that she can feel by constructing her own tree on a heavy piece of cardboard.

Make a *wildlife poster* by letting your preschooler cut and paste magazine photos of elephants, giraffes, and other animals on a large piece of construction paper. Or, create *mixed-up wildlife pictures.* Find pictures of lions and tigers and bears. Your preschooler will say, "Oh, my!" when you cut the pictures and let him rearrange them back together to make silly animals: a crocodile with a rhino's head or a zebra with a camel's hump.

Put a nickel in a jar each time your preschooler turns off a light someone left on or spots a dripping faucet. This way he will learn that conservation does save money.

Resources for Section Seven: Science - Nature

FOR ADULTS

Golden Field Guide and Nature Guide Series, Golden Press. Inexpensive, colorful, and in-depth books that contain basic information on: weather, ecology, non-flowering plants, insects, mammals, pond life, birds and trees.

Pint-Size Science; Finding-Out Fun for You and Your Young Child, by Linda Allison & Martha Weston. Little, Brown, 1994. Your child is a natural scientist, and that's because science is exciting and fun to do! This lively paperback gives adults creative ideas for using the equipment you have on hand to help your children think, participate in interesting activities, and enjoy exploring their world.

Square Foot Gardening, by Mel Bartholomew. Rodale Press, 1981. An excellent, illustrated resource for beginning gardeners with tips on saving space and work time. The book focuses on small, outdoor gardens, but has a thorough section on indoor gardening as well.

Bubbles Rainbows & Worms: Science Experiments For Pre-School Children, by Sam Ed Brown. Gryphon House, 1981. Preschool teachers and parents will find this book useful in suggesting simple activities with plants, water, the senses, etc.

A Sense of Wonder, by Rachel Carson. Harper & Row, 1956. A delightful account of wonders shared between aunt, nephew and the outdoors. From the author of the best seller, *Silent Spring.*

Sharing the Joy of Nature: Nature Activities for All Ages, by Joseph Cornell. Dawn Publications, 1989. This practical handbook contains a variety of activities for parents to use with their children. Each experience helps you observe and interact with different living things in our environment.

Don't Know Much About Geography: Everything You Need to Know About the World but Never Learned, by Kenneth C. Davis. William Morrow, 1992. A lively and informative book that proves that it's never too late to learn.

The Peterson First Guide to Birds, by Roger Tory Peterson. Houghton Mifflin, 1986. A simplified field guide to the common birds of North America, this is an introduction to the delights of birding. Also :*The Peterson First Guide to Wildflowers, Insects, Weather, etc.*

Peterson Field Guides: Trees and Shrubs, by George A. Petrides. Houghton Mifflin, 1986. 646 trees and shrubs are described and illustrated in full color. There are detailed descriptions of shape, arrangement of leaves, height, color, and identification of different species.

Hug a Tree And Other Things To Do Outdoors With Young Children, by R.E. Rockwell, E.A. Sherwood, & R.A. Williams. Gryphon House, 1983. This helpful book contains tips for parents and teachers on organizing an outdoor experience. It includes lists of resources and specific outdoor activities for ages 2 years and up.

FOR CHILDREN

Changes, by Marjorie N. Allen & Shelley Rotner. Macmillan, 1991. Using color photographs of flowers, trees, animals and people, the authors show how things in nature change as they grow and develop.

Crinkleroot's Guide to Knowing the Birds; Crinkleroot's Guide to Knowing the Trees, by Jim Arnosky. Bradbury Press, 1992. These are lively and informative nature guides. The first covers such important basics such as what to look for when you spot a bird, where birds live, and how to attract them to your yard. The second book helps you identify trees and their leaves. It tells the reader to get to know the trees individually. In that way, "whenever you walk into the woods, you'll be among old friends."

Dinosaurs to the Rescue! A Guide to Protecting Our Planet, by Laurie Krasny Brown & Marc Brown. Little, Brown, 1992. This book is entertaining and informative, featuring dinosaurs who guide the reader in ways to help the environment.

Alphabet Garden, by Laura Jane Coats. Macmillan, 1993. A little boy takes an alphabetical tour through his garden by entering through his <u>A</u>rbor, and enjoying the flowers, animals, and insects he finds there, with each letter of the alphabet. The story ends as he gathers a handful of <u>Z</u>innias.

Grandpa Art: Insect Songs; Grandpa Art Sings About Birds, written and performed by Arthur Custer. The Sun Group (1133 Broadway NY, NY 10010), 1992. These audiocassettes feature award-winning musician Arthur Custer, who has composed music for over 300 juvenile productions. The songs are easily sung by children aged 4 to 8, and are informative as well as entertaining.

My first Book of Questions, by J. Daniel, et al. Scholastic Cartwheel Books, 1992. This useful book of 60 *easy answers to hard questions children ask* deals with many questions about science. For example: *How do fish breathe? What makes leaves change color? How does an egg become a chicken?*

The Desert (1992); The Forest (1991); The Ocean (1992); and *The River (1991),* by Susan Deming. Chronicle Books. Rather than reading them page by page, the reader <u>unfolds</u> each of these 4 nature books to reveal a panoramic view of the environment. The detailed illustrations show the animals and plants to be found in each location, with labels for each, making each book a fascinating field guide for your young naturalist.

The Empty Lot, by Dale H. Fife. Sierra Club/Little, Brown, 1991. When Harry Hale inspects an "empty lot" that he owns in order to sell it, he is surprised to learn that that the lot is not so empty after all. It is inhabited by birds, insects, and small animals.

My First Nature Treasury, by Lizann Flatt. Sierra Club Books for Children, 1995. This profusely illustrated book provides an exciting exploration of nature for young children. It depicts the major families of animals and plants and how they grow, along with a variety of environments such as a rain forest, a desert, a tundra, etc.

In the Snow: Who's Been Here? by Lindsay Barrett George. Greenwillow, 1995. Two children walking along a trail in winter find clues as to what animals had been there before the children arrived. They observe the tracks of a ruffled grouse, hear the song of the cardinal as it flies away, see the nest of a family of gray squirrels, and more. The paintings are so real that you feel you can almost stroke the feathers of the grouse, or touch the rough bark of the tree.

Recycle, by Gail Gibbons. Little, Brown, 1992. "A Handbook for Kids" that explains the process of recycling from start to finish.

Brother Eagle, Sister Sky, A message from Chief Seattle, paintings by Susan Jeffers. Dial, 1991. The artist, Susan Jeffers, tells us at the end of this book that, "The origins of Chief Seattle's words are partly obscured by the mists of time." They were spoken in his native tongue, transcribed into English, and adapted over time. But what matters is that his words inspire a compelling truth about caring for the environment. The illustrations and text celebrate his message.

Looking Down, by Steve Jenkins. Houghton Mifflin, 1995. If you were out in space, looking down at the earth, what would you see? The imaginative collage pictures in this beautiful wordless book show you our planet out in space; then they move closer and closer to earth. Each illustration shows more and more details until you can focus in on... a ladybug!

Birds (1993); Flowers (1993); The Tree (1992), and *Vegetables in the Garden (1994),* created by G. Jeunesse, et al. Scholastic Cartwheel Books. These four books in The First Discovery Series help preschoolers explore nature as they turn the brilliantly colored glossy pages. Transparencies reveal nature's changes in a bird's plumage, show the roots of a chestnut tree, or let the reader peek inside the petals of a crocus, or the root of a carrot. Unique and creative.

How a Seed Grows, by Helene J. Jordan. *(A Let's-Read-And-Find-Out Book™).* HarperTrophy edition, 1992. In language young children can understand, the author explains how seeds grow into plants, and describes an experiment you can make planting bean seeds and watching them grow.

Johnny Appleseed, retold and Illustrated by Steven Kellogg. Morrow, 1988. Illustrating the story with lively, action-filled pictures, Kellogg tells the tale of the man who became a legend as he spread his love of apple trees through the western frontier. (Also published in a Mulberry Big Book edition, 1996.)

A Child's Book of Wildflowers, by M.A. Kelly. Four Winds Press, 1992. This is an informative introduction to 24 wildflowers commonly found in North America. Not only are you helped to identify the wildflowers, but you learn their significance in history, along with some suggestions for using the flowers in special ways. The illustrations are by the noted naturalist painter Joyce Powzyk.

Hoot Howl Hiss, by Michelle Koch. Greenwillow, 1991. With bright, simple pictures and just a few words on each page, this book can be enjoyed by the youngest preschoolers. They can hear about the sounds made by a variety of animals, and try to imitate those noises themselves.

The Carrot Seed, by Ruth Kraus. Harper & Row, 1945. A classic story about a little boy who plants a carrot seed. The members of his family all tell him that the seed won't come up, but the little boy knows in his heart that it will. He cares for his seed and one day a marvelous carrot grows.

My First Book of Nature: How Living Things Grow, by Dwight Kuhn. Scholastic Cartwheel Books, 1993. All living things grow. In this book, children learn how 30 living things grow: for example, mushrooms, guppies, and humans. The book is filled with interesting color photographs.

Be a Friend to Trees (*Let's-Read-And-Find-Out Science® Stage 2*), by Patricia Lauber. HarperTrophy, 1994. Trees are nice. They are also useful — for everything from making pencils to building houses. People and animals eat many parts of trees, and trees provide oxygen for us to breathe. This book explains these concepts and offers ways for children to be a friend to trees.

Alison's Zinnia, by Anita Lobel. Mulberry Books edition, 1996. Using names of girls and flowers from A to Z, the author/illustrator dazzles the eye with gorgeous paintings.

How Do Apples Grow? (*A Let's-Read-And-Find-Out Book™*) (*1993*); **Why Do Leaves Change Color?** (*Let's-Read-And-Find-Out Science® Stage 2*) (*1994*), by Betsy Maestro. HarperTrophy. Children are always asking , "Why?" These two books explain simply, yet scientifically, how apples grow from bud to flower to fruit, and what happens to the leaves when in autumn they turn such brilliant colors.

Awesome Animal Actions; Baffling Bird Behavior; Freaky Fish Facts; and Incredible Insect Instincts, illustrated by Paul Mirocha. HarperFestival, 1992. These four books are part of the series: *Amazing Nature Pop-up Books.* In each book you will read about unique creatures and see them come to life in three dimensional scenes.

Have You Seen Birds? by Joanne Oppenheim. Scholastic, 1986. Written in a lilting style, this book describes different kinds of birds and how they sound.

Spring, by Fiona Pragoff. Aladdin, 1993. Colorful photographs and simple text make this book a lovely introduction for young children to the wonders of nature in the spring.

Our Yard Is Full of Birds, by Anne Rockwell. Macmillan, 1992. A little boy describes the colorful variety of birds that come to his garden all year long. The detailed paintings by Lizzy Rockwell can help children looking at this book to watch for the birds in their own yards.

Nature Spy, by Shelley Rotner and Ken Kreisler. Macmillan, 1992. With handsome color photographs, this book examines a child's close-up view of nature, as she observes a seed pod, a bird's feathers, or a turtle's shell.

Insects and Crawly Creatures; and *Night-time Animals, Eye-Openers Series,* by Angela Royston. Aladdin, 1992. With color photographs, and text simple enough for youngsters to understand, these two books introduce children to insects such as the bumblebee, butterfly, and grasshopper, and nocturnal animals such as the bat, owl, and fox.

See How They Grow: Duck; and *See How They Grow: Frog,* written and edited by Angela Royston. Lodestar/Dutton, 1991. The first book shows the development of a duck from the egg stage to six weeks old; the second shows a frog's growth from the egg stage to over a year old. The books are illustrated with color photographs, and written in clear and simple language.

Let's Look at the Seasons: Springtime, by Ann Schweninger. Viking, 1993. The wonders of spring are explored in this appealing book, with information about indoor and outdoor gardens, spring flowers, and baby animals.

How To Be A Nature Detective (Let's-Read-And-Find-Out Science® Stage 1), by Millicent E. Selsam. HarperCollins, 1995. "Nature detectives find tracks and clues that answer these questions: What animal walked here? Where did it go? What did it do? What did it eat?" This book guides children in ways to understand animal tracks and what they tell us.

Where Does the Garbage Go? (Let's-Read-And-Find-Out Science® Stage 2), by Paul Showers. HarperTrophy, 1994. For children who are curious about where the garbage truck takes all that trash, and how it can be turned into energy, this book provides interesting answers.

A Tree Is Nice, by Janice May Udry. HarperTrophy edition, 1987. This winner of the Caldecott Medal sings the praises of trees: they fill up the sky, they are nice to hang a swing in, or to lean your hoe while you rest.

Egg! by A.J. Wood. Little, Brown, 1993. "A dozen eggs, what will they be? Unfold each page and you will see!" After reading the text, the reader may guess the name of the creature that hatches out of the egg. The opposite page unfolds to reveal the answer.

What's Alive? (Let's-Read-And-Find-Out Science® Stage 1), by Kathleen Weidner Zoehfeld. HarperCollins, 1995. For young children, it is not so simple to make the distinction between living and nonliving things. This book helps to point out the differences.

Section Eight
Trips
With
Your
Preschooler

Section Eight
Trips with
Your Preschooler

Introduction

Fascinating journeys can start right in your own neighborhood. To a young child, a stroll down the street to see a road under construction can be a thrilling experience. There are sights he has never seen before — like huge bulldozers moving piles of rocks, and sounds that are noisier than anything he's heard before — like a jackhammer drilling through the concrete.

The authors of this section tell how you can expand a young child's world with a trip a few blocks away to see a fire station, or across town to see a museum. They offer practical hints for planning your journey, and suggestions for enhancing the learning experience.

In addition you can peruse a list of children's museums to visit on your next vacation.

SECTION EIGHT
TRIPS WITH YOUR PRESCHOOLER

Chapter 40
Neighborhood "Trips" with Your Preschooler

Pegine Echevarria

Trips Provide New Learning Opportunities

My 2 $\frac{1}{2}$ year old and I often go on "trips" in our town. Down the block they are doing road construction, so one morning I decided to pack a breakfast picnic and go with my son and 7 month old daughter on a "trip." The picnic consisted of coffee in a thermos for me, juice for my son and some fruit. My son's reaction was unrestrained enthusiasm! "BULL-DOZER," he yelled. As we approached the workers he was awed by the machines. The men were on their coffee break and one of them had a conversation with Kenneth about the big wheels. He loved it. He got to stand in the bulldozer's shovel, touch the wheels, and throw some rocks. When we got home we called daddy at the office and had a whole excited conversation about his "trip." The rest of the day was filled with lots of imaginary play about the men and their machines.

Trips provide new learning opportunities

Preschoolers truly benefit from being taken on well planned and organized excursions by their parents and caretakers. Trips open up the world for children, encouraging the introduction of new vocabulary and providing a treasure of material for conversation and discussion. Whether you are in a small town or a large city, there are a variety of trip experiences that can be planned for toddler and preschooler. Feedback as to the value of these trips comes easily through the child's comments, new vocabulary and imaginary play, all of which usually incorporate some aspect of this new experience.

Strategies for planning a trip

Keep it Simple. The opportunities for day trips are endless. However, the most important thing to keep in mind when planning a trip for a preschooler or toddler is to keep it simple. A child in this age group is focusing on small bits of information. He looks at life piece by piece — not as a whole. Therefore, it is best to concentrate on one aspect of the trip. In my son's case, it was the bulldozer pushing the rocks. The cement truck will be seen another day.

Take Children's Needs into Consideration. In order to have an enriching experience, the trip must be well prepared. The needs of the child must be met. Children at this age get tired and need their rest. Trips should be planned around their nap times. The morning is the best time since the child is well rested and ready to take on the world. Preparing food for the trip is a consideration. Picnics are wonderful because they add excitement to the outing. Instead of eating at a table, picnics add a variation to the routine. The food should be kept simple, like sandwiches and crackers. Don't forget to pack some food for yourself. The length of the trip, including travel time, should be kept to a 2 1/2 hour maximum. Children of this age have a limited attention span and cannot concentrate on one subject for long periods of time. Children like to return to their toys, their room and their "space." For them, returning home reinforces the sense of self and provides them with a feeling of security.

Introduce Your Child to Community Workers. As parents we have the task of introducing society to our children. If we introduce our children to the various service organizations of our communities, we can help them formulate their opinions of the world in a nonthreatening manner. We introduce the police officer and his vehicle as helpers in our society and not as someone our children should fear. Speaking to him and seeing him up close, makes the police officer a "real person" and not just some intimidating official in a uniform.

Questions Help Your Child Verbalize the Experience. The use of questions during the trip helps the child verbalize what he is seeing, tasting, touching, hearing, and feeling. (See the suggested questions listed with each trip.) Questions should be geared to the child's comprehension level, for instance, "Is the truck's wheel bigger or smaller than you?"

Children with working parents can enjoy trips too
Working parents can plan trips for their small children and their caretakers or grandparents. If everything is prepared and planned by the parent beforehand, most caretakers would love to have the opportunity to accompany the child on these fun excursions. When mommy and daddy return home at the end of the day, the child will have a great deal to talk about before bedtime. The trip has not only enriched the child's life, but the parents' life as well. There is nothing as refreshing as viewing the world through the eyes of a child.

SOME SUGGESTIONS FOR NEIGHBORHOOD TRIPS:
FIRE HOUSE, PET STORE, CONSTRUCTION SITE, POLICE STATION

FIRE HOUSE

Preparation: A child carrying homemade cookies to a fire house is irresistible. Baking these cookies with your preschooler gets conversation going about the fire house and fire engines.

Suggested Questions: How do we put out fires? Why are the engines bright colors? What noise do fire engines make? When do the firemen turn on the siren?

Comments: **Call ahead.** At the station, point out to your preschooler the sliding bar and explain that the firefighters sleep at the station. Concentrate on the fire engine. Point out the ladder and hose and tell what they are used for. Show your child the special clothes that are worn. It's usually a big hit if they can sit inside the engine and ring the bell, but don't push it if your child doesn't want to.

Reinforcement Activities:
• Point out fire hydrants and their purpose. Play a game going home: *I see a fire hydrant; do you?*
• Have your child color a large white paper the color red. Using a black magic marker, draw the cab of the fire truck and a firefighters driving the truck. Wrap the paper around an empty milk container and place it on its side. Draw in the wheels with the marker. Using this fire truck, have your child describe your trip to the station to someone.

PET STORE

Preparation: Read one or two books on pets and baby animals. (See Resources, page 317.) Point out animals that people have as pets. If your family owns a pet, discuss with your child how you acquired the pet.

Suggested Questions: What colors are the animals? How many legs do they have? What sounds do they make? Where do they live? Who takes care of them? What do you do to take care of them? What kind of food do they eat? What do they feel like when you touch them?

Comments: Find the store that has the most extensive collection of animals or one that concentrates on one species (a parrot store or an aquarium store). Ask the staff if your child can pet the dog, cat or rabbit.

Reinforcement Activities: A great activity is to become the animals. Mommy and child (or daddy, grandpa, etc.) make believe they are the animals. "Hop like the bunny." "Walk like the turtle." "Run like the puppy." Have your child tell you what to be. When daddy or mommy come home, give them a fish kiss, puppy kiss or bunny nose kiss.

CONSTRUCTION SITE

Preparation: Using one of your child's toy trucks, point out the different types of trucks that are around. Talk about dump trucks, cement trucks, bulldozers and cranes.

Suggested Questions: What is the bulldozer doing? Why does the cement truck go around and around? What are they building? What does the crane do? What are the men doing? What tools do they use?

Comments: If there isn't a construction site nearby, there may be road work being done. Children love seeing big machines at work and they especially love to use their imaginations to make believe they are driving the heavy equipment, or that they themselves are the big machines.

Reinforcement Activities:
• At home, let your child dig in the sand or dirt as though he were the bulldozer.
• Give him water and flour, put it in a sealed clear (nonbreakable) jar and have him roll it like a cement truck to see the flour and water mix like cement.

POLICE STATION

Preparation: Discuss police officers and police cars. Talk about the ways to identify a police car. Discuss what policemen wear that lets you know that they are police officers. If your child has a toy police car you can use it to develop conversations about the police and their equipment.

Suggested Questions: How is the radio different from our radio at home? What do you think all the radio's buttons are for? Who sits in the back? Why? When does the policeman turn the flashing lights on? What color are they? What makes his car special? How does the siren sound?

Comments: **Call ahead.** Let the desk officer know you only want to see one aspect — the police car for example. Sometimes the officers get over-zealous and want to show everything and sometimes they are awfully busy. If they are busy, ask to see something even if it is just the belt an officer wears. Police officers also appreciate homemade cookies made for them, although a box of store bought donuts tied with a bow also makes their day.

Reinforcement Activities: Talk with your child about the trip—the things she liked best, things she didn't like, what was special. <u>Write it all down.</u> Have several pieces of white typewriter paper folded in half. Using a black marker, write on each page one short sentence that your child said about the day. Fasten the papers at the fold with paper fasteners so it becomes a book. Read it to your child. During the next couple of days, scan the magazines and cut out or have your child cut out pictures that go with the book. Let your child glue the pictures. She will love reading her book over and over. This activity should be done over a few days and should only last 5 to 10 minutes at the most. The key for the parent is preparation. The reward is priceless.

Chapter 41
The Wonders of
Children's Museums

John D. Allen

Children's Museums
can provide
the foundation
for lifelong curiosity.

A young child enters a Native American village and looks curiously around him. He steps through the low doorway of a rough shelter and peers into the gloom.

Right there in front of him are some brightly colored jars and bowls. He seizes one with delight. Suddenly another interesting item catches his eye and the jar slips from his hand and drops to the hard-packed earthen floor. But the jar does not break. It is not a real clay jar, and the child is not in a real Indian village but a replica of one that existed in 1900.

He is in the Discovery Center in Fresno, California where children can actually walk into Native American houses and experiment with toys, tools, and clothing.

Children's Museums provide exciting experiences

That's just one of the exciting kinds of experiences that your preschooler may be involved in when visiting a children's museum where interaction with the environment becomes a powerful learning tool. Rather than being told "don't touch" — children are invited to become directly involved with hands-on activities. This difference from traditional museums can be seen in the names children's museums use for their displays, such as Discovery Center and Science Playground.

Children like hands-on activities

Here is just a small sampling of the many activities preschoolers can experience in children's museums across the country. The Southeast Museum in Brewster, New York, has an exhibit where children can play with traditional toys and try on clothes from the 1800s. They can roll marbles through chutes and pinwheels, and spin whirligigs. Toys like these have fascinated children for hundreds of years, and they still have the power to entertain and instruct.

The Arizona Museum for Youth in Mesa , has an art center where preschoolers can express their creativity by making sculptures using soft materials. Or they can try their hand at "painting" a still life picture using Velcro®-backed art elements. When a preschooler produces a "painting" in this way he is filled with delight at his newly discovered talent.

Other exhibits at children's museums include man-made caves and animal dens which children can crawl into and pretend that they are wild animals. At the same time they are learning what an animal's home looks like. Some children's museums have huge play areas with houses, cars, trucks, boats, and planes. Here a child can use his imagination to be a driver, or a pilot, or to create his own village. Many children's museums also have a room full of large, brightly colored blocks and other building materials which preschoolers can use to build imaginative homes.

Preschoolers learn in many ways

They have active imaginations and naturally seek to learn through experimentation with the world around them. While you, as parents, can encourage learning through toys, books, and everyday experiences, children's museums can be another important resource. Here museum staff provide active, creative learning experiences in safe, stimulating environments.

At a children's museum children have control over what activities they wish to try. They use their imaginations, hands, and eyes to discover answers rather than having answers given to them: learning is active rather than passive. They learn to analyze patterns and colors, materials and shapes, similarities and differences, and to discover how things work. These experiences will help enrich future classroom learning and lay a foundation for lifelong curiosity.

Planning Your Museum Visit

John D. Allen

Plan Ahead

Find out what children's museums — or museums with children's programs—are available in your area, or in the city where you plan to vacation or visit (see listing on pages 310-316). Call any local museum and they should be able to give you information on children's museums in the area you are interested in. Also, your library should have a copy of the American Association of Museums' *Official Museum Directory* which lists children's museums. The book *Doing Children Museums* (see Resources, page 317) provides detailed information on children's museums.

Call or write to the museums in which you are interested and have them send you a brochure detailing their exhibits. Make sure that you find out what age group each program is intended for. Many children's museums have programs for several age groups so that they are of interest to both preschoolers and older children. (Don't forget that zoos, arboretums, and nature centers are also "museums" and that many have children's programs.)

Before the visit decide what you can realistically plan on seeing. Allow enough time because children who become absorbed in a discovery room may want to stay for awhile. Plan to visit the museum when you and your child are fresh; this will reduce the possibility that fatigue and restlessness will become a problem.

Enjoying the exhibits
When you are at the museum, let your preschooler move at his or her own pace. Do not feel that you have to see every exhibit, or even everything in one exhibit. Children not only learn differently, they have different interests and temperaments. One child will "jump" from one thing to another while another will stay engrossed in one activity for a long time. For instance, if a child loves things that move and make noise he might spend most of his visit with a bright mechanical toy and not even pay any attention to other toys. However, if you do see something your child might enjoy but hasn't noticed, point it out at an appropriate time.

Enhancing the learning experiences
You will have opportunities to help your preschooler learn from his museum visit. You can pick an interesting object and talk about its size, color, and shape. Then you can compare it to things that your child is already familiar with. If you are viewing an exhibit on animals, you can ask questions such as, "How big are they?" "Are they all one color?" and "Do they have smooth or furry coats?"

If your preschooler asks you a question, try to answer it with a question. This will help him think about it, and make him feel good if he can come up with the answer by himself. For example, if he wants to know why an Indian needs to wear an animal skin, you can ask him first why anyone wears a coat, and then why an Indian might need to worry about getting cold.

After the visit

The museum visit is a valuable opportunity to learn more about your preschooler's interests. Surrounded by the many exciting experiences found in a discovery center, children will focus on only those things which interest them most. By watching your child you will be able to decide what kind of toys and books you should buy. Many children's museums have well stocked gift shops with products that relate directly to the exhibits.

For example, if your preschooler shows an unexpected interest in sculpting, you'll want to add modeling clay to your shopping list. Or, if he is fascinated by the dinosaur exhibit, children's books on this subject will feed his curiosity. Interested in old-fashioned clothes? Use dress-ups at home for pretending. A blanket spread over the dining room table will make a suitable "animal den" for your imaginative youngster.

Future visits

Do not think of the museum trip as just a onetime visit. Regular visits can provide your preschooler with time to become accustomed to a new environment and gradually to build new skills. It is worthwhile to explore the museum every few months at least. Because your child's fine motor skills (use of the muscles in the fingers), reasoning skills, and perceptions will have changed in that time, another visit will reveal whole new areas to explore.

Children's Museums You can Visit on Your Next Trip

This list of children's museums is fairly comprehensive and up to date. However, because museums have special hours and days that they are open, you should contact them in advance. Your local library or museum will be able to supply addresses and telephone numbers. The children's museums will even let you know what exhibits and special programs will be available on the dates that you plan to be there.

Alabama

Birmingham: The Discovery Place of Birmingham
Gadsden: Center for Cultural Arts
Mobile: Exploreum
Montgomery: Montgomery Art Museum & Children's Museum "Artworks"
Tuscaloosa: Children's Hands-on Museum

Arizona
Mesa: Arizona Museum for Youth
Tucson: Tucson Children's Museum

California
Bakersfield: Lori Brock Children's Museum
Chula Vista: Chula Vista Nature Interpretive Center
Fresno: The Discovery Center
Hayward: Sulphur Creek Nature Center
La Habra: Children's Museum at La Habra
La Jolla: The Children's Museum of San Diego
Los Angeles:
    Gulliver's City Children's Museum
    The Los Angeles Children's Museum
Palo Alto: Palo Alto Junior Museum
Pasadena: Kidspace, A Participatory Museum
Penn Valley: Museum of Ancient & Modern Art
Rancho Mirage: Children's Museum of the Desert
Roseville: Kaleidoscope Discovery Center & Bev Bos Discovery School
Sacramento: Sacramento Science Center
San Francisco:
    Randall Museum
    The Exploratorium
San Jose:
    Children's Discovery Museum of San Jose
    Youth Science Institute, Alum Rock Discovery Center
San Mateo: Coyote Point Museum for Environmental Education
Saratoga: Youth Science Institute,
        Sanborn Discovery Center
Sausalito: Bay Area Discovery Museum
Walnut Creek: The Lindsay Museum

Colorado
Denver:
    Children's Museum of Denver
    Hall of Life

Connecticut
Manchester: Lutz Children's Museum
New Britain: New Britain Youth Museum
Norwalk: The Maritime Center at Norwalk

District of Columbia, Washington:
Capital Children's Museum
Museum of the National Guard
Rock Creek Nature Center
The Children's Museum of Washington

Florida
Cocoa: Brevard Museum
Delray Beach: Cornell Museum at Old School Square
Melbourne: Space Coast Science Center
Miami: Miami Youth Museum
Panama City: The Junior Museum of Bay County
Plantation: Young at Art Children's Museum
Sanibel: The Shell Museum & Educational Foundation

Georgia
Marietta: Cobb County Youth Museum

Hawaii
Honolulu: Hawaii Children's Museum of Arts, Culture, Science & Technology

Iowa
Bettendorf: The Children's Museum
Cedar Rapids: Science Station

Illinois
Alton: Alton Museum of History and Art
Chicago:
    Balzekas Museum of Lithuanian Culture
    Chicago Children's Museum
    Kaminski Polish-American Archives
    Spertus Museum
Morton Grove: The Art and History Association
Wilmette: Kohl Children's Museum

Indiana
Bloomington: Bloomington Youth Garden-Nature Center
Indianapolis: The Children's Museum
Mishawaka: Hannah Lindahl Children's Museum
Muncie: Muncie Children's Museum

Kansas
Kansas City: The Children's Museum of Kansas City
McPherson: McPherson Museum

Kentucky
Lexington:
    Lexington Children's Museum
    The Living Arts and Science Center
Louisville: The Louisville Visual Art Association/Main Library

Louisiana

Baton Rouge: Louisiana Arts and Science Center
Lake Charles: Children's Museum of Lake Charles
New Orleans: Louisiana Children's Museum
Shreveport:
    Grindstone Bluff Museum & Environmental Education Center
    Stoner Arts Center

Maine

Portland: Children's Museum of Maine

Maryland

Baltimore: 1840 House
Brooklandville: Cloisters Children's Museum
Galesville: Ann Arundel Natural Science Museum

Massachusetts

Acton: The Discovery Museums
Boston: The Children's Museum
Holyoke: Children's Museum at Holyoke
North Easton: The Children's Museum in Easton
Somerville: The Somerville Museum
South Dartmouth: Children's Museum in Dartmouth

Michigan

Ann Arbor: The Ann Arbor Hands-on Museum
Battle Creek: Kingman Museum of Natural History
Detroit:
    Children's Museum
    Youth Heritage House
Middlevale: Historic Bowens Mill
Midland: Midland County Historical Society

Minnesota

Duluth: A. M. Chisholm Museum
St Paul: The Children's Museum

Missouri

Chesterfield: River Hills Visitor Center
Hermann: Historic Hermann Museum
Independence: 1859 Jail Museum & Marshal's Home
Kansas City:
    Kaleidoscope
    The Kansas City Museum
Mansfield: Laura Ingalls Wilder-Rose Wilder Lane Museum & Home
Springfield: Medical Museum Health Education Center
St. Louis:
    Eugene Field House and Toy Museum
    The Magic House

Montana
St. Ignatius: Flathead Indian Museum

Nebraska
Kearney: Kearney Area Children's Museum
Omaha: Omaha Children's Museum

Nevada
Las Vegas:
    Las Vegas Art Museum
    Lied Discovery Children's Museum

New Hampshire
Bethlehem: Crossroads of America
Nashua: The Nashua Center of the Arts
Portsmouth: The Children's Museum of Portsmouth

New Jersey
Cherry Hill: Garden State Discovery Museum
Lincroft: Monmouth Museum
Newark: The Newark Museum
Paramus: The New Jersey Children's Museum
Rutherford: Meadowlands Museum
Short Hills: Cora Hartshorn Arboretum
Trenton: New Jersey State Museum

New Mexico
Deming: Deming Luma Mimbres Museum
Farmington: Farmington Museum
Santa Fe: Santa Fe Children's Museum

New York
Auburn: Cayuga County Agricultural Museum
Brewster: Southeast Museum
Garden City: Long Island Children's Museum
New York City:
    Bronx:
        Lehman College Art Gallery
        North Wind Undersea Institute
    Brooklyn: The Brooklyn Children's Museum
    Manhattan:
        Children's Museum of Manhattan
        Metropolitan Museum of Art
    Staten Island: Staten Island Children's Museum
Painted Post: Erwin Museum
Scotia: Scotia-Glenville Children's Museum
Troy: The Junior Museum
Utica: Children's Museum of History, Natural History and Science at Utica
Watertown: Sci-Tech Center of Northern N.Y.

North Carolina
Charlotte: Nature Museum
Rocky Mount: Rocky Mount Children's Museum

Ohio
Canton: The McKinley - National Memorial;
Discover World; Museum of History, Science & Industry
Cleveland: Cleveland Children's Museum
Oberlin: Little Red Schoolhouse

Oklahoma
Bartlesville: Bartlesville Museum in the Price Tower

Oregon
Ashland: Pacific Institute of Natural Sciences
Dalles: The Wonder Works, A Children's Museum
Medford: Southern Oregon Historical Society
Portland: Children's Museum
Salem: The Gilbert House Children's Museum

Pennsylvania
Lancaster: Hands-on House, Children's Museum of Lancaster
Philadelphia: Please Touch Museum
Pittsburgh: Pittsburgh Children's Museum
Stroudsburg: Quiet Valley Living Historical Farm
Williamsport: Peter J. McGovern Little League Baseball Museum

Rhode Island
Pawtucket: Children's Museum of Rhode Island

South Dakota
Geddes: Geddes Historic District

Tennessee
Johnson City: Hands on! Regional Museum
Kingsport: Netherland Inn House Museum & Boatyard Complex
Knoxville: East Tennessee Discovery Center
Memphis: The Children's Museum of Memphis
Oak Ridge: Children's Museum of Oak Ridge

Texas
Archer: Archer County Museum
Austin: Austin Children's Museum
Cuero: Dewitt County Historical Museum
Fredericksburg: Children's Discovery Center
Henderson: The Depot Museum

Texas *(continued)*
Houston
Houston Fire Museum
The Children's Museum of Houston
Laredo: Laredo Children's Museum
Midland: Museum of the Southwest

Utah
Salt Lake City: The Children's Museum of Utah

Vermont
Essex Junction: Discovery Museum

Virginia
Charlottesville:
Children's Museum
The Virginia Discovery Museum
Chesapeake: Chesapeake Planetarium
Portsmouth: Portsmouth Children's Museum
Richmond: Richmond Children's Museum

Washington
Eatonville: Pioneer Farm Museum
Puyallup: Paul H. Karshner Memorial Museum
Seattle:
Pacific Arts Center
The Children's Museum

Washington, D.C. (see District of Columbia)

West Virginia
Charleston: Sunrise Museums, Inc.

Wisconsin
Delavan: Clown Hall of Fame & Research Center
Madison: Madison Children's Museum
Ripon: Ripon Historical Society
Wausau: Leigh Yawkey Woodson Art Museum

Resources for Section Eight:
Trips with Your Preschooler

FOR ADULTS

The American Association of Museum's Official Directory of Museums. National Register Publishing Company. This is the most complete guide to American museums and is indexed by subject and location. It can be found in the reference section of most large libraries.

Doing Children's Museums: A Guide to 265 Hands-on-Museums, 2nd, rev. ed., by Joanne Cleaver. Williamson Publishing, 1992. An excellent guide to all aspects of visiting a children's museum with your child. Includes a directory of museums listed by state with indexes of museums by subject matter, special services, etc.

Open the Door Let's Explore More! Field Trips of discovery for Young Children, by Rhoda Redleaf. Redleaf Press, 1996. This book is filled with activities to do before, during, and after field trips to reinforce learning while having fun.

Where's The Me In Museums: Going to Museums with Children, by Mildred Waterfall and Sarah Grusin. Vandamere Press, 1988. The first chapter of this brief but comprehensive guide explains how to make children and yourself comfortable in the museum setting. The following chapters offer useful advice on visiting art, science, history, and children's museums.

How to Take Great Trips with Your Kids, by Sanford and Joan Portnoy. The Harvard Common Press, 535 Albany Street, Boston, MA 02118, 1984. This book offers the basics of long and short distance travel — a must to read before traveling with children.

FOR CHILDREN

The Children's Play Museum, by P. Adams. Child's Play International, Ltd., 1979. Children learn how history museums contain objects which were once used in everyday life. Once page shows the objects on display and the next shows them in use.

My Visit to the Dinosaurs, by Aliki. Thomas Y. Crowell, 1985. A little boy goes to a museum and sees the dinosaur skeletons. The descriptions of various types of dinosaurs are written so that young children can understand.

Machines at Work, by Byron Barton. Crowell, 1987. A variety of big machines are pictured in bright, clear colors, along with construction workers and their tools in this appealing book.

Visiting the Art Museum, by Laurene Krasny Brown and Marc Brown. Dutton, 1986. A mother and father take their three children to an art museum. Even their oldest boy, who wanted to stay home to watch television, finds that museums are fun and have something for everyone. Excellent tour of a museum for all ages.

Lost in the Museum, by Miriam Cohen. Dell, 1983. On a school field trip to the museum, Danny and Jimmy wander off to see the dinosaur and soon they are completely lost in the huge building. After many exciting adventures they find their way back to their class.

General Store, by Rachel Field. Greenwillow, 1988. Originally written in 1926, this book was reissued with new illustrations by Nancy Winslow Parker. It tells of a little girl who wants to own a general store one day, and dreams of all the items she will sell.

Dinosaurs, Dragonflies & Diamonds, All About Natural History Museums, by Gail Gibbons. Four Winds Press, Macmillan, 1988. This book tells about natural history museums in clear and simple language, with information on what you might find there, what goes on behind the scenes, and how a new exhibit is made.

Once Around the Block, by Kevin Henkes. Greenwillow, 1987. Annie is bored waiting for Papa to come home from work, so her mother suggests a walk around the block. Annie talks with several neighbors, meets the mailman, and returns home happily to find Papa waiting for her.

Sam Goes Trucking, by Henry Horenstein. Houghton Mifflin, 1989. Color photographs illustrate a nonfiction book about Sam's day with his trucker father.

Katie's Picture Show, by James Mayhew. Bantam Books, 1989. Katie visits an art museum. This book teaches the most elementary observations that can be made of painting, such as the subject, the colors, etc.

Whose Hat? by Margaret Miller. Greenwillow, 1988. This book presents hats of many different occupations, such as fire fighter, police officer, nurse, and construction worker. Children will enjoy the game of guessing whose hat is in the color photograph. When they turn the page, they will find the answer.

Help For Mr. Peale, by Barbara Morrow. Macmillan, 1990. This book is based on a true story. In 1794 the collection of stuffed birds and beasts as well as paintings were to be moved from the home of Charles Willson Peale to a museum in Philadelphia. But how were they all to be moved? Mr. Peale's son Rubens saves the day with his creative solution to the problem.

Lets's Get a Puppy, by Caroline Nessm. HarperFestival, 1994. A little boy wants a dog for his birthday, and the whole family offers advice about the kind of puppy to buy. When they get to the pet shop a puppy chooses him.

William the Vehicle King, by Laura P. Newton. Bradbury, 1987. William brings out all of his cars, trucks, and blocks, to construct a superhighway on his rug.

Curious George and the Dinosaur, by Margret Rey and Alan J. Shalleck. Houghton Mifflin, 1989. The mischievous chimp George, and his friend Jimmy visit a museum. George has a delightful time in an exhibit, but his activities horrify the museum director.

Come to Town, by Anne Rockwell. Crowell, 1987. With simple text this book describes the bear family's trip to town to visit the school, supermarket, library, and office building, and details what is happening in each place with colorful illustrations.

The Pop-Up Book of Big Trucks, by Peter Seymour. Little, Brown, 1989. In addition to learning interesting facts about many kinds of trucks, such as: dump trucks, concrete mixers, and fire engines, you can actually pull a tab to see the load of sand pour out, turn a wheel to see the concrete flow down the chute, and raise and extend the aerial ladder on the fire truck!

Grover and the Everything in the Whole Wide World Museum, by Norman Stiles and David Wilcox. Children's Television Workshop, Random House, 1974. Grover goes to the museum but finds he must go outdoors to find everything in the world.

Where Are You, Ernest and Celestine? by Cabrielle Vincent. Greenwillow, 1986. Ernest and Celestine become separated at the museum. But after franticly searching for each other, they have a happy reunion.

Section Nine
School

Section Nine
School

Introduction

On the first day of kindergarten, I found a friend.

Many children do have a happy experience on the first day of school. But there are youngsters who have difficulty with this new adventure, and it helps to have some preparation.

The chapters in this section suggest ways to familiarize young children with the schoolroom and school routine. The authors discuss how school can be an enriching experience for all children, including those with handicaps.

One chapter explains how teachers and parents have much to learn from each other, and much to give to each other. When they work together closely, the children are the beneficiaries.

Chapter 42
Preparing for a
School Experience

Judy Keshner

*Can you remember
how you felt
on your
first day of school?*

"Starting school!"... Such emotions come to mind at these words; such complex feelings.

Can you remember how you felt on your first day of school? Were you excited? Scared? Upset? Nervous? Happy? Did you want to go or did you want to stay at home? Was the school a familiar place or an unknown one?

Whether your child is starting preschool or kindergarten, your attitude will have an effect upon his feelings about starting school. If you think that this new experience will be a happy and positive one, your child will be more likely to think so, too.

Preparing your child for school

Getting there:
 • *Walking to school on a nice day is a good experience to share.* Point out where the crossings are, count the number of blocks you walk, notice the world around you.

 • *If your child will be taking a bus to school, find out the bus route and follow that.* This routine, if done often, will ease your child's concerns about where home is in relation to school. It's very helpful for children to be able to visualize relationships and distances between two places.

 • *Visit the school playground, preferably when the children are at play.* Talk about how this area will be part of the daily activities once school begins.

 • *Visit the room that your child will be in and let her see all the exciting, fun things that she will soon be able to play with.* (Make a note about all the different play areas, so that you both can talk about them at home.)

Communicating school routine to your child
 • *If she's entering kindergarten the schools most likely will have a program set up to orient children and parents to the school and its policies.* These orientations usually take place during the spring before a child will enter kindergarten, and might consist of a parent meeting or "tea," a visit to the school or classroom for the child, and a meeting with school personnel who will be involved with your child in some way. There may be several visits or just one.

 • *If your child will attend a preschool, you should learn all about the school's routine:* hours for arrival and going home, activities, snack time, storytime, outdoor play, etc.

Communicate the following day's routine the night before, so that your child knows what to expect, especially when there is a change in the routine: holidays, field trips, etc.

Establishing a home routine

• *Several weeks before school starts establish a routine that will work for your family during the school year.* Experiment with bedtimes, getting up times, breakfast, and getting dressed routines, etc. See how long each takes and try to find a routine that's relatively stress free and smooth.

A child who awakens with a smile on his face will be much easier to deal with than one who must be awakened to get ready for school. How long does it take to get out of bed, washed, dressed, and have breakfast? Would an earlier bedtime make the morning routine smoother? Take time to prepare for the first day of school.

Preparing for separation

• *If you and your child have a problem separating, take time to get used to being apart.* Start slowly, for short periods of time, and gradually lengthen the time away from each other to equal the length of the school day. Always show your child when you will return on the clock, and be sure to be on time. Continue to do this when school begins. Always be where you said you would be.

Your child will be sensitive to how you feel about separation. If you are worried about leaving him, discuss your feelings with the director of the school, or your child's teacher beforehand, to seek reassurance. If your youngster is feeling anxious or upset, let him know you understand that saying good-bye may be difficult.

Expect there to be some separation anxiety even in the best of relationships. And it might continue even if your child loves school, especially when the routine is changed due to weekends, holidays, and vacations.

Communicating with the teacher

• *Think about information you want to share with the teacher to help her get to know your child.* Write this down along with any concerns you have and address these points when school begins. You will find this helpful when meeting with the teacher.

After your child starts school

(You can also use these suggested activities <u>before</u> your child starts school)
• *Begin to spend some time alone with your child each day or evening.* Make this quality time, something he can count on, no matter how busy you are.

Continue to have at least ten private minutes with your child after school starts. That way, no matter how many children you have or how rushed your day is, this child will know that "his time" with you will be there. It's a perfect time for sharing the day's events, problems, excitements. Storytime, and an overview of the next day, are nice, relaxed ways to end the child's day. And Mommy's (or Daddy's) lap is a great place to do all this!

• *Read to your child every night.* Pick books that tell about experiences and adventures with a little anxiety or problem solving that end with the child triumphant, or the character conquering fear. Anything that has to do with confronting a difficult situation and surviving it will help with the excitement/nervousness that starting school brings. (See Resources, page 337.)

• *If you have a chalkboard or large chart paper, you could write a message each night that your child will find when he wakes up.* (Even if you have to read the entire message to him — he'll be pleased that the message was "just for him.") Using words and pictures, the message could say, "Good Morning, Joey. Today is a (beautiful, rainy, cloudy) day. We are going to (school, grandma's house) today. What would you like for lunch? Love Mommy." After a while, you may be finding written answers and a two-way conversation in print will begin. This encourages writing skills and language development. Even the youngest child can communicate using scribble writing. Eventually he may recognize those words that you use every day in your message.

• *Continuing an awareness of language and print, point out signs in the street, labels on food in the supermarket.* Make all trips an adventure. Food in the shopping cart can be sorted by sizes, shapes, cans, boxes, those that need to be refrigerated and those that don't, colors, types of food, non edible items, letters on labels, etc. Just use your imagination. The variety is endless. Ask your child for sorting ideas. Get his creative juices flowing.

• *When you go to the pool, beach, park, or playground, ask your child what he thinks might be found there.* After experiencing the outing, summarize what was done, how it felt. Compare this to the original conversation. "Did we see what we thought we'd see? Were there any surprises? Where else can we go to see similar things? What did you like best? What did you like least?" Get your child used to conversations involving critical thinking. "What if..., how else..., another way to..." are some beginning phrases to stimulate ideas.

• *Encourage imaginative statements and scenarios. Write fairy tales together and illustrate them.* Change the endings of books that you read together. Become authors and illustrators. Your child can dictate a story for you to write and he can then draw the pictures to go with the words. *(Don't expect the artwork of preschoolers to represent real people and objects.)* Some young children prefer drawing first and then adding the words. You can put together a writer's box or briefcase filled with different sizes and colors of paper, crayons, pencils, markers, pens, scotch tape, and safe, child-sized scissors that your child can use whenever he feels like writing, drawing, or both. Help him write letters to friends and relatives. He'll be thrilled when he receives answers.

All of these activities help a child to understand the connection between language and print. They foster reading skills and are great fun!

Try not to "over-program" after-school activities
After-school activities such as sports and performing arts have their place as long as they don't take up too much of children's free time. Don't overlook the importance of leaving your child enough time for creative play and socialization with friends outside of the school.

Planning in advance should make your child's entry into school as smooth and stress free as possible for the entire family. Further participation throughout his school years will allow everyone to enjoy this wonderful experience.

Chapter 43
A Special Child
in the Preschool

Elizabeth Kuhlman

*An enriching experience
for all children.*

Because he was born with cerebral palsy, Scott cannot stand alone or walk. He uses a wheel chair. He has been mainstreamed into a class of four year olds who are not handicapped. Today his teacher has placed him on the floor in the middle of the block area. He is building a city. He cannot move to get blocks off the shelf himself, so he enlists the help of other children. As he talks about his city, he captures their imagination. Soon, every child in the class is engaged in city building, and every wooden block, LEGO®, and construction set in the room is incorporated.

Softly, the teacher begins to sing a familiar spiritual:
"Oh, what a beautiful city..."
The children join in,
"Oh, what a beautiful city...
Oh, what a beautiful city...
Twelve gates into the city...
Hallelujah!"

When handicapped children are mainstreamed into regular preschool classes with thoughtfulness, sensitivity and careful planning, all involved — children, teachers, and parents find their lives enriched.

However, the decision to mainstream should raise questions in the minds of parents. These questions are important to you as a parent, whether or not your child has a handicap.

Questions that all parents should ask:
Will my child be safe? Space and activities in any preschool classroom must reflect careful planning for safety for all children. If a child with a vision, hearing, or mobility problem is to participate in the program, the staff should be able to explain to you what special plans they have made to insure that child's safety. Every program should have an emergency first aid plan. If a child has a health problem such as epilepsy or heart disease, special first aid procedures must be posted for that child. Also, that child must be included in the plan for the safe evacuation of the building in the event of fire or other such emergency. Special procedures must be practiced to insure that a child with hearing, vision, mobility or language problems gets out of the building safely.

How will my child adjust to this new experience? Going to preschool for the first time creates some anxiety in every child and every parent. A good preschool program plans sensitively for the first days of all children, creating an atmosphere of warm acceptance, and allowing a gradual, comfortable separation between parent and child. This is particularly important for a child with special problems.

Will my child be recognized and treated as an individual with individual talents and needs? A preschool classroom should offer a variety of activities and allow children to make choices that suit their particular styles and developmental levels. A good preschool teacher directs herself to the various styles, skills and needs of each child in a group, even when all children are doing the same thing (listening to a story, for example).

Handicapped children share with all children the ability to explore and learn from a preschool environment which is both stimulating and orderly. They also need happy, satisfying relationships with people outside their families. The staff of a preschool program which includes a handicapped child should be able to explain how they will plan activities to accommodate the individual developmental strengths and needs of each child in the program.

Will our children get along with each other? One of the most important things that happens in preschool is that children learn how to make friends. In a preschool class where handicapped children are successfully mainstreamed, friendships flourish despite marked individual differences. In a program where teachers set an example of warmth and acceptance children show an amazingly creative ability to work around differences which might create barriers to adults: often they teach staff and parents a thing or two about tolerance and adaptability.

Chapter 44
What Preschool Teachers and Parents can Learn from Each Other

Bette Simons

*...sharing the caring
of young children
is a learning experience
for all the adults
who are involved...*

When it's time for children to leave preschool for grade school there are often tears in the eyes of both parents and teachers.

In the office, parents may leave books inscribed with their child's name. In the yard, a tree may get planted. Mothers and fathers are grateful for what their children have learned and they, the parents, have learned things as well.

Teachers and directors value the notes of thanks parents leave them. The children who are leaving may talk eagerly of the summer camp they will attend or the kindergarten they are headed for. But the teachers may remember that they changed diapers on this child, and held that one crying during the initial entrance into the center. They may remember they helped another child through a phase of biting or empathized with a parent through a family crisis. Teachers are grateful for having been a part of the children's lives. They have learned things from families that will enrich their teaching for years to come.

What is it that parents and teachers might have learned from each other? How does it happen that sharing the caring of young children is a learning experience for all the adults who are involved?

WHAT PARENTS CAN LEARN FROM PRESCHOOL TEACHERS

Learning to help their child who is starting school
As soon as a child is enrolled in a preschool a parent begins to learn many things from a teacher. One parent may worry, "Will this teacher understand how bad I feel leaving my child?" Another parent may think, but not say out loud, "Have I chosen the right place, even though I must get child care quickly for that new job I will start?"

Experienced teachers inform parents right away about the importance of helping their child adjust to their new environment before leaving them. Teachers know that parents must tell children when they do leave so as not to create the anxiety that comes if a parent disappears when the child is busy playing. Parents also learn that once the child has adjusted, the longer a good-bye, the greater the tension. When parents learn these things, they soon find children eager to go to school.

Learning what to do when problems arise
Mothers and fathers will find there are periods of time when children complain: "I don't want to go to school," or "I don't have any friends." These times can be very worrisome. When the parent lets the teacher know of these concerns, a conference may be called for to talk things over. The

teacher, based on her vast experience, can assess the situation. If the preschooler is having a difficult time at school, might it be due to changes at home?

If the child seems to be socializing well and having a normal amount of successes and disappointments, the teacher can recommend that the mother or father observe the child during the day's routine. This helps the parent understand that children have ups and downs in their relationships at school, and that they learn and grow from these experiences. The teacher might also suggest that a parent's attitude should be that of a good listener. This helps children figure out their own problems. Every crisis at home or school can make a child a little stronger.

Learning about child growth and development

A child is the most precious thing a parent has. Parents need to be reassured when the child is having a period of growth that is bumpy. A preschool teacher may have had extensive experience with one age group — such as teaching two year olds for many years. A mother may only have one child and find the behavior of a two year old startling. If a child bites or gets bitten, or won't share toys, parents can feel upset. Teachers can reassure them by saying, "In my experience, I have found that children this age behave this way. He'll learn. I'll help him."

Teachers often see behaviors that seem out of the "normal" range. They can describe to parents the child's behavior and, if they agree that it's necessary, make recommendations for testing. Developmental delays or disabilities usually profit from early intervention. There are speech teachers, neurological pediatricians, and professionals that test children.

Learning about special children
Preschool teachers can teach adults as well as the children to have a place in their hearts for exceptional children. When children are cared for in a group, parents may often worry that their child is not getting enough attention, so children with disabilities, children with behavior problems, children who do not accept limits easily and children with little impulse control, often seem to take too much of a teacher's time. Teachers are obligated by state and federal laws to try to make space for challenging children.

Learning how to manage behavior
A teacher shows parents that she doesn't need clowns, balloons or tricks to manage the behavior of children. Instead she has information and ideas up her sleeve. While many parents find that the event of giving a birthday party is stressful, watching a teacher work daily with as many as 12 children is instructional. She moves the group with fantasy: "Lets go outside like crickets." She sings directions during potentially stressful times, "Whistle while you work, clean up time has come." She alternates periods of activity with periods of quiet. She holds the attention of a group with something interesting, like a bunch of worms from the garden, or a puppet who whispers things to her.

Teachers are good models for discipline. Nothing makes children as anxious as an environment that is not predictable. Teachers demonstrate how the cautious two year old becomes the confident five year old by her consistency in being there for the children, having a set schedule and routine, and adhering to school rules. "No hitting," means a sand shovel will be removed from the child who hits. Parents who give many warnings but have a hard time following through, can learn by watching a good preschool teacher be consistent about what will happen during the day and what is expected of children.

Learning about preschool philosophies
Preschool philosophies vary, some stressing early academics, others current early childhood educational theories: letting children learn through active play, giving them adequate space, developmentally appropriate materials and activities, and providing warm interpersonal relationships between children and teachers.

A parent may be concerned that his child will not do well in grade school because the focus is on learning through play — and not on academics. This is the time when the teacher can explain the reasons for the preschool's educational philosophy.

WHAT PRESCHOOL TEACHERS CAN LEARN FROM PARENTS

Children come from families of differing economic levels and cultural backgrounds. Teachers can learn how different families live in different circumstances. During a home visit when a teacher observes the child's life style, she better understands the behavior of the child. She may also see sibling relationships that make it clear why a child behaves a certain way in school.

When teachers observe interactions between parent and child they invariably learn something useful. One parent may often stroke or hug a child affectionately; another uses words more. This gives a teacher a clue as to how to help a child who is tired or under stress. One child may need a back rubbed, another may need to hear, " Your mother is having her lunch now and thinking about what you are doing."

During conferences a parent can explain the stresses in the household or tell about abilities the child has that the preschool doesn't know about.

Learning to deal with parents' feelings

Teachers who are used to children's tears and know how to comfort, might also watch the faces of mothers or fathers who are feeling keenly the hard task the family has of separating to go to preschool. Teachers' natural empathy can extend to parents as well as children.

"That seems very worrisome to you..." is needed by the parent. Empathy is the best way to show parents the preschool understands that a parent has entrusted what is most precious in the world to the teachers there. Getting skillful at helping adults gives preschool teachers inner strengths.

Learning to use parents as resources

Parents can be a source of learning to schools in may ways. A father who is in the navy can come in his white dress uniform. He is sure to inspire marching to "Anchors Away" or other martial music the next day. A mother who is a dentist can show the children how to brush and floss. A dad may be a musician who plays the guitar for a school sing. A mother who is an experienced gardener can help a teacher who isn't. The mother shows how to plant bean seeds and tells the teacher when to water. Every parent who shares a skill with the class helps the teacher use this information in the future.

Parents enrich teachers' knowledge in deeper ways when they show teachers something about a culture the teacher is unfamiliar with: a parent who can explain the importance of the Kwanzaa festival, or the meaning of the Purim holiday, or who introduces Filipino food for the graduating kindergarten.

Inviting parents to share their skills, their cultural ways, special holidays, or information about the work they do makes teaching enjoyable as well as informative. When teachers and parents share the caring they learn together for the benefit of all children. It does truly take a community to raise a child.

Resources for Section Nine: School

FOR ADULTS

Learning to Say Goodbye: Starting School and Other Early Childhood Separations, by Nancy Balaban, Ed.D. Plume/New American Library, 1987. The author, an early childhood specialist, offers wise advice and proven strategies that turn goodbyes into good growth experiences for both the child and parent.

Good Day Bad Day: The Child's Experience of Child Care, by Lyda Beardsley. Teachers College Press, 1990. Writing about two fictional child care programs, the author uses her experiences as an early childhood consultant and researcher to compare the child's experience in a superior program to one in a low-quality center.

Sharing the Caring: How to Find the Right Child Care and Make It Work for You and Your Child, by Amy Laura Dombro and Patty Bryan. Simon & Schuster, 1991. A valuable resource for parents, offering practical advice about how they can work effectively with caregivers to ensure a positive experience for their child. Amy Dombro is also an author of a chapter in this book.

Starting School: A Parent's Guide to the Kindergarten Year, by Judy Keshner. Modern Learning Press/Programs for Education, 1992. The author provides parents with helpful sugggestions to prepare their children for a happy, successful school experience. She also has contributed a chapter in this book.

Resources for Early Childhood: A Handbook, edited by Hannah Nuba, Michael Searson, & Deborah Lovitky Sheiman. Garland, 1994. This comprehensive guide to early childhood contains informative essays about all aspects of child development, along with annotated resource lists helpful to parents and educators.

Scenes from Day Care: How Teachers Teach and What Children Learn, by Elizabeth Balliett Platt. Teachers College Press, 1991. The author records in detail the small events that happen in day care in order to focus on the question of what kinds of experiences should occur in quality day care.

Two to Four from 9 to 5, by Joan Roemer as told to Barbara Austin. Harper & Row, 1989. A book about the adventures of a daycare provider that reads like a novel. You will find it difficult to put down.

Teacher/Parent Communication: Working Toward Better Understanding, by Elizabeth J. Webster and Louise M. Ward. Preschool Publications (1-800-726-1708), 1992. The authors are specialists in the field of parent communication. In this guide (in the series *Early Childhood Fundamentals*) they discuss how parents and teachers are important to each other and how they can communicate more effectively.

Working with Parents of Young Children with Disabilities, by Elizabeth J. Webster and Louise M. Ward. *Early Childhood Intervention Series.* Singular Publishing, 1993. Webster and Ward, who contributed to several chapters in this book, give the reader the benefit of their considerable background in the field of counseling and psychology. They offer many examples of parents' own words and stories to guide professionals in their work.

Behind the Playdough Curtain: A Year in My Life as a Preschool Teacher, by Patti Greenberg Wollman. Charles Scribner's Sons, 1994. An engaging story of a dedicated preschool teacher and the children and families that her life touches.

FOR CHILDREN

This Is the Way We Go to School, by Edith Baer. Scholastic, 1990. A book in rhyme about the different means of transportation children use around the world to get to school.

Sue Lee Starts School, by Dr. Lawrence Balter. Barron's, 1991. One of the series of *Stepping Stone Stories,* written to help young children understand their feelings, this book discusses how Sue Lee and her mother prepare for kindergarten — and what happens there on the first day. A special page for parents follows the story.

The Witch Goes to School, by Norman Bridwell. Scholastic/Cartwheel, 1992. When your next-door neighbor is a witch and you are late for school, you might be as lucky as the children in this story and get a ride to school on a broomstick. The witch is invited to stay in the classroom for the day, with imaginative, funny, positive results.

When Daddy Came to School, by Julie Brillhart. Albert Whitman, 1995. A little boy tells in rhyme about the wonderful time he had on his third birthday — when Daddy came to spend the day at his preschool.

Someone Special, Just Like You, by Tricia Brown. H. Holt, 1984. A photo book which emphasizes that all children, in spite of disabilities, have the same kinds of feelings.

The Best Teacher in the World, by Bernice Chardiet and Grace Maccarone. Scholastic, 1990. Bunny is thrilled to be chosen by her teacher, Ms. Darcy, to take a note to Mrs. Walker. But the little girl gets lost on the way to Mrs. Walker's room. She feels just terrible, but Ms. Darcy, the best teacher in the world, teaches her that it's all right to ask questions when there's something you don't know.

The New Teacher, by Miriam Cohen. Aladdin edition, 1989. Why did their teacher need a baby, when she had the whole first grade! But she left, and today there was going to be a new teacher. The children in the playground wonder what she'll be like, and Jim makes up mean riddles about her. Then they meet her, and by the time the morning is over... they all know she is going to be just fine.

We Play, by Phyllis Hoffman. Harper & Row, 1990. With just a few words in rhyme to tell the story, this book captures the fun and loving atmosphere in a caring nursery school. The pictures by Sarah Wilson depict playful toddlers hugging, bumping, dancing, and reading.

When You Go to Kindergarten, by James Howe. Mulberry Books edition, 1995. This book is an ideal introduction to a new experience. With color photographs of boys and girls in real school activities: playing with blocks, painting, reading, and making friends with everyone including the teacher, who will be "your best grown-up friend at school."

Alice Ann Gets Ready for School, by Cynthia Jabar. Joy Street/Little Brown, 1989. Lively and full of enthusiasm, Alice Ann shops for new shoes, a lunch box, and notebooks. Just a little anxious the night before, will she miss the bus? Will she find her classroom? Alice Ann is ready early on the big day — and on her way to school!

Willy Bear, by Mildred Kantrowitz. Aladdin Books edition, 1989. A little boy, going to school for the first time, talks to his teddy bear about his feelings, and sets the bear by the window to wait for him to return.

Leo the Late Bloomer, by Robert Kraus. Windmill Books/Thomas Y. Crowell, 1987. In this story, Leo, a tiger whose father worries that he can't do things yet, blooms "in his own good time."

Going to My Nursery School, by Susan Kuklin. Bradbury Press, 1990. With color photographs of young children at a quality nursery school, photojournalist Kuklin follows a four-year-old boy through the activities and routines of the day. Includes an informative section for parents entitled, *What to Look for in a Nursery School.*

School, by Emily Arnold McCully. Harper Trophy edition, 1990. In this wordless book, the littlest mouse in the family decides to follow the older mice to school to see what it is all about.

Monster Goes to School, by Virginia Mueller. Albert Whitman, 1991. Schools for monster children seem filled with familiar activities. The children have playtime, storytime, music time, and naptime. Little Monster makes a clock, showing all the different "times" they have at school. Lynn Munsinger's drawings of the monsters show them to be appropriately weird yet appealing.

First Day of School, by Helen Oxenbury. Puffin Pied Piper edition, 1993. This author/illustrator of many fine children's books, tells about the first day of nursery school with humor and understanding.

About Handicaps, by Sara Bonnet Stein. Walker & Co., 1984. A book for parents and children about a friendship between two boys, one of whom has cerebral palsy. Annotations on each page give parents background and guidance in answering their own child's questions.

Jesse's Daycare, by Amy Valens. Houghton Mifflin, 1990. Jesse goes to daycare at Sara's house while his mom goes to work. This gentle story parallels Jesse's activities at daycare with his mom's activities at work.

Section Ten
Kids
and
Computers

Section Ten
Kids and Computers

Introduction

I am writing this on a computer.

It's a great tool for me, but are computers good for young children?

The author of this section tells us the good and the bad about computers and kids. She differentiates among various types of computer programs and makes note of several important questions to help adults decide if a program they are considering is a good choice.

Make way for the future! Computers will be as important for today's children as the telephone was for their parents.

But let's not let computers take the place of the natural world, the enjoyment of art and books, and the warmth of human relationships.

Chapter 45
Kids and Computers

Neala Schwartzberg

*A good program
is a tool to let children
learn, play, and discover.*

"It lets kids work on their own," explains Terry, "but I'm not sure it involves enough thinking."

"I envy my children, in a way, because of the computer," says Sharon wistfully. "I had such trouble with math when I was young. I had difficulty grasping concepts my six year old has easily mastered."

Another mother summed up her attitude..."At least I know she's not watching television."

We hear about computers and kids, about how important it is for children (and adults) to become "computer literate." But are computers always good for young children? And how can we use computers wisely as "thinker toys" rather than high-tech baby-sitters?

The good and the bad about computers and kids
Kids are naturally curious. They poke into everything and ask a thousand questions. The world is a new and exciting place, and they are the eager explorers. Computer programs can be their vehicle for this adventure, presenting them with a rich stream of experiences, knowledge and concepts.

A good program is a tool to let children learn, play and discover. But computers can not and should not replace other activities. Kids need to bake cookies, play with blocks, and cuddle up while an adult reads them a story. They need to cut out shapes and draw pictures. Kids need to poke in the dirt and watch the bugs. They need to look at duck weed on the pond and collect falling leaves.

Using computers wisely
So how do the adults in a child's life help a youngster: 1) use them constructively, and 2) become comfortable with computers? Each year more and more computer programs are produced for children. And it is easy to become overwhelmed by the selection available. How can a parent decide if a program is a good choice? Here are several questions to ask about the programs you are considering:

Can the program be used without adult supervision?
You may not want your preschooler to glue himself to the computer without you, but a program for children should be user-friendly. Your youngster should be able to use it without having you stand by flipping through the pages of the manual.

Do you have the equipment to use the program?
All software programs require certain equipment in order to run properly. Make sure your computer has the features that the program requires. If it doesn't, and can't handle other desired programs either, decide whether it is worth upgrading your equipment. If you have a color monitor, but only have a black and white printer you may not want to get a drawing program. Those magnificent screen creations won't look quite so colorful when rendered in shades of gray. Music programs need computers with sophisticated sound capability. Do you have a joystick for programs which recommend a joystick?

Almost all the new programs come on CD-ROM. If your computer is a bit older you may not have CD-ROM capability and may need to upgrade. Also, if you use a disk drive, make certain the program comes on a disk that is the correct size for your computer. Floppy drives come in two sizes. The 3.5" size is currently standard, but some older machines have the 5.25". Before you buy a program, make sure it will fit.

Does your computer have enough RAM (Random Access Memory)? This is the "working memory" of your computer, the amount of information it can handle. If your computer doesn't have enough memory, the program simply will not run.

Is it targeted to your child's age?
Does it allow room for growth? A youngster's mind grows quickly and a good computer program will expand with her. It's okay to buy a program which is good just for the moment, but you don't want to spend serious money on a program which your youngster will outgrow in 6 weeks.

Does the program encourage thinking skills, or is it rote drill and practice?
Again, there is nothing wrong with some drill and practice when a child is learning letters, numbers, etc., provided the whole experience is enjoyable. Computers are endlessly patient while children practice new skills, and they generously reward youngsters for their achievements. But kids need to practice thinking, too. Don't become so concerned about academics that there is no whimsy, no creativity, no "what ifs." Children need a balance in their experiences, and in their computer programs.

Do the music and graphics support the content or distract from it?
Some programs seem to add on things to make it more glitzy but they have little to do with the purpose of the program. In fact, some of those features can actually distract your child and make it harder to focus on the important information.

Is this a program for just one child or can two children use it at the same time?
Some programs encourage or at least allow kids to work together. If you
expect to have two children (whether friends or siblings) using the
computer at the same time, you may want to consider this in selecting
software.

How interactive is the program?
A good program should offer the child different kinds of activities and
encourage him to explore and learn. Clicking on things is very nice, but
what will the child experience as a result of just clicking on objects? And
will it support and reinforce the information, expand the information, or
just distract her?

Are the programs you are considering different from each other?
How do the content and skills required overlap and reinforce each other?
Do you want programs that stress new skills and information — or do
you want programs which approach the same content from different
perspectives? Reading programs and interactive book programs may
overlap in the skills targeted for development. Problem solving and
science may also overlap. Check the package and decide if each offers something unique. You can decide that you want software which overlaps in
order for one to reinforce the knowledge and skills of the other, but you
need to consider that as an issue. You don't want to come home with $200
worth of programs and discover they are all about the same.

Types of Computer Programs

Neala Schwartzberg

Many of the computer programs seem to be divided into subject area.

Academic programs stress academics. Many of the drill programs for learning letters, words and sounds are inventive and fun. There are also programs which allow children to choose among several activities; listen to the story, learn about the vocabulary words and concepts, listen to songs and play games. *Joey can listen to the computer read him a story and watch the words crawl along the bottom of the screen. The characters and objects in the story fill the rest of the screen. Whenever he wants, Joey can click on these objects and learn more about them.*

Math programs, stressing counting and early math skills are also frequently found on the shelves. Science programs for children allow youngsters to experiment with "making" weather, creating machinery, exploring the body (whether human or otherwise).

Painting and drawing programs allow youngsters to create their own pictures, color them in, even animate them as well as use special effects. *Jason is working on a drawing, but he seems to enjoy taking the large paintbrush and making huge brush strokes across the screen. His sister Amy loves to use the pattern brush which "paints" shapes across the screen the way her brother paints solid color.* Although *music* programs are more difficult to find they allow children to create music for different instruments. Other programs incorporate music as part of the activities allowing youngsters to explore sounds and music.

There are programs labeled *"problem solving."* Their goal is to encourage children to explore and investigate. Kids click and drag with the mouse to construct roads, build different objects and machinery and more.

Other programs are organized by *location* and interest rather than academic skill. These take place on farms and airports and encourage children to learn a little bit about everything in that location. Kids can learn the objects, vocabulary, how things work etc. *Sabrina is fascinated by the farm machinery and often clicks on them with her mouse to learn more about what they do and how they operate.*

These programs can get very expensive. Take a few minutes to decide what your youngster likes to do, what skills and interests she already has, and what skills and interests she might want to cultivate. Develop a rough plan of the kinds of programs you want to buy before you go to the store. You can certainly change and adjust, but it will give you a starting place.

Making computer time part of family time
Computers should never replace family activities; they should make them richer. If you are exploring art, computers can be one of the ways you and your youngster create. It doesn't replace painting a picture or drawing with crayons. It is simply another medium to use.

Integrate computer activities with more traditional parent-child time. Use a computer to create a picture book. Some programs allow you to create text around the graphics. Take the pictures from some of the coloring book programs and write your own story about them. Make birthday cards and posters. Take some of the science in the software program and see it "live" in your backyard or kitchen. Take trips to some of the places your child "explored" through the computer.

Discuss how the computer version is similar and different from the "real thing." Use the computer to enrich your life and your child's life, not to replace it. And most of all...enjoy.

Resources for Section Ten:
Kids and Computers

MAGAZINES

FamilyPC, published monthly by Ziff Davis, and *HomePC,* published by CMP Publications. Both family-oriented computer magazines feature software reviews. They are available at book stores and newsstands. They may also be carried by local libraries. Because of their family orientation, many of the programs reviewed are educational or "edutainment" programs ("edutainment" is a new category of program which seeks to educate children while entertaining them).

Green Eggs & RAM is a monthly newsletter published by Bit-by-Bit Computer, Inc.. 1-800-588-6807, that focuses on using computers in early child-hood settings. It explores such important topics as: developmentally appropriate computer activities and techniques, choosing software, etc.

BOOKS

Newsweek Parent's Guide to Children's Software is an innovative combination of CD-ROM which contains reviews of fifty top titles to provide a glimpse into the program itself, and a book about children's software with reviews and "report cards."

Teachers, Computers & Kids: Recipes for Success in Early Classroom Settings, by Suzy Crowe and Elaine Penny. Bit-by-Bit Computer, (1-800-588 6807), 1995. This book offers strategies for early childhood educators to integrate computer play into early childhood settings. It includes information about developmentally appropriate software, and fun activities to engage in away from the computer.

Young Children & Computers, by C. Hohmann. High/Scope Press (1-800-40-PRESS), 1990. This paperback explains how to get started using computers in preschool and kindergarten, what equipment and software are needed, and how computer activities fit into the daily routine.

High/Scope Buyer's Guide to Children's Software, 11th ed., by C. Hohmann, B. Carmody, & C. McCabe-Branz. High/Scope Press (1-800-40-PRESS), 1995. This comprehensive guide reviews over 600 software programs for use in preschools, child care centers, public schools, libraries, and homes.

KidWare: The parent's guide to software for children, by Michael C. Perkins and Celia H. Nunez is published by Prima Publishing, Rocklin, CA., 1995. The book reviews software for children ages 2 to 7 and 8 through 13. The software includes math and science, reading, thinking, creative play (art, design, music and writing) and multisubject programs.

Young Children: Active Learners in a Technological Age, by J.L. Wright & D.D. Shade, eds. NAEYC (202-328 2604), 1994. This volume was written by experts on children and technology on topics such as choosing developmentally appropriate software, benefiting children's cognitive/ social development, and helping staff to use new technologies confidently. (Order #341)

CREATORS AND DISTRIBUTORS OF SOFTWARE FOR CHILDREN

Many companies offer a line of programs for children. The following is a partial list of those who will provide toll free product information:

Broderbund, 1-800-521-6263, is the source for *The Playroom, James Discovers Math,* and *Dr. Seuss's ABC.*

Knowledge Adventure 1-800-542-4240 offers several programs for kids including *Casper: Brainy Book, Jump Start Preschool* and others.

Maxis SoftwareToys for Kids 1-800-336-2947. The people who brought adults SimCity provide these programs for children.

Sony, 1-800-922-7669, offers *Mr. Wonder's Greatest Toyshop on Earth.* For children ages 4 -9. By selecting one of 96 toys on the toy shelves children learn about energy, weather, living things, environment and sound plus painting and "making things."

Virgin Sound and Vision, 1-800-814-3530, have available several CD programs for kids, and a sample disk.

SOFTWARE CATALOGS

In addition to purchasing programs from stores, mail order catalogues offer many of the major software and CDs:

The Edutainment Company, 1-800-338-3844, offers hundreds of non-violent Edutainment titles for children and adults on diskette and CD-ROM.

MediaPhiles, 1-800-268-6991, specializes in CDs for children and adults.

About the Contributors

John D. Allen is a consultant in museum education, most recently working on a project for the North Carolina Museum of History.

Thomas Armstrong, Ph.D., is the author of *In Their Own Way, Awakening Your Child's Natural Genius, 7 Kinds of Smart,* and *The Myth of the A.D.D. Child.*

Barbara Baskin, Ed.D., is President of the Mother Child Home Program, a preschool literacy program with domestic and international replication sites. Dr. Baskin, formerly with the Child and Family Studies Program, State University of New York at Stony Brook, now heads a consultant service for parents of gifted children.

Nancy F. Browning, Ed.D., is an Assistant Professor of Reading at Lincoln University in Missouri.

Laura Carey is an Environmental Educator at Rogers Environmental Education Center in Sherburne NY, and is enrolled in the Environmental Studies program at the School of Environmental Science and Forestry in Syracuse NY.

Mitzie Collins, B.A., Eastman School of Music, is a specialist in music for children. Her popular record for children is called *Sounds Like Fun.*

Laura Daigen-Ayala, B.A., M.S., is coordinator of the Spanish Department at Central Park East Secondary School in NYC.

Janet Dengel is the mother of three children, Linda, John, and Paul. She is a free-lance writer and editor of *KIDS Magazine* in Westwood NJ.

Amy Laura Dombro is an infant/toddler specialist and consultant. She is coauthor of *Sharing the Caring: How to Find the Right Child Care and Make It Work for You and Your Child,* Simon & Schuster/Fireside, 1991.

Pegine Echevarria, M.S.W., lectures and consults on parent issues. She conducts Minority Motivational Seminars, and has written a book, *For All Our Daughters: How Mentoring Helps Young Women and Girls Master the Art of Growing Up,* published by Chandler House Press, 1998

Betty Farber, M.Ed., is President of Preschool Publications, Inc., and was the Editor and Publisher of *Parent and preschooler Newsletter* for 11 years. She has taught and directed early childhood programs in St. Louis, MO, and Memphis, TN, and was Instructor and Early Childhood Coordinator at LaGuardia Community College of the City University of NY.

Lester Feldman is an amateur ornithologist who has spent his professional life as an Art Director for a NYC/international advertising agency where he created many ad campaigns during his almost 40 years there. A dozen of his TV commercials are in the Museum of Modern Art collection of "classics," and he's won the gold and the silver medals from the Ad Club of New York

Marilyn Gilbert is an elementary school Enrichment Program teacher in Port Washington NY, where she does enrichment lessons for all classes, grades Kindergarten through 5th, as well as lessons for students with above average intellectual ability in grades 3 through 6. Gilbert is coauthor (with Lois Kipnis) of, *Have You Ever...Bringing Literature to Life Through Creative Dramatics*, published by Highsmith Press.

Michael Glaser has been presenting environmental science to children for 30 years, at schools, camps, museums, and nature centers. He is the author/illustrator of the picture book, *Does Anyone Know Where a Hermit Crab Goes?*

Tara Greaney is Director of the Children's Center at Cravath, Swaine & Moore in New York City.

Dr. Ellin Greene is a library educator and consultant in library services for children. She is the author of *Books, Babies and Libraries: Serving Infants, Toddlers, Their Parents and Caregivers*, American Library Association, 1991, *Storytelling: Art and Technique*, Third Edition, R.R. Bowker, 1996, and *Read Me A Story: Books and Techniques for Reading Aloud and Storytelling*, Preschool Publications, 1992, as well as ten books for children.

Sallie Hillard went to the University of Memphis with a Master's Degree from Vanderbilt University. She was a clinical supervisor and instructor for more than 20 years and was respected and loved for her ability to help students grow and succeed.

Carol B. Hillman is an Adjunct Professor, Early Childhood Education, Westchester Community College, Valhalla, NY and Adjunct Lecturer in Education, Manhattanville College, Purchase, NY. She is on the Board of Trustees, Bank Street College of Education, New York NY. Hillman is the author of *Before the School Bell Rings,* published by Phi Delta Kappa Educational Foundation, 1995.

Ellen Javernick has been a preschool director and teacher of young children. She writes for numerous periodicals and has written ten books, including, *What If Everybody Did That,* and *Ms. Pollywogs Problem Solving Service.*

Judy Keshner is a grandmother of three and was a kindergarten teacher for 28 years, recently retired. Keshner is the author of *The Kindergarten Teachers' Very Own Student Observation and Assessment Guide,* Modern Learning Press, Rosemont NJ, 1996 and *The Kindergarten Program — A Teacher's Guide,* for Valley Stream NY District #24, 1995.

Elizabeth Kuhlman, M.A., M.S., is an Early Childhood Special Education consultant.

Dr. Lila Lasky was formerly a Professor of Early Childhood Education, and Early Childhood Parent Involvement Coordinator, NYC Board of Education. She is the coauthor of *Art: Basic for Young Children,* published by NAEYC. Now retired, she is enjoying gardening, photography, computers, and her two-year-old grandson.

Michael K. Meyerhoff, Ed.D, is the executive director of The Epicenter Inc., "The Education for Parenthood Information Center," a family advisory and advocacy agency located in Wellesley Hills, Massachusetts.

Anne Moriarty is Owner/Director of Creative Learning Center in Olney, Maryland. She and her husband have three teenage daughters.

Norma Nathanson is Head Teacher at Caedman School in New York City.

Elizabeth Bernard Pettit is the Director of The School for Education in Dance and the Related Arts in NYC. She is the founder of Holiday Hill for the Arts in Gladstone NJ, and cofounder of Viewpoint Gallery in NYC.

Rae Pica is a movement consultant and author of 10 books and numerous articles. She conducts movement and music workshops for parent and early childhood groups throughout the country.

Laura Robb is a teacher and educational consultant, and the author of dozens of articles for parents and teachers. She is the author of *Whole Language Whole Learners: Creating a Literature-Centered Classroom,* Morrow, 1994.

Neala S. Schwartzberg, has a Ph.D., in Developmental Psychology and has written extensively on children and parenting. Her articles have appeared nationwide and have been reprinted in several anthologies. She is a regular contributor to several publications on health related topics. Dr. Schwartzberg has been the editor of *Parent and preschooler Newsletter* since January 1997.

Lois Ross has been teaching music at Public School 189 in Brooklyn, NY (elementary level) for 21 years. She has attended Orff workshops each year which have contributed greatly to the creativity of her lessons.

Bette Simons writes about preschool children and the adults who care for them, based on her experience as a training teacher in the Preschool Laboratory of California State University, Northridge, as well as in her own child care center in Woodland Hills, CA.

Diana Stanley, a former kindergarten teacher, is an editor/writer from Oklahoma City OK, who teaches a course in *Writing the Magazine Article* at Rose State College.

Sandra Stroner Sivulich has been teacher librarian at Pearl River Middle School, Pearl River, NY, since 1994. She previously was teacher librarian at West Nyack, NY Elementary School, from 1989 to 1994. She coauthored, with Randall Enos, *New York is Reading Country* — a manual on summer reading programs for New York public libraries.

Louise M. Ward was on the faculties of the University of Alabama and the University of Memphis. She contributed articles and book chapters in her field and is now Associate Professor Emeritus at the University of Memphis. Ward is the coauthor of *Teacher/Parent Communication: Working Toward Better Understanding,* Preschool Publications, 1992.

Elizabeth J. Webster holds a Ph.D. in Developmental Psychology and is Professor Emeritus, University of Memphis. Dr. Webster is the author of many books and articles on counseling parents. She retired to Deerfield Beach FL, where she is taking a creative writing course and has volunteered to tutor public school students. Webster is the coauthor of *Teacher/Parent Communication: Working Toward Better Understanding,* Preschool Publications, 1992.